I0209463

"I've coached over two hundred pastors, and no one knows holistic health for pastors better than Luke Thomas. You'll find his writing engaging, theologically rich, and scientifically astute. You'll walk away with practical steps to boost your health and ministry."

—John Fooshee, CEO,
People Launching

"This holistic approach to a flourishing life for leaders is smart, practical, and achievable. I didn't think I could change, but this book broke the ground for me to feel the best I have in 20 years."

—Jamey Nettles, Lead Pastor,
Summit Crossing Community Church, Limestone, Athens, Alabama

"Page after page of *Leadership Durability* is like sitting with a coach who both experientially understands and empathetically cares about the real danger of burnout in ministry. In these chapters, you will find a highly practical diagnostic and treatment-based compendium of wisdom by a pastor for pastors."

—Joseph Swords, Lead Pastor,
The Exchange Church, Clio, Michigan

"I have a handful of books I regularly pass out to leaders. This book is going on the list. It's a must-read for leaders wanting to grow toward healthy leadership. In a time when leaders are burning out at a rapid pace, Luke's wisdom is sorely needed."

—Bubba Jennings, Lead Pastor,
Resurrection Church, Tacoma, Washington

"Luke does a great job of highlighting the role of self-care and energy in leadership. Oftentimes, we're told to steward a lot of things like money and other resources, but rarely are we told the importance of stewarding our energy to keep us from burnout. Leadership is tough and there are many things vying for our attention, and the reality is none of us are omni-gifted. Without intentional self-care, we won't finish well. *Leadership Durability* gives you the tools you'll need to thrive and finish well."

—**Jerome Gay,** Lead Pastor,
Vision Church, Raleigh, North Carolina

"Leader, you are on a path that is probably unsustainable. You probably don't believe that, but it is true. The good news is we now have a resource that takes all the research that few of us can even comprehend and applies it directly to the tired leader. Luke knows what he teaches and, unlike so many health and fitness zealots, he doesn't approach the topic from a sense of superiority but from a desire to help. *Leadership Durability* will help set a sustainable course in your life. The chapters on sleep and fitness alone are worth the price of the book. Pick it up!"

—**Rick Gilmartin,** Lead Pastor,
Holy Cross Presbyterian Church, Staunton, Virginia

"When it comes to leadership, Luke understands that for a leader to be healthy, they must be healthy in all areas. Every leader needs to read this book—those who need to rebound from burnout, as well as those wanting to prevent it."

—**Jeremy Hager,** Pastor,
Providence Road Church, Norman, Oklahoma

"As someone who has hit rock-bottom on the burnout scale, Luke's battle scars bleed out onto every page in the form of life-giving wisdom for his brothers-in-arms. Like Luke, 'I'm never too far from burnout,' and all too often, I operate in dangerous patterns that are worn like badges of honor. But this is not sustainable. I desperately need my pride exposed and the lies I'm prone to believe uncovered. I need hope that it is possible to reset my life, and I need clearly defined exit strategies to break the cultural mold I so naturally fit into. And that's exactly what *Leadership Durability* provides."

—**Jeff Martin,** Lead Pastor,
Redeemer Community Church, Johnson City, Tennessee

"The material presented in this book offers firsthand insight from a pastor with street-cred concerning burnout and fatigue. We have much to consider when God calls us to place much on the line. I appreciate this work and the reorienting it brings."

—**Chris Harris,** Lead Pastor,
Legacy West, Knoxville, Tennessee

"As both a pastor and triathlete, I resonate with Luke's attention to both the spiritual and the physical side of leadership health. I couldn't stop saying, 'yes, that's me,' or 'yes, I've felt that before.' Such directness and grace to the leader who is strong yet knows their need for God. Luke doesn't offer a silver bullet approach to health, and that's a great thing."

—**Shawn Stinson,** Lead Pastor,
Redemption Church, Charlotte, North Carolina

LEADERSHIP DURABILITY

THE DEFINITIVE GUIDE TO OVERCOMING BURNOUT AND BUILDING RESILIENCY

LUKE THOMAS

FOREWORD BY ELLIOT GRUDEM

LUCIDBOOKS

Leadership Durability
The Definitive Guide to Overcoming Burnout and Building Resiliency
Copyright © 2019 by Luke Thomas

Published by Lucid Books in Houston, TX
www.LucidBooksPublishing.com

All rights reserved. No part of this publication may be reproduced, stored in a retrieval system, or transmitted in any form by any means, electronic, mechanical, photocopy, recording, or otherwise, without the prior permission of the publisher, except as provided for by USA copyright law.

Unless otherwise indicated, Scripture quotations are taken from the ESV® Bible (The Holy Bible, English Standard Version®), copyright © 2001 by Crossway, a publishing ministry of Good News Publishers. Used by permission. All rights reserved.

Scripture quotations marked (The Message) are taken from *THE MESSAGE*, copyright © 1993, 1994, 1995, 1996, 2000, 2001, 2002 by Eugene H. Peterson. Used by permission of NavPress. All rights reserved. Represented by Tyndale House Publishers, Inc.

ISBN-10: 1-63296-295-0
ISBN-13: 978-1-63296-295-9
eISBN-10: 1-63296-298-5
eISBN-13: 978-1-63296-298-0

Special Sales: Most Lucid Books titles are available in special quantity discounts. Custom imprinting or excerpting can also be done to fit special needs. Contact Lucid Books at info@lucidbookspublishing.com.

*To Paula, my bride, who picked me up off the
mat of crumbling despair, preached the gospel to my
parched soul, and nursed me back to vibrancy.*

TABLE OF CONTENTS

SPECIAL THANKS

I began researching and writing material with the single goal of helping a few random sick leaders find health. It seemed so many others were experiencing the same thing I was. At that time, I was also surrounded by many voices that encouraged me to produce this book, speak, and coach others orbiting burnout and overall leadership sickness.

Along this path, I was greatly shaped and held together by my friend John Fooshee. For years, he has been both a heavy voice and a good friend, and he knew when to be which.

I also couldn't have done this without the support and prodding of Elliot Grudem and the other men of the Leaders Collective—Jamey Nettles, Rick Gilmartin, Jason Tucker, Bubba Jennings, and Jerome Gay. Without Elliot's life-altering guidance and shaping through the Leaders Collective, I'd still be meandering in sickness.

Finally, I'm thankful for the people and pastors of Legacy Church. Not only did they afford me the time to write this book and coach other pastors, they encouraged and expected it. I couldn't have done it without all of them.

FOREWORD

All of my work is with pastors. Some consider me a pastor to pastors. I spend the majority of my time helping pastors flourish. Luke Thomas and the teachings in this book are an integral part of the work I do. I get Luke in front of pastors as often as I can. What he shares is so important and so neglected that I strongly encouraged him to write this book.

There's a fairly common problem with books like this one that are written with the noble aim of helping others. They are often written by someone who has suffered or failed in a specific way, found their way out of it, and in a well-meaning attempt to tell their story and help others facing similar difficulties, they assume their experience should be normative for others.

"Do what I did and it will be OK," is the simplified version of the advice they offer.

There's some value to that. You don't want to pursue health or longevity based on the theoretical advice of someone who hasn't done it. But there's also a danger. The author often can't get past themselves to see or consider you. Their advice doesn't sound much different from the platitudes offered by your high school football coach: they might sound good, but don't help much when you put them into practice.

This is not that kind of book. Luke's story is very much part of this book, but Luke isn't the focus. His love for Jesus and his fellow pastors are. As I read *Leadership Durability*, I heard the voice of a pastor (Luke) talking to me about work, health, self-care, and rest. And I saw him talking to me with a huge smile on his face, telling me what he's telling me because he loves me, Jesus, and Jesus's church.

Like any good pastor, Luke meets us where we are and reminds us there's a better way to do life and ministry. He reminds us Jesus has more for us than we thought possible. Jesus didn't design us to do ministry until we find ourselves completely depleted. He's a good manager of our time. He doesn't want us to be super obedient in the work of ministry by being super disobedient in caring for personal health or ignoring his commands to rest. He wants us to do the work he's given us to do, not give ourselves to what Hilary of Tours called "a blasphemous desire to do God's work for him."

And Luke wants this for us too. That's why he's written this much-needed book. I've personally benefited from it. I hope you will too.

—Rev. Elliot Grudem
Founder and President, Leaders Collective
Raleigh, North Carolina

INTRODUCTION

U p, Up, Down, Down, Left, Right, Left, Right, B, A, Start. If you're familiar with the almighty Konami Code, I'm in good company. If you aren't, it only means you're not a nerd and have likely done something productive with your life. The Konami Code is the cheat code one would hurriedly bang into the 1980s Nintendo controller before the opening screen of the game *Contra* in order to get 30 extra lives. It was humorously and secretively programmed into the game by the developers. My friends and I would spend entire summers using this code so that we could repeatedly beat the game. After all, if I lost a hero here or there, I always had a couple dozen remaining. You can always play a game a bit more carelessly when you have endless lives. *I know you already know this, but there is no cheat code for staying alive in ministry leadership.* There is no quick hack to endure the stressors and trials of leadership. We just don't have 30 lives.

The book you're holding has chunks of my life in it, and not my most favorite bits and pieces. I wrote this a couple years after a battle that nearly claimed my career in the ministry as a lead pastor and church planter. It certainly claimed my health for a few years. In all honesty, I never wanted to be a voice in the area of leadership self-care—I'd rather be helpful in another key area of leadership—but I feel God placed me in such a place at such a time with such a suffering so that I could be of some help to you.

Upon reconstructing my smoldering life, I found myself where you may be now, in a sort of *liminal space*. Liminality is the broken middle. It's the uncomfortable and transitional environment where you obviously cannot retreat to where you were, but you haven't really "made it" to where you need to be. Liminality is that thin place between the past and the future, or as Samuel Chand refers to it, the "hell in the hallway."[1]

My hell in the hallway didn't have bookshelves stocked with material instructing someone in how to overcome burnout, chronic fatigue, or "leadership sickness." My hell in a hallway was more lonely, filled with well-meaning people whose advice was either focused solely on my *physical* frame or on my *spiritual* health. I wanted a more integrated solution, one that addressed my whole being without cutting me into chunks or departments. My hope is that in your difficult and liminal hell in the hallway, I can provide a resource and voice.

Rounding all the bases of burnout and returning to resilient leadership was a gift of God to me, and I pray that as you read this, it never escapes you how sweet God is to you in this season. It may be hard and even odd for you to imagine God being noble and benevolent when it feels so hellish, but it's the path and posture of a leader. As God reduced me to ashes and raised me back up, I felt as Job did at the end of his story: "God I had heard of you, borrowing secondhand experiences from others, but now I know you myself" (Job 42:5). Rebuilding your health shouldn't just change your heart rate, nutrition, and calendar; it should surgically alter your very theology.

More curation than creation, I attempted to synthesize and adapt from great minds and voices rather than render all unique material. Like an art gallery, I attempted to curate and display thoughts and moments for your leadership survival and for your flourishing. I did this with the intention that this not be the only book on the bookshelf of your hallway leading you to long seasons of creative and fruitful leadership, but that it may be the first. Each chapter certainly deserves its own book, but this can at least be a toolbox you revisit as you depart from liminality into a more vibrant and durable season.

May God's grace be with you in this season, and may you go forth satisfied in God above all other pursuits.

PLAYING HURT

THE X'S AND O'S OF BURNOUT

It's not livin' that you're doin' if it feels like dyin'.
—Ray LaMontagne, "Old before Your Time"

I have to admit that I don't know much about playing football at the middle linebacker position. Seriously, I wouldn't even know how to put shoulder pads on without a video tutorial, yet I feel I could sit and reminisce with the best of them. It has become obvious to me over the last several years that leaders in the ministry share common sufferings with those on the football field waiting for the ball to be snapped.

We live in an exciting time in football history when the so-called up-tempo, hurry-up, or no-huddle offense is blooming. What was a fad or gimmick in the National Football League in the 1990s has ripped through college football at a rapid pace. Now, it's rare to have a matchup where at least one team isn't prepared for the hurry-up offense. It's been a pretty controversial innovation. Many fans are excited about it, while the other nation of fans deems it the death of football. Steve Shaw, the Southeastern Conference's coordinator of officials, considers it a "Democrat-Republican issue."[1]

For those who aren't familiar with this innovation, the offense (the team with the ball) forgoes a conventional huddle and gets into a predetermined formation in order to begin the next play with little time between plays. The offense doesn't need to be lightning quick; it only has to *threaten* to be quick any time it pleases. The defense (the team trying to get the football back) has no time to catch its breath, get set, or make casual substitutions. It has to stay ready with little or no break. The hurry-up offense essentially takes the wind out of the defense, never letting them get their heads on straight or gear up for the next play.

Bucky Brooks, who used to play receiver for one of the first up-tempo offenses, described it well: "When a no-huddle/hurry-up attack operates at optimal speed, the defense is at the offense's mercy, and defensive coordinators are rendered helpless on the sideline."[2] Even the officials have to jog briskly to keep up, and the NCAA is experimenting with adding an eighth official to compensate for the increasing speed of the game.[3]

The key for us in Brooks's statement is that the defense is at the mercy of the offense. That is where I feel a kindred spirit with those elite athletes. If you have been in leadership for long, like 16 minutes, you, too, understand what it means to be at the mercy of the offense. Leadership can feel like the whistle keeps signaling the next play, and there is no time to put the mouthpiece back in before getting hit again. No substitutions are coming. There is no time to stop our eyes from crossing. Out of breath. Demoralized from the last collision. On our heels. Weak in the legs. Readying ourselves for the next play. Oh yeah, and all this is happening live before an audience—a critical one. Dr. Dan Allender commented wisely in his book *Leading with a Limp*, "So here's the hard truth: if you're a leader, you're in the battle of your life. Nothing comes easily, enemies outnumber allies, and the terrain keeps shifting under your feet."[4] Well said.

I have personally weathered the hurry-up offense for the majority of my time in leadership, feeling beaten and wondering if there would ever be a time when I could collect myself and regroup. Wave replaces wave. Crisis replaces crisis. The struggle of ministry leadership can smother almost anyone. And the struggle with the weight and pace of leadership isn't behind closed doors. Our families observe its effects, as do those we lead. It kneecaps our work, friendships, family, calling, creativity, and health. We become disillusioned with why we're leading at all, and for too many, that leads to burnout.

"Burnout"

Notice that I'm putting "burnout" in quotation marks when first introducing the term. That's because it has become overused in leadership circles to describe anything from temper tantrums to hospitalization, so it has largely become an empty diagnosis. It's very similar to shin splints, an injury runners get. It seems like no one knows exactly where shin splints come from or how to get rid of them—they just are.[5] For the purpose of this book, we'll describe burnout as simply the state in which we have run our resources dry. Depleted emotionally and physically, we have burned our last match.

I continually see burnout in leaders, especially younger ones, due to overreaching and overworking to the point that basic and rudimentary self-care is neglected, and the body is broken. Like a car careening through flimsy guardrails on a cliff, we bust through the biological fences God has created for us, breaking his gift to us. We'll call this type of burnout hurry-up sickness.

If we overcome this kind of burnout, the effects can linger and take one to three years to see our body fixed physically—but only for someone who is very resolved and disciplined. For those who aren't so determined, there may be brief seasons of improvement due to a hack or quick fix, but it's usually followed by another nosedive in the next tough season. Similar to those who experience a heart attack without recognizing it as such, many leaders break their bodies repeatedly during their time in leadership, oblivious as to why it's happening.

Leadership burnout comes complete with goofy theories and cures. I've heard some unhelpful advice about how to get rid of it as though it were a cold or computer virus. Burnout, however, has claimed more victims in the pastoral ranks than infidelity. Pastors and leaders are exiting their roles every day because of this *thing* that has gone wrong inside of them, and they don't know how to fix it. Even worse, churches aren't teaching those coming into leadership how to avoid burnout in a holistic and realistic way. We dole out knee-jerk advice like "take a nap" or "drink juice." That's not horrible advice in itself, but it's a bit like spitting on a bonfire to try to put it out. My goal is to help you specifically and practically craft a lifestyle that leads you from the damage you've no doubt done to your body as a leader and build resilience in your leadership. The applications in this book won't make you impervious to burnout, but they will make you more resilient as you contend with the relentless waves of crises and heavy emotional costs.

I hope to help not just those contending with burnout but also those training others to lead. As a leader called to train leaders, I am convinced and resolute that self-care must be part of any discipleship training, residency, or assessment. Christ did this with his disciples in an obvious way,[6] but too much of our training focuses on a leader's competency to do the job of the ministry, and we fail to teach others that being good stewards of their own health and *being ministered to* is as important as *ministering to* others. We cannot keep failing in that area.

My hope is to guide you through your innovative response to the hurry-up offense as you contend with the reality of burnout. No two people reading this book are the same, so you must develop your own response to the pace and demands of your specific role and calling. I want to help you customize your response to the no-huddle offense so you don't fall out of leadership, destroying your health and family in the process.

Where's Waldo?

If you've read this far, you'll likely resonate with one of these postures:

1. *You feel totally fine.* You've wondered if you were getting close to burnout, but because it hasn't happened yet, you find yourself ignoring the possibility. You say it's something that happens to others who are out of shape or less gifted. You might be wondering why you're even reading this book, and you probably won't go to the self-care breakout at the next conference.

2. *You're hitting some potholes.* It's as if something inside you is breaking emotionally and physically, and you can't fix it. You don't know what to do, so you keep pushing, applying bandages and hoping it will all get better. But it hasn't been getting better. You may even own a couple of good books that have helped, but the break inside of you feels systemic, not seasonal.

3. *You have already burned out.* You're wondering how long it will take to get back to normal. You don't need convincing that this is real. You aren't even sure what *normal* is supposed to look like, but you know it isn't where you are now. You remember better days, and you're trying to get back to that place. You're in a liminal state, between two places.[7] One you never want to go back to; the other you cannot find.

I have been in all three categories. As someone who has always been in shape and thought only little sissies burn out, I blew it all off for more than 15 years, starting churches and campus ministries. I skipped all the self-care-oriented sessions at conferences, which wasn't hard because there really weren't very many. I'd also shelve the books dealing with the subject because, after all, they were for a lighter weight class than I was in. I focused only on what was going to help me put new tools in my tool belt.

I've actually been in the throes of burning out for the majority of my ministry career. Most of my days could be measured in various degrees of hurry-up sickness, but because I was serviceable, I never came off the field to recharge. I kept pressing. I never saw burnout coming, and when it hit me, I had no idea what to do or even how to describe it. I could not put into words what was going on, and I had no tools to fix the problem. Even once my IQ caught up, it took years to establish a new lifestyle and walk out of the damage I had done. By God's thoughtful grace, I am no longer there.

Hello, My Name Is Burnout

In 2011, the Monday after Easter, I made my introduction to burnout. As the anonymous quote says, "Man and moment have met." I felt fine the night before. I never saw it coming. We had a good Easter service in the midst of a good year in a fun, young church plant in an unbelievable city. Even with the hits of ministry, I was living the dream. It was my third church plant to pioneer and by far my favorite. I remember celebrating with my friends over what God had done on Easter and then passing out after binging on a couple episodes of whatever was the TV rage. Several hours later, however, with light pouring into my window, I couldn't get out of bed. It wasn't a Cameron-from-*Ferris-Bueller's-Day-Off*-can't-get-out-of-bed event; I was *physically* unable to get out of bed. And even worse, I didn't *want* to leave my bed. I had deep sorrow and pain on the inside and began crying for no apparent reason (okay, maybe I *was* like Cameron). I felt weak, confused, and, to be honest, a bit embarrassed. For two days, I lay in my bed unable to sleep, eat, get dressed, or describe what I was feeling.

I've always prided myself on being a strong, disciplined, and militant individual with little need for external motivation. I've competed in several Ironman triathlons with more than a decade of endurance racing and have always been in great physical form—I thought. I wasn't a sugar addict, didn't drink soda or sweet tea, and tried to eat something green every day. As I lay there trying to make sense of my apathy, I tried to deduce what was wrong. Was it my sleep? Diet? Why did I feel like this? Was I being a sissy? Why was I still crying? What should I tell my wife? Did I break something inside of me? Who can I talk to about this? Will the other pastors make me retire? Is this how it all ends? How will I get ready for Sunday?

I had burned out—officially. If I had been playing defense against a relentless offense, the medics were now carrying me off in a stretcher. There may have been warning flags here and there, but I didn't take any of them seriously. I was beginning to sense the increasing danger but couldn't solve the problem. I felt like David in the 69th Psalm.

> Save me, O God! For the waters have come up to my neck. I sink in deep mire, where there is no foothold; I have come into deep waters, and the flood sweeps over me. I am weary with my crying out; my throat is parched. My eyes grow dim with waiting for my God.[8]

For a few months, I dorked around with various self-imposed remedies I gathered from the Internet—sleeping in, doing a cayenne pepper cleanse (I wouldn't advise it), and eating more salad. Then I listened to my wife and got checked out by a professional. The doctor's name was Dr. Holliday (no kidding, like the gunslinger), and I sat there puffing my chest out and bragging of my fitness as he took spit and hair samples to develop a thorough profile. He wasn't impressed with my hypermasculinity, and he wasn't impressed that it was my first physical since high school sports.

My test results revealed I had broken some vital parts of my body, and Doc Holliday gave it to me like a gunslinger. My adrenal glands, which we'll discuss in a moment, were functioning at approximately 20-percent capacity. My cortisol level was almost nonexistent, and my testosterone figure was so poor that it looked like a mistake. Doc let me know I had better innovate and make changes or I was going to get worse quickly. I wanted to argue and blow him off, but the numbers were staring me in the face, and 20 percent isn't 100 percent. My days of pretending were over. It didn't matter how fast or long I could run or how many times I could flip a dumb truck tire. I had cold hard data objectively measuring my body's failure. I got more tests and a second opinion, but all the tests agreed; I had broken this body God had lovingly given me.

Innovation Begets Innovation

What's interesting about college football is the reciprocal innovation that defensive coaching staffs all over the country have. Beyond the X's and O's of where players need to be positionally, the overall cardiovascular fitness and stamina of players in defensive positions have had to evolve. Denzel Devall, a linebacker for Alabama's Crimson Tide from 2012–2015, once talked about the new warp-speed offenses and how he had to make changes. An article about the hurry-up offenses stated, "Devall said losing weight was a primary goal this offseason as linebackers need to be quicker on their feet to play in space against fast teams."[9]

And there you have it—innovation begets innovation. That is the way it is. When a challenge comes, innovation responds with an answer. That is the hope of this book, because whether you like the up-tempo challenges of your calling and role or not, it's not going to slow down. Your current frustrations will only be replaced with newer, bigger, and more complicated ones. We as leaders need to innovate and make foundational changes in how we see leadership self-care. To be more blunt, *innovate or die,* because what you're doing now simply isn't working. Agreed?

Throwing Haymakers

To borrow from another sport's analogy (because what other decent analogies are there?), you can tell you're getting close to burnout or are already there when you begin throwing haymakers.

A haymaker is a punch devoid of all skill and accuracy. It's thrown when the fighter is all out of gas and desperate to end the bout. It's a kitchen-sink effort when all other punches have missed and you're getting too tired to stand upright, simply wanting it all to end. It's named after the farm machine that knocks down newly cut hay to speed up drying. The angle of the arm in a haymaker punch looks like the sickle-like machine. It's the punch pugilists toss when they are getting tired and desperate. If you've ever watched or been in a middle-school fight, that's what *all* the punches look like. The haymaker is meant to end the fight quickly.

When leaders execute their roles and their callings are overdrawn, they begin throwing haymakers with the wrong kind of desperation. They just want the challenges to go away and the win to come quickly, but they are too tired and emotionally winded to be patient and rely on God. Fatigued leaders are performing everything very raw. Like forest fires, many of the messes leaders deal with are started by people, so tired leaders want not only for the mess to go away but eventually the people as well. There isn't much accuracy or strategy to their leadership, and it now has an overly emotional edge to it. Worn thin, these leaders have no stamina for the variables that pop up, so they get sloppy and impatient.

Those we are called to care for and lead feel the brunt of haymakers when they get in the way. When ministry leaders work while overdrawn, they preach when they're mad and get even from the pulpit. Instead of loving those who are bleeding, they turn on them and even abandon them. These haymakers roll over the staff or leaders in meetings when there is pushback or disagreement. Because these leaders are in this bad place, people pay the price. From the kiddos at home to the barfly you are trying to bring the gospel to, they all feel like they are on the receiving end of a very tired and poorly thrown punch.

For years, it was the only punch I knew how to throw. Actually, the culture of church growth I was accustomed to *engineered* leaders to burn out. I grew up thinking it was noble to burn out for Jesus. I even remember notable leaders in my life saying things like "Imma burn out for Jesus." I believed that if I pushed hard enough for God, he would surely take care of my health. I mean, why wouldn't he? "Take care of God's house, and he'll take care of yours" was a common statement. I worked under the assumption that we are always in the red zone.[10] Always go-time. Always a crucial season. Never a time to gear down, never time to rest. After all, there is way too much on the line, right? I was always convincing myself that I could rest later, process later, go on a diet later, sleep later, vacation later, play with the kids later, and, yes, even spend time beholding Jesus later.

I once heard Tim Keller, pastor and theologian, tell a roomful of leaders that, like ducks, we all find a duck-mother to follow—someone whose voice resounds with us. I have many duck-mothers. In fact, I have a Mount Rushmore full of them. As of this writing, only one remains in healthy leadership, and the rest had to get out after throwing too many unsuccessful haymakers. Take an honest appraisal of how you are handling others. It is a key indicator of your leadership health.

Up-Tempo Assessment

I suspect I'm not alone. I suspect you might have one foot in your hurry-up sickness as you read this. In all the great books written on leadership sickness and burnout, many of the symptoms overlap, and others are barely mentioned. I have combined and made simple many of the ones I have found to be true. Be honest with yourself as you read these symptoms, noting where you resonate with other leaders and what they have described.

You're likely burning out right now if:

- *You are having great difficulty getting to sleep and staying asleep.* Even when exhausted, you can't get to sleep. Some days, you wake up too early and others too late. It's also not uncommon to wake up very early in the morning trying to solve a problem. There doesn't seem to be any real consistency except that your sleep consistently stinks. You may also be on a prescribed medication for your poor sleep.

- *You have been unable to get out of bed*, either from depression or a deep, unexplainable, internal fatigue. Gone are the days of springing out of bed optimistically. Getting up takes a long time and is often accompanied by a smothering sadness and a disdain for the day's itinerary.

- *You're crying at odd times for reasons you can't quite explain.* You can only describe it as an emotional intensity. It can come or go with no reason. You don't tell people about this because it's confusing and embarrassing. There is no predicting or forecasting when it will happen. That may be particularly alarming if you're not typically given to crying.

- *You have acid reflux more often than not.* I realize that reflux can come through various key routes, but it seems like you have lava coming up your esophagus far too often. You're probably taking something over the counter for it. You tell others it is a food thing, but you suspect it's probably more.

- *You loathe people who require heavy lifting.* I used to call them bleeders, people who never contribute or help and only make a big mess. When their names come up in conversation, you immediately start twitching and want to wrestle them in the front yard. Anger and mockery have replaced compassion—and you didn't used to be like that.

- *You're chronic.* You have chronic illnesses you've been perfecting over time, like arthritis, respiratory infections, chronic bronchitis, and chronic allergies. The body's ability to churn out necessary chemicals is very low, degrading your resilience in stress-related work.[11]

- *Your sex drive is all but gone.* I'm not specifically talking about erectile dysfunction as much as I am overall sex drive. You love your spouse, but to be honest, you'd rather be a buddy and not invest the time and energy to woo and connect on a sexual or deeply emotional level. She, of course, has already told you that. You hear commercials on testosterone treatments and wonder if that's your answer.

- *Your immediate reaction to bad news is to go overboard.* Running toward the worst scenario in your pessimistic imagination, you feel everyone is out to get you and everything is coming apart. The victim costume becomes your favorite one to wear. Your spouse and friends now hate telling you bad news for fear that you will throw a tantrum.

- *You ignore those with pervasive needs.* They simply aren't sheep worth shepherding anymore. They are making too many messes, and they're not helping you build your dream, so you leave them behind. You outwardly call it stewardship, but even you know better. You remember a different version of yourself years back.

- *You have no creativity left.* You're going through mechanical motions, not feeling inspired to create or imagine anything anymore. You have resorted to making counterfeit reproductions off the creativity of others. You're becoming a creativity sloth, unable to render new material, only able to borrow or plagiarize.

- *You hunt for alone time.* You aren't pursuing solitude but rather escape and isolation. They're different. But after being bubble-wrapped from others, you never feel fulfilled. Being sheltered from all problems seems like a perfect place, and you dream of escaping.

- *Your heart rate races at odd times, even while lying down.* You might notice it in the evenings or early mornings. The variability in your heart rate has nothing to do with your activity level, and you can't figure out why it's all over the place. You might even experience what feels like a panic attack.

- *Your hands and feet are always cold or sweaty.* It is a symptom of a high alert state where your body is rerouting your blood. If that is consistently the case, there may be a problem with how your body is acknowledging and navigating danger. Poor circulation isn't always an innocent phenomenon.

- *You're always clenching your hands or teeth.* You have to remind yourself to relax in order for it to actually happen. Sounds odd, but just like cold hands, clenched hands or jaw reveals a state of alert in times of danger or tension. A clenched jaw, of course, can contribute to tension headaches you may be having.

- *You have thoughts of suicide, divorce, or ditching leadership.* I'm describing thoughts that go beyond a mere glance. You're daydreaming of anything but the role you're in or the spouse you're with. If this is you, my friend, you are burning out. You have likely not told others about these thoughts for fear they will make a big deal of them.

- *You can't make simple decisions.* You used to be an executive, finding it thrilling to chart a course through tough waters, but now you are petrified, continually hitting the same walls of indecision and frustrating everyone around you. "Simple problems refused solution,"[12] and you are paralyzed in your constantly looping thoughts.

- *You're emotionally fragile.* Anytime an emotional deposit is warranted, you sprint in the opposite direction. You just don't have it in you. It's not that you don't see and acknowledge the need; you just know you can't meet it. In fact, you don't have a very impressive emotional IQ around your family, either. Ask them.

- *All food is becoming comfort food.* Feeling entitled by your difficult role, you are abusing food in order to bring satisfaction to yourself. You may even reason that you aren't overweight or obese, yet we both know gluttony isn't a weight thing—it's a comfort grab.

- *You are no longer enjoying alcohol to the glory of God.* You now *need* wine or beer to shift down a couple gears. You tell others that it's not a problem and you are free to partake, but then again, you know *free* is the last thing you are from handling alcohol. You call drunkenness *tipsy* and feel entitled to relax at the end of a hard day, but now all days are hard.

- *Your medicine cabinet makes you look like an octogenarian.* I'm not talking about supplements but meds you needed a prescription to get. You've been working on a nice collection of medications, with many of them covering your lack of past self-care. You don't know what to throw out, and you may feel stuck.

- *You see compulsive behaviors come out of nowhere.* Whether you're talking to yourself incessantly, triple-checking everything, micromanaging, or having bouts of paranoia, you are certainly in the anxious category. You may have a personality like that, or you may be finding that it has come out of nowhere. The nervous tics are now obvious.

- *You're being worn down by minor-league temptations.* What used to be easy to run from is now conquering you. And what used to bring you pleasure no longer does. Shifting affections and disciplines reveal a tectonic slide of the soul seen in major burnout. If you don't believe me, read the news. Leaders are tripping on things they used to step over.

- *You have chronic neck and back pain.* I realize there are various reasons such pain can occur, but it's widely documented that stress causes tension in specific areas. Unless you've been in a bad accident or hit the squat rack every day, you might be a victim of unnecessary muscle tension from pervasive stress reaction.

- *Brain fog is so normal that you can't remember not having it.* You are also easily distracted. Of course, that gets worse as the day moves ahead. It takes forever to read something, and you can't remember it later. You forget people's names and feel .64 seconds behind everyone around you. You likely blame it on sleep.

- *You act like a donkey to those around you.* In other words, it doesn't take much to get a reaction out of you. Even small things provoke you to go nuclear—things that wouldn't have provoked you in the past. Temperament is a fair measure of leadership health.

- *You are sick a lot.* It doesn't matter if the flu bug is all the way across the county; if someone has it, you get it. You especially feel it in the sinuses. Whenever the seasons change, you can set your watch to getting a bug. Always taking something over the

15

counter and always unable to fight off even the smallest things, you can't seem to ever win.

- *You have belly fat.* We'll go over this in another chapter, but belly fat is the product of cortisol-induced fat storage. A beer belly is more accurately a *stress belly.* Do all the sit-ups you want, and it won't go away unless you make some systemic changes in both diet and overall lifestyle.

I left a bunch out but did the best I could to combine some of the major warning signs. If you have more than a few of the above warning lights going off, you're likely already in a case of hurry-up sickness or in mid to late adrenal fatigue syndrome (AFS).[13] I know some of you aren't totally convinced this is you and were able to massage some of the above symptoms to accept a lie. So I thought I'd add some other indicators that might show you why you are headed for burnout soon, if you aren't already there.

You may be headed for burnout in the very near future if:

- *You are among the majority.* About 90 percent of pastors feel insufficiently prepared or trained to cope with the demands that come with ministry,[14] and 70 percent say their self-esteem has declined since they began the ministry.[15] Around 67 percent of the general population carries damage from hyperstress.[16] That is a large majority of us. Don't be fooled. You aren't better than the leader next to you.

- *You're already prone to anxiety.* Certain personalities are given to burnout a bit faster than others. It's not that you are weaker than other leaders; you simply have a different flavor of suffering from which you can glorify God. Personalities that normally contend with an unsettled heart must beware of burnout to a more serious degree.

- *You eat garbage.* You tell other people you eat pretty healthy, but that's because you think eating iceberg lettuce with your Chik-fil-A qualifies as healthy. You're eating on the run at stoplights and taking green pills to give you what your food should. Adding to the madness, you don't track what you eat or put a meter on it, so you have no idea how much garbage you're eating. Good job!

- *You have a C-posture.* Literally, your spine is shaped like a C, complete with shoulders that roll in and a spine that rolls out. Your head droops forward, opening your jaws ever so slightly. Because of that, one of the nagging injuries you've collected is a back that chronically tweaks and aches.

- *You guzzle significant amounts of coffee, soda, and sweet tea.* When we abuse coffee, we accelerate our failure. Yes, I said abuse. *Significant* means more than 8–10 ounces per day. A Grande at Starbucks is 16 ounces to put that in perspective. Just because it comes in a single cup from a barista doesn't make it okay.

- *You are starting to creak, pop, and snap.* Your small nagging injuries are now looking more like career-ending injuries. Inflammation lingers, and injuries don't heal like they should. It's not a matter of whether you have inflamed injuries, but rather how many. You have likely chalked it up to just getting old.

- *You go to bed consistently after 11:00 p.m.* No, you aren't a night person—you are a poor planner. Biology has ingrained in you a circadian rhythm, regardless of your preferences. Just because we think clearly and are productive in the evenings doesn't mean we should try to rewire the way our body was designed to function.

- *You are lacking in the hope and vision departments.* You are becoming disillusioned, and the version of you that was once idealistic and hopeful has been replaced by a more morose and pessimistic version. You now play conservative and fearful.

- *You're a mouth-breather.* Remember that drooping head and agape mouth? That supports most of your predominate mouth-breathing. It may even take an inordinate amount of concentration to breath from the diaphragm with a correct breathing posture. Breathing is something you do on accident, not with any design.

- *You don't plan or execute sabbath rest consistently.* Whether it's a shaky theology or poorly guarded rhythms, you have no moments, days, or seasons when you *aren't* producing, fixing, or solving. Rest is more of an episodic or occasional thing for you. When you aren't working, you've noticed that you also aren't resting. You don't know how anymore.

- *You have no accountability.* Alone, you have no voices telling you that you're running too hard. You may have people you are 30 percent to 60 percent honest with, but not 100 percent honest. Conversely, you have people who are only partially honest with you. Your pride convinces you that accountability is a liability and an exercise in telling half-truths well.

- *You sit on your butt all day.* If you're average, you're sitting 13 hours per day. That is an orthopedic car wreck for your joints and spine. I know you have tried standing workstations, but you don't really prefer them. That has more to do with leadership self-care than you realize.

- *You feel alone.* No matter how many of your closest relationships tell you they understand, you are certain they don't. You think you are unique or misunderstood. Self-pity causes you to create even more distance between you and those in your immediate spheres. Surrounded by allies, you have no confidants.

- *You have no sense of balance in schedule or rhythms.* In other words, you don't give much thought to what drains and fills your tank.[17] You find yourself draining your tank much more than filling it. Your answer is typically related to time. "If I just had more time," becomes your anthem.

- *You can't manage a calendar.* You overbook and bloat your calendar so there is no breathing room. Of course, that assumes you use a calendar. If you do, it may not be a key or essential part of your routine, and you have no idea how to steward it properly or make it serve you. It might be just a weedy garden that you refuse to tend to in an intentional manner.

- *You cannot say no.* You say yes to everything and see every concern as your personal responsibility. As an older and more seasoned leader once said to me, "Luke, you keep grabbing bags with holes in them." You cannot discern what is good from what is best, so you treat everything as the best thing.

- *You have no identity or role.* The definition of your role is always cloudy, and you never feel quite like you're driving in the right lane. As you try to do what you feel called to do, you're sucked into other roles. You're grinding through the daily work you cannot stomach. You feel trapped and don't know what to do.

- *You are working in a war zone.* Your position at your current gig has you in knots, and you feel like the leadership above you or around you is domineering. What started out as exciting has turned into something that resembles staying alive. You might be thinking about ditching leadership altogether.

- *You don't use your gym membership.* You're that person. You might even have some kettlebells in your garage, but your good intentions have run out of gas. You can't seem to find your pirated P90X, and you don't really care. Even your fancy smartwatch is telling you to simply walk more. Walk.

- *You are unduly pasty.* You get no sun or nature as you camp in whatever Starbucks has plugs. Vitamin D is something you take in pill form, and the nature you experience is mostly on the Discovery Channel. Nature is a mythical thing that your ancestors had to brave.

- *You are boring.* You have no hobbies or anything that isn't work. I'm not talking about wrecking your family in order to restore the old Camaro in the backyard. But what about doing something you enjoy and giving all the glory to God—something that isn't work? If you say that your ministry, church, or Jesus is your hobby, then you automatically fail this part.

- *You are absent.* You rarely appear where you're needed most. The dinner table, Little League practice, and daddy-daughter dates never have the pleasure of your attendance and attention. If you aren't sure this describes you, just stop reading and go ask your kids and spouse. Thought so.

- *Your spouse isn't appealing to you.* You simply aren't as attracted as you used to be. You might have some remaining sex drive left in you, but it's aimed improperly. You are now fighting the urge to think of what it would be like to be married to someone else.

- *You're a teenager when it comes to media and technology.* Seriously, you are checking your e-mail at stoplights and sitting on the toilet 11 minutes after you are done so you can retweet people who don't know you so others who don't know you can read it and retweet you. What on earth has happened to you?

- *You're throwing haymakers.* You can spiritualize it, of course, but you are being intense and aggressive more for your satisfaction than for building up people. You weren't always like this, of course, but now you feel it's necessary to get the greater good done. You are now building a theology that endorses your brutal and tyrannical leadership.

- *You are proud.* You believed your mom when she said, "You are special." You think you are impervious to failing leadership health. It could never happen to you because you *feel* fine. You think it only happens to a small subset of leaders you secretly judge inside. You fail to see the finiteness of your capacity.

Own It

Tim Keller stated it wisely:

> To deny your hurt—to tell yourself you are just fine, thank you—means you will likely pay a price later. You may find yourself blowing up, or breaking down, or falling apart suddenly. Then you will realize you were kidding yourself. You hurt more than you thought you did.[18]

Maybe this is you, winded and kidding yourself. Maybe you're throwing impatient punches. If you are burning out, your first step is simply *owning that you've personally failed.* Even if you are a victim of another leader, an illness, or a bad circumstance, you need to own your response to it.

Even though our culture bristles at this truth, you are accountable for how you respond to stressful situations. External stressors may be out of your control, but how you respond to them is on you. Own that the problem is worse than you think and that a nap or short vacation is insufficient to fix it. Own that you haven't been truthful with others or yourself. Own that you can't fix it with a bandage and that you've underestimated the decline in your health. Dr. Richard Swenson admonishes us well, "If you are underslept, overweight, and unexercised, it is your job to change."[19] Our body, our responsibility.

Additionally, stop shifting the blame. Your job or role didn't do this to you. It isn't your church's fault. It's not the bleeding folks that message you all day long. It's not your detractors and critics. It's not the finances. It's not the city in which God has placed you. It's not your spouse's fault for not giving you what you want on time. It's your fault for not leading yourself well. Stop shifting blame and own your leadership sickness.

The Many-Headed Monster

Before we get into strategies, it might be helpful to break down burnout into its main causes.

Bad theology generates burnout. It specifically relates to how you see God, his church, your city, and your personal role in the whole equation. Poor theology that drives poor leadership ends in bad burnout. A warped theology simply keeps us from properly interpreting crisis or suffering. In my story, my theology needed a serious change. Not because I was a heretic in what I preached but because I was heretical in how I lived and led.

Dissatisfaction with God's glory in Jesus leads to burnout. When Jesus doesn't satisfy, we will find a replacement to satisfy us. Many who burn out are coming apart because they're expecting a church or ministry to be their savior. Burnout found me intoxicated with what I could build to my own glory, security, and approval. Walking away from burnout came through my fascination and satisfaction with Jesus.

Burnout comes through simple ignorance about how the human body responds to stress. Even when God began to heal my theology and my heart grew quieter and less hurried, I still had many lifestyle ruts that needed attention. I was ignorant about much and lazy with even more. I simply needed a new leadership IQ. Even as an athlete who went to school for pre-medicine, I had no functional understanding of how to steward my health as a leader. A leader's biology needs special attention.

Burnout comes when we mismanage our energy and time. I see burnout happening to leaders who don't know how or where to properly position projects, meetings, shallow tasks, reading, rest, deep work, sleep, and fitness. Even full calendars can have rhythms that are disproportionate and oddly arranged. All the right furniture is in the room, but it's oddly placed with no flow. When I began to walk out of hurry-up sickness, I needed help moving the furniture around.

Report Card

Leaving Doc Holliday's office in 2011, I was jolted enough to address change. With the help of my church's pastors and my wife, I immediately applied some very drastic changes and sought the help of various professionals. That evolved into research for leadership sustainability. I resourced physicians, researchers, and experts in the areas of health, diet, fitness, sleep, productivity, and leadership.

I have to be honest. I'm never too far from burnout. Hurry-up sickness walks alongside me more than it does behind me. I don't have the panacea for burnout or the answer to leadership longevity. I only know what I have applied and what has worked effectively for me and others. I cannot pretend to address all the various reasons for burnout or attempt to interpret your specific situation. But I will do my best to shoot for the bulk of the bell curve and speak to what I am seeing on a growing scale among ministry leaders. The vast majority of burnout cases are preventable.

Since April 25, 2011, I've become far healthier than I was in my 20s. My sleep is consistently between 7 hours and 45 minutes and 8 hours and 15 minutes with no alarm clock necessary. I simply roll over and spring out of bed. My body fat has dropped to half of what it was in my most competitive form. I've entered my 40s faster and stronger than my 20s or 30s. My leadership vision, hope, and creativity have increased. I have sensed a sweeter and more compassionately relaxed posture with those around me. My wife has sensed it, too. I've learned how to rest well—and work harder.

Anecdotally, I have stopped having acid reflux and back pain, and I don't snore anymore. My sex drive is healthier than ever before. My leadership role has better shape and protection now, and I find myself staying true to what God has called me to do. I have radically shifted how I manage energy and have seen my rhythms and calendar serve my calling. My theology has also improved as I see God and his good news for us in a clarity that leads me through crisis *and* stasis. My leadership reformation has brought health to not only my body but also my relationships and the way I care for Jesus's church.

Through this process, I have been able to teach and lead our local pastors to see warning signs in me and ask wise questions at appropriate times. They have been a great help in assessing my heart, fears, pace, and load. They also know when I am making excuses and not being realistic. My bride also knows what some of my warning signs look like, what I might need, what my escapes are, and how to communicate with me or the pastors around me regarding my health.

Looking back, that burnout experience I had in 2011 may have been the best thing that could have happened to me, my family, and our church. I whined a bunch at the time, but now, after working with many leaders regarding their self-care, I can see God's sweetness. He was not only breaking me down to bring me to health but allowing me to walk a trail where I can lead others. God has been very kind and helpful. I hope it will be the same for you.

BENT TREES
WHO BURNS OUT?

There are two ways to cope with pain. One is to put your head down and grunt through it. I didn't know the other way.

—Dean Karnazes, ultrarunner

I grew up in West Texas where there are no trees taller than a toddler, so it was a huge adjustment for me when we first moved to East Tennessee. One of my early lessons as a missionary there was how to "ride the lightnin'." It isn't illegal, and it doesn't have anything to do with moonshine. Ride the lightnin' is climbing a young tree to the height of maybe 30 feet, at which point it slowly and gradually droops and bends down to the earth, dropping you off like an elevator. It sounds stupid, I know, and I laughed at it until I tried it. Now, I can't quit. It's hard for me to walk by a tree without appraising in my mind (1) how high I could climb it before it bent, (2) who's recording this, and (3) if my insurance is up-to-date.

Daring your friends to climb higher and higher on trees is burned into my wilderness experience, especially when everyone has their phone out ready to birth the next viral video. Sometimes, however, we find a dud, picking a tree that is too young. After a couple of not-skinny guys ride the lightnin', the tree has no reflex. With no resilience,

25

the tree stays bent. If we had waited for a day or two between climbers, the tree would have slowly found its natural form. Of course, we don't have the patience for that, so we look at the bent tree, grieve for about seven seconds, and move on to the next tree.

That is a helpful picture of burnout. For many, there is a lot of stress traffic, leaving little chance to reset, so resilience comes up short, and people look a little bent. Our capacity to handle stress is also similar to filling a bucket, and people fill our stress buckets faster than anything else. You see, stressors in life are bankable over time. "It is important to remember that all stresses are additive and cumulative," said Dr. James Wilson, an expert in adrenal function. "That is, the number of stresses, whether or not you recognize them as stresses, the intensity of each stress and the frequency with which it occurs, plus the length of time it is present, all combine to form your total stress load."[1] Even if this week has been easy sailing, you are still carrying the effects of stress that have been lacquered on over the last weeks, months, and, in my case, years.

I occasionally bump into leaders who have a pretty healthy lifestyle and can combat the accumulative stress response. Their trees might bend like crazy during certain seasons but always seem to reform to the original upright position afterward. They have high stress traffic but are also resilient. But many of the leaders I know are simply walking around bent. Their bodies and souls are never given the adequate time and resources they need to be nurtured and refreshed. For the sake of our metaphor, there are too many people ridin' the lightnin'. They can't hold anyone else because they are bent sideways. At that point, there has been significant damage to the brilliantly designed response system God has entrenched in us. We have begun to break God's architecture of our very form.

It's important to note that I am not suggesting we don't bend the tree. We're called to work hard and march straight into stressful situations. In fact, I'll make the case later that our negligent lifestyle is keeping us from working hard. I'm not going to go into a thorough defense of working hard to God's glory but would like to assert that sloth and laziness aren't the keys to beating burnout in leadership. Charles Spurgeon said it well:

> Anxious to serve his Master, he finds his strength unequal to his zeal; his constant cry is, Help me to serve You, Oh my God. If he is thoroughly active, he will have much labor; not too much for his will, but more than enough for his power, so that he will cry out, I am not wearied of the labor, but I am wearied in it.[2]

Weariness isn't the enemy; weariness is a result of working hard. Too many of us, however, aren't wearied *in* what we do but wearied *of* what we do. It's the difference between being tired and being burned out. One occurs when we honor God's gift and calling; the other happens when we abuse and break it. If you have been abusing your body's emergency response system, you are not far from quitting. You must allow time for the tree to reestablish its right form before you keep allowing others to climb it.

Sign Me Up!

Everyone has physical reactions to the challenges of this jagged world. To feel stress isn't a sign of failure or weakness; it's a sign of humanity. Even the Type B, laid-back, middle-born child sleeping on the beach in the middle of the workday has stress from time to time, but there is a certain personality that thrives on it. It's most likely you—the classic Type A.

The term *Type A* was coined by doctors and sociologists in the mid-twentieth century to describe who was at a higher risk for heart disease. But it has become helpful when describing how we're wired. Dr. Richard Swenson does an excellent job of describing the Type A personality.

> The type A personality is commonly characterized as "driven." Type As have a drive to control others, an aggressiveness and competitiveness characterized by a need to win. They think multiple thoughts and do multiple actions at the same

time....Their carburetors are set on high, and they surge into overdrive at the slightest provocation. Most people find a vacation relaxing, but type As often do not. Relaxing is one of the most stressful things on their agenda, which is why they seldom do it. Progress and type As feed on each other. They are very productive people and usually the leaders of companies or institutions.[3]

I would like to note, however, that the Type A personality has been overdramatized by culture to look like a wood-chopping, ex-astronaut, spiral-throwing, Navy SEAL, with a full beard. Because of that description, many folks (maybe even you) don't see themselves as Type A. The truth is that statistically, most of us have a heavy shade of Type A in us. I have heard some cultural commentators project that upward of 70 percent of us are Type As. It's actually the Type B personality that is much rarer. You may not be on the far end of the spectrum, but statistically, you are a Type A personality. I'm betting it's part of the reason you're reading this book.

Most business leaders, church planters, entrepreneurs, and pastors are raging Type As. I am a card-carrying member myself, although my spiral needs some work. I recall as a young man reading an account of Sir Ernest Shackleton's voyage on the *Endurance*, an ill-fated trip that has become a classic for both sailors and business leaders. I've read about his adventure to Antarctica more than a dozen times.[4] The first time I read it, I was grabbed by the poster Shackleton posted around town recruiting men to go on the voyage to the middle of Antarctica. Here's what it said:

> Men wanted for hazardous journey, small wages, bitter cold, long months of complete darkness, constant danger, safe return doubtful, honor and recognition in case of success.[5]

I immediately resonated and read it to my bride who thought it was dumb. I thought it was brilliant. I would have loved signing up for something like that because of the Type A in me. Safe return doubtful. Constant danger. Sign me up! But that isn't the story for all Type As.

You don't have to be an uber soldier or CrossFit champion to be that kind of leader. You just need to be one who loves to execute action in dangerous conditions and begin things against the odds. That, as it turns out, lends itself to great expansion, growth, start-up companies, and entrepreneurial endeavors, but it also lends itself to hurry-up sickness. We thrive and drink too deeply of the very chemicals our body needs in order to periodically replenish.

Is *Ambivert* Even a Word?

The Type A club isn't for extroverts only, by the way. Our membership is made up of introverts as well. That's because introverts (which I find myself evolving into as I age) have stressors that just happen to be more people- and crowd-oriented. Whether our stressors are people or not, driven personalities start, lead, pioneer, compete, challenge, and sign up for endeavors that are in "constant danger," as Shackleton put it.

Just as most people are some shade of Type A, most of us walking upright are not true extroverts or introverts—we're ambiverts. I know, it sounds like I just made up a word, like Napoleon Dynamite's liger,[6] but I didn't. That term is as cutting edge as 1927 when it appeared in a book written by a sociologist named Kimball Young. Ambiverts find themselves very comfortable around people *and* in solitude. They can be locked in a bad party full of strangers *and* alone in a cabin in the woods for a few days. It just depends on the day and the duration. Carl Jung famously said, "There is no such thing as a pure extrovert or a pure introvert. Such a man would be in the lunatic asylum.[7]

That might be news to you, especially if you've taken the Myers-Briggs Type Indicator or another personality test. Tests that assess personality are widely misinterpreted when they show extroverts as stronger than introverts in the realm of leadership. Chances are that you are *both*, and that is exactly why you're in leadership. In fact, most successful leaders in the world aren't purely extroverts as we once might have thought. The best leadership arises from introversion as much as it does from extroversion. So stressors may change shape for us, but we all have a bucket full of them.

Occupational Hazards

Before we go full nerd into the biochemistry of what happens when we burn out, I'd like to do a police sketch of our roles as leaders so we understand a bit more why burnout is so prevalent. The commonality in leaders who aren't resilient is striking. Maybe you can resonate with some of these similarities.

We empty ourselves. Leaders who invest in others empty their personal contents often and thoroughly. They do this for good and broken reasons and even to the detriment of their own health. There is nothing wrong with digging deeply for the one God has put before you, even when you are tired and overdrawn. Personally, I have truly enjoyed watching the Lord's strength in my weakness and his Spirit speak truth with love and wisdom where I had none to give. I think that is part of how we see God move through our calling. When leading poorly, however, we may over-invest because we need their approval, we need to be needed, we need to avoid other issues, and so on. But no matter the reason, we certainly know how to empty ourselves.

Emptying ourselves to provoke the flourishing of those around us was displayed well by Jesus. It's a Christ-shaped picture that shows the cross holding a better shepherd who spent himself for our benefit, even though it brought him death. We have this mark on us, but lowering ourselves and dying for the flourishing of others is not an ascetic call to break and abuse the faculties God has given us. We will, of course, have seasons where we are more empty and overtaxed, but burnout reveals leaders who never balanced their lives so they can lead for a lifetime. I can say this confidently because Jesus never burned out. He never fell to anxiety or hurry-up sickness. He didn't blow out his adrenal glands or lose his mind from years of neglecting rest. Jesus didn't take Ambien or think sleep was overrated. If Jesus invested and emptied beyond what we could and yet never ruined his health, then we may be doing things wrong when we do.

I remember the first time I heard the flight attendant tell us to put our own oxygen mask on before we helped the one next to us, even if it was a child. I remember thinking, *That's selfish and cowardly. A true leader would walk around holding their breath if need be in order to make sure everyone else is taken care of first.* Now, I see some validity in that directive. I can't help others if I'm sucking wind and turning blue. Too often, I have neglected my self-care to the detriment of others. I, like many leaders, have tried to operate with surgical accuracy on the lives of others when I am in deep need. That will lead to burnout if we don't navigate it well.

We are alone. Many years ago, when raising money for church planting, I sat with a tenured, solid pastor. I felt like things were positive until he quipped, "Luke, I remember my first church plant. I'd at times go out to the trainyard just to watch the trains go by." At that point, I was thinking, *Great! This guy is about to tell me how suicidal the whole thing got, and I didn't need that.* But he finished his story like this: "I just wanted to see something moving that I didn't have to push." It turns out that he was just joking, but the look on his face betrayed him. The only laughter was forced nervous laughter. It wouldn't be a joke if there wasn't at least a ribbon of truth to it.

Currently, our church operates with a pastoral plurality, which means I am not alone. The other pastors and I carry equal authority and weight, yet we defer to each other in key areas and have specific roles.[8] My role as the lead vision and teaching pastor is a vocational role, meaning the church pays my salary. Plurality is a big conviction for us, and we are resolute to build and plant more churches in that fashion. It's not my church—it belongs to Jesus. With all of that out front and said, although I am not alone, I *am* alone.

Because in America the guy who talks the most is the boss, I am seen as the senior pastor of our church. Most of our core people understand the nuances of our leadership model, but the culture-at-large does not. That means I catch a load of warfare the other pastors do not. The pastors around me understand most of the trials I go through, but not entirely. They can't totally understand them because they don't hold the same position. That aspect of leadership is a big reason many lead pastors tap out of their role. They simply are finished being alone. They feel like Elijah in 1 Kings 19, despairing of life and wishing they could just quit or die.

We can hide our pain. Because leaders can hide behind the fluidity of their schedules, many leaders are able to disguise their spiraling conditions. That may not be as easy for those who aren't in high leadership positions, but because of this overall freedom, it's easy to insulate their true selves from the views of others. That is why we are shocked when we hear about a leader fouling out of the ministry or committing suicide. We think to ourselves, *I never knew that guy struggled with that. I never saw that coming.* Wayne Cordeiro said, "I was able to mask it pretty well. Not many knew. I still preached well and even included enough humor to have a good stage presence. But there was a growing disconnect between who I was up front and who I was in private."[9]

One of the more liberating truths I learned as a young pastor is that I can be free to struggle as a leader in real time in front of others. In fact, countless people have told me they have found freedom because I have been vocal and vulnerable with my pain. God has not called us to lead because we are perfect. He called us because he called us, and his will is inscrutable. I often remind people, "I am not a pastor because I am better than you, I am leading because God has called and equipped me to do it." It won't drive people away; it draws them close. If the only time you admit failure in your life is in the past tense, something you used to struggle with years ago, then you are still wearing camouflage with a "compulsive desire to present a perfect image to the public so that everybody will admire us and nobody will know us."[10] Hiding out and disguising our needs and wrinkles is a quick way to get burned out.

We have busy minds. Our minds don't really clock out. I have had jobs that allowed me to clock in and clock out. But top leadership doesn't always allow us to do that. A. W. Tozer observed, "The heart's fierce effort to protect itself from every slight, to shield its touchy honor from the bad opinion of friend and enemy, will never let the mind have rest."[11] That sounds about right to me. Even when I'm home crushing my kids at *Mario Kart*, I'm thinking about that last phone call. I've clocked out, but not really. I'm eating with the family or trying to fix the garbage disposal, and yet I'm already working on the new budget and what I'm going to say to that troublemaker when I see him.

Busy minds struggle to find rest but not to find anxiety. As we repeatedly loop the same crises in our heads, we are trying to master our universe. It's a struggle to believe God is in control and that he is good. The more scenarios we roll over and the more outcomes we predict, the less we are satisfied resting in God's plan. We feel God is not paying enough attention to our struggle, so we grow toxic in how much attention we give to that struggle. A mind that cannot find rest from what only God can control is flirting with burnout.

We are disappointers. Armchair quarterbacks always throw straight. If you've been in leadership longer than 16 seconds, you already know that. You can hit it out of the park on Sunday, preach your finest sermon, baptize a ton of people, announce a new church plant—only to receive an e-mail later that night claiming nothing new is happening. I'll have more on why you're even checking your e-mail on Sunday night later, but you get the point. You can't make everyone happy. That should not shock us, as Jesus and Paul experienced the same thing. Both of them were found by the people in their circles to be, well, disappointing. Christ said it would most certainly happen to us as well.

We hunger for everyone to be joyful about what God is doing, recognizing the Spirit's work in their midst, yet many will be blind to everything but our failures. They see our failures in high definition. Disappointing others is part of a leader's normal routine, making burnout possible. Have you ever paid attention to how US presidents look before and after their presidential terms? The most drastic I can recall is Barack Obama. Entering his first term, he looked vibrant and ready, youthful and eager. As he left after his eighth year, he still had a smile and cordiality, but it seemed like all his hair had turned grey. I think he aged 20 years in those two terms. It's tough when you'll never make everyone happy and when every decision is ridiculed.

We have amnesia. I call it stress amnesia. We get to a place where in total futility we throw our arms up and say, *Something must change. This needs drastic remedy and help!* But after a while, things settle down, and so does the urgency of the remedy. In times of peace, we rarely think about and apply battle strategies, but in times of war, we find ourselves regretting that we didn't have things properly in place. Stress amnesia is why many couples, during intense moments of fighting, promise they'll go to counseling with their spouses, but after a week or so of peace, outside help is just a memory.

We quickly forget what the pain tastes like once it's gone. When the pain returns, we almost hate ourselves for once again hitting the same potholes. In response, we quickly point to the great things happening around us, convincing ourselves that everything is not so bad after all. After a long time of ignoring weaknesses, we approach burnout. It's inevitable.

We have Sunday. Unless you play for the NFL, where else does someone invest so much output in a single day? So many leaders put incredible attention on a small block of Sunday, spending double-digit hours on sermon development, volunteer management, and a host of other things that must happen. I for one don't believe the Sunday gathering is the most important part of a church family, but I'd be dishonest to say that Sunday doesn't kick my butt. Come Sunday night, I'm wiped out, and the tree is thoroughly bent. It's rare to come across a leader with high Sunday output who also has a well-guarded resilience protocol. It shouldn't be Wednesday afternoon before you feel human again. That's insufficient and unnecessary.

A common adage I've heard too many times is that preaching one sermon levies the same emotional tax as running a marathon. I've done a bunch of both and can attest that preaching requires much more. Many pastors float into the Sunday gathering unprepared because they didn't handle Saturday well, only to drain themselves on Sunday. After Sunday, there is no real game plan to rest and reset. That is why so many self-medicate in areas that only compound the problem. Forty to 50 weeks of doing that will quickly lead to burnout—and poor preaching.

We're young and reckless. In other words, we sacrifice immediate common sense for the greater good. Ron Sellers, president of Ellison Research, found this in his work.

> The youngest ministers are the heaviest, the most likely to skip meals, the most likely to eat unhealthy foods, the least likely to get exercise, the most likely to go without sufficient sleep, the least likely to take vitamins, the most likely to eat fast food, and the most likely to report problems sleeping. It might be argued that these are eager young ministers out

trying to change the world, or at least to build their careers. But it's tragic that they apparently are sacrificing their own health for these purposes.[12]

When younger, I threw most caution to the wind and burned the candle as fast as possible, believing I was indestructible for Jesus and that he "had my six."[13] I was young and idealistic, but as much as I've grown, my wiring as a leader still has me looking through idealistic and, many times, reckless glasses. It's deep in us as leaders, and if left unchecked, it will lead to burnout.

We are switch hitters. Our calling to care for and make disciples has us transitioning quickly between settings requiring various emotions. We leave weddings to officiate at funerals. We leave a church discipline issue to handle a new believer's refreshing excitement to evangelize. Hospitals, lunches, staff meetings—the settings are endless. One minute we're in an extroverted setting, and then we shift gears and enter a time of solitude.

Burnout, as we'll see, occurs when we overtax hormones and chemicals, which can happen rapidly when we change settings and moments so drastically. The constant ups and downs that are implicit in our role nudge us ever closer to burnout. Being cognizant of which moments tax us more than others is a step in the right direction. Even better is sticking to a routine that is preemptive in spacing out those overly taxing moments.

We are starters. Many leaders are better daddies than fathers. What I mean is that we are better at beginning things than we are at nurturing them. One thing I continually notice in leadership is that the more things I start, the more I have to manage later. Cordeiro wisely said, "I drove hard on all cylinders, not realizing that being an entrepreneur means that everything you initiate, by default you must add to your maintenance list."[14]

I also find that we have just enough skills to pick a fight we don't know how to finish. For example, many pastors can gain traction to get their church to a certain size, only to run out of skills to lead well when it gets bigger. My first church and campus ministry plants grew from zero to no more than 200 before I left to pioneer or help with another one, so the depth of my experience falls within that size. Once my current church hit that number, I realized I needed to be a better so-called father and nurture the work with an expanded skill set. Burnout can advance in our lives when we are frustrated that we can't manage what we've started or delegate others to manage it for us. Elliot Grudem, an expert in leadership resilience who started the Leaders Collective, uses a helpful metaphor. "It takes a warrior," he said, "to start and grow something in a harsh, uphill setting, but it takes a king to govern and administrate it well." I find that it's hard for me, as well as many others, to put down the sword and pick up a scepter.

We're emotionally stupid. What I mean is that our EQ/EI—emotional quotient/emotional intelligence—is low.[15] You may not have even heard of an EQ, but you've got one, and it may be in the cellar. Many leadership gurus believe EQ is more important in dynamic leadership than IQ. Your EQ is driven by your awareness of your own emotions and your ability to manage them well. These first two chapters are, in fact, a dive into how accurately you can assess yourself, how you respond to crisis and stress, and how healthy your overall leadership is. Knowing *how* you tick will help you mitigate the effects of stress as you understand *why* you feel the way you do. A high EQ allows an honesty that combats the frustration we can feel inside when we respond to particular stresses. Brennan Manning, in his book *Abba's Child*, wrote, "Whether positive or negative, feelings put us in touch with our true selves. They are neither good nor bad; they are simply the truth of what is going on within us. What we do with them determines whether we live lives of honesty or deceit."[16]

For example, it was years before I understood why it hit me so hard when families left our church. I know that it hits all leaders, but it incapacitated me. I'd stew on it for months. I'd internalize it and replay it when most of the other leaders around me had moved on. My EQ was low, and my leadership was drained because of this. Now, I'm a bit faster to recognize this, and it allows me to contend much better. It's imperative that you not only react properly to crises and the stress of the up tempo calling you, but you must also be able to decode *why* you struggle in certain areas. That will reveal how you view and enjoy God.

By no means is this list complete, but I think you get the point. Many of the things that make us great leaders can also bend us toward burnout.

Athletic Overtraining

To help you understand even more how your body reacts to your leadership, let's pull a page from the playbook of advanced sports science. Many of the biomarkers and biochemical reactions that can be measured in professional athletes have a similar analog to leaders. Medically and scientifically, our burnout looks an awful lot like an athlete who has drastically overtrained. The two phenomena aren't identical matches, but they're close enough for us to gain immense insight. Science has, in fact, already shown that stress response is higher for the organizational leader, the pastor, or the entrepreneurial leader than for the professional athlete, so the comparison can be helpful. Millions and maybe even billions of dollars have been spent in the science of athletic performance, and we can borrow chunks of it where it pertains to how our bodies respond to over-taxation.

Some have said that if you visit Olympic Village where the athletes live and party during the Olympics, you will smell cough drops and VapoRub. That's because in order to peak or get ready for the most important moment of their lives, the athletes have had to dance on the razor's edge of overtraining. Often, they are unable to gauge their overall feel and fitness, so they end up sick. It still amazes me that many of the world records that are set are, in fact, set by those with sniffles and fevers. They have jeopardized the basic principles of training to be at their best form at the right time. They have overtrained, and their immune systems are shot as they reach too far. Leaders and top entrepreneurs suffer from the same thing, which is why many of them get sick on their first or second day of vacation. They have overreached and worked berserko hours in order to get out of town, and now it's all humidifiers and tissues.

Not only do our immune systems mimic those of an advanced athlete, but so do our nervous and endocrine systems. We'll look at that in the next chapter. What I want you to see is that as we understand what happens to athletes when they push too hard, so it is with us—only much worse. As taxing as physical overload is to our bodies, emotional or mental stress affects us even more. That is counterintuitive due to how tired we are after the gym or a 5K run, but a physically demanding load is easier on us than an emotional one.

To illustrate that point, Dr. Swenson shares a study he found in which researchers placed a poor soul on a treadmill for a cardiac exam. Despite the pace, the patient's cardiovascular readings were stable. That changed, however, when they asked him to subtract seven from 777 serially for about four minutes. So running on a treadmill is pretty miserable, but not as miserable as doing subtraction while running in place. The findings were pretty telling; his blood pressure rose 40 points. Dr. Swenson accurately interprets the test for you and for me by noticing this: "Biochemical stress parameters are more affected by psychological stressors than by physical stressors.... Chronic uncertainty, sustained levels of increased vigilance, or struggling with a mental task are more stressful than chopping wood."[17]

Essentially, you can be a professional mover, or apparently a wood chopper, and have less stress damage to your body than someone starting up a business from behind a desk. If your sedentary role includes routines where you feel out of control, damage is being done to your body, even if you don't necessarily feel it. To illustrate this, Tim Chester and Kevin DeYoung mention the same study, revealing that commuters experience a greater stress response than riot police and those who fly fighter jets.[18] That's because fighter pilots and riot police at least *feel* as if they can gain control of the situation or that they have a fighting chance. If you don't have control, or even a semblance of control, then even sitting can destroy you. Sitting can degrade your body more than running if you are sitting under an emotional load. You have probably experienced this. Haven't you accomplished some Marlboro man moment like roping cattle, building a fence, or fixing a roof, only to be tired but not burned out? And haven't you made it to the south side of a staff meeting feeling like a puddle on the floor?

My great uncle, Walter Tucker, was a brave Army chaplain who served multiple tours in Vietnam. After that intense ministry experience, he wrote about his leadership among the soldiers on the battlefront. I find his words to be helpful now.

> In my lifetime I have dug ditches, picked and chopped cotton daylight to dark, swung a pick and splitting wedge for hours at a time, wept with friends in hospital rooms and conducted hundreds of funeral services. But taking the most distressing of news to family members, especially during wartime, made all the other physical and emotional experiences appear calm by comparison.[19]

I think there is wisdom in this. Our role is bloated with the kind of work that is mistaken as easy or calm because we aren't covered in sweat. Nothing can be further from the truth. You are perfect for burnout.

For the last few years, I have devotedly measured my heart rate variability (HRV), which is nerd code for the variation in time between heart beats. It doesn't simply measure the rate but also the variation within the rate using a complicated algorithm. It analyzes the overall health of the autonomic nervous system, something athletes use to know how hard they can push before crashing their systems. It essentially measures how healthy my fight-or-flight system and my rest-and-digest system are and how well they're playing together. I have a version of this technology that appraises me every morning and gives me a simple number that lets me see where I'm at. It shows me how tapped out my nervous system is so I don't continue to tax it unnecessarily. I'm not a professional athlete that uses this to arrange my training, but I do use it as a gauge on my dashboard to arrange (or rearrange) my calendar for that day or week. What I have learned is that I get the most troublesome readings (telling me to cease and desist) not after hard workout days but after (1) a huge meeting that didn't go well, (2) Sundays that were difficult, or (3) arguments or rough patches with my wife. I get the worst readings when I have never broken a sweat.

Recently, I was able to visualize this graphically, and the results anecdotally back the research I'm purporting. Interestingly, in 2016 when I completed an Ironman triathlon[20] in just over 12 hours, I only received a take-it-easy reading the next day. But when I had to manage a church discipline matter that went sideways a couple months later, I got a stop-immediately-and-find-a-hammock warning the next day.[21] My body was telling me to slow down and find a way out of fight-or-flight mode so I could reset.

Even though I'm using high technology to paint a picture, this physiology isn't new. Roland H. Bainton in his masterful biography of Martin Luther wrote:

> "Panic invaded his spirit. The conscience became so disquieted as to start and tremble at the stirring of a wind-blown leaf. The horror of nightmare gripped the soul, the dread of one waking in the dusk to look into the eyes of him who has come to take his life. The heavenly champions all withdrew; the fiend beckoned with leering summons to the impotent soul. These were the torments which Luther repeatedly testified were far worse than any physical ailment that he had ever endured.[22]

As you can see, I'm building a case. If leaders in the church respond similarly to athletes under strain and are tempted to overreach, then we should borrow from their time-tested protocols. There aren't millions of dollars being spent on research for leadership health in the ministry, but there is on athletic recovery and health. I believe we can look over their shoulders and couple it with what God has already told us. That is what I am attempting to unpack in the chapters ahead, but first I'd like to look at what you're doing to your body so you can see the size of the hole you may be digging.

SHE-BEARS
WHAT ON EARTH IS HAPPENING TO ME?

When you live on monster island, someone's
breathing fire every day.
—Mark Wetmore, legendary running coach

I live in a postcard at the foot of the Great Smoky Mountains National Park, which is awesome if you are an outdoorsy person. My hammock and trail-running shoes are pretty much always accessible in the truck. A few weeks ago, while relaxing with my feet in a noisy stream, I saw a half a dozen deer to my right and a group of wild turkeys to my left. I fully expected to see a unicorn in that moment because it's as close to paradise as I've ever been. I am incredibly thankful to God for bringing me to a place like this, especially since I am a runner. Most runners are stuck running on man-made trails of concrete built for strollers and rollerbladers that didn't get the memo, but when you have a mountain range in your backyard, you can run for hundreds of miles and barely see anyone.

Once I was running alongside my son on a remote trail called Jake's Gap. I don't know who Jake was, but I'm thankful for his trail. My teenage son was trying to keep me behind him, and my vanity was trying hard to be within trash-talking range. In trail running, you have to keep your eyes looking ahead *and* at the ground in front of you. One misplaced step and you can be eating dirt faster than you can blink.

You'll also be laughed at by your teenage son. It requires more focus and nimble feet than road running, and I have scar tissue to prove it.

Rounding a blind corner, I saw something that made my blood run cold—an enormous female bear. I grabbed my son who didn't see the bear, and we both stopped mid-stride to see the animal turn and face us head-on from 10 to 15 feet away. We were so busy looking down at roots and rocks that we neglected to see the she-bear and nearly ran into her. Being downwind and quiet, we had startled her, and she felt a bit threatened. She lowered her head, struck the ground with her paw, and made a guttural sound I'd like to forget. Of all the wild bears I have seen, I have never seen a bear of this size. I'm pretty sure I cussed.

As we did all the things the magazine articles tell you to do and backed away, I silently worked on my awards speech for the parent-of-the-year award for dragging my teenage son out in the middle of nowhere and into a grumpy bear. It took a while before she stopped following us and moved off the trail. Although she threatened a charge, she never attacked. God was very sweet to us that day, and it will be a story we'll always share. Now when I run Jake's Gap, I either tie a small bell to my leg or clap every few feet, looking like a tourist. Because no matter what *National Geographic* says about black bears, I think the she-bear would win a bar fight.

I tell that story in order to build an illustration for what happens to your body when you encounter an event with significant load to it. You have your own version of the she-bear—that *thing* you didn't anticipate, ambushing you from that *angle* you didn't even see, which happened to be on that *day* you never expected. Or maybe you did expect it, but you were so worn out and tired from the previous day that it felt like your walls were too short and stumpy to protect you. Maybe you can relate when I say that what was a two on my Richter scale last month is now a nine because it's Monday after a titanic Sunday and I stayed up too late watching Jack Bauer[1] hit people on Netflix. Maybe it's more gradual and not so sudden. Maybe you have an overwhelming dread that follows you step-by-step no matter where you go. Unable to do anything without seeing the bear, you are constantly at a level of emergency response.

Whatever the situation, you are looking at a she-bear, and although you don't know what to do, your body knows exactly what to do. It's the brilliance and thoughtfulness of God. As a radiant architect, God engineered our biochemistry to cope and engage danger as well as excitement and anticipation. Let me explain using the same she-bear example.

Stress's Flavors

God created you to react in emergency situations in a different gear than what you use for normal living. Stressors don't have to be nefarious but can actually be good things that bring elation. In fact, as leaders, we can be a bit addicted to the process of reacting to stressors to achieve success. There are two bodily responses to pressure in our world. One is eustress (eu = good), and its evil brother—for our purposes, anyway—is distress.

Distress is exactly what it sounds like. For me, on that crazy day on Jake's Gap, I was distressed to see the freaked-out bear. That is what most of us actually mean when we say, *I'm so stressed out right now.* Distress is what we experience when a family leaves the church in a not-awesome way, when your guest preacher is a no-show (or shows up but was so bad you wish he had been a no-show), or when you find out the budget has been swerving off course. Although distress can move us to executive and decisive action, no one really enjoys this type of stress, and when it stacks up cumulatively, it turns into hyper stress. Hans Selye, a Hungarian endocrinologist, taught, "It's not stress that kills us; it is our reaction to it."[2] That is particularly true with built-up hyper stress that snowballs.

Eustress, however, is a bit different. It energizes and psyches us up for a good challenge, or a roller coaster. Dr. Richard Swenson said, "This is what employers consciously induce in a work environment to make employees productive—a kind of creative tension. Some people love this feeling, thrive on it, and almost become addicted to it."[3]

Eustress carries feelings of hope, optimism, vigor, excitement, creativity, and meaning, whereas distress is associated with despair, anxiety, confusion, depression, and pessimism. Eustress is our body perceiving a challenge and feeling that we aren't too far from achieving it. Distress is pretty much the opposite. Sometimes, like in skydiving or public speaking, the same stressor brings both responses. In either case, the complex human body is ready for action. God in his kindness has chemically and biologically stacked us so we can respond efficiently to whatever stressor comes our way.

It's What's for Dinner

Here is a very important fact to know regarding these two stress reactions. Your body's internal chemistry cannot discern the difference between good stressors and bad ones. It simply reacts the same. In either distress or eustress, our body's cogs and gears set themselves in motion so we can meet the load of the stress head on in order to survive. It is commonly referred to as the fight-or-flight reaction. It's not by accident that we feel differently when we become alert due to various stressors. In fact, the stressors we feel around us aren't all that bad—they move us to action. We simply wouldn't get very much done without external stressors, especially if we're in leadership.

I've heard about making lifestyle changes that include cleansing *all* stressors from our life in an attempt to be happier. Although I agree that much of our stress is unnecessary, it's nevertheless a part of leadership. You cannot design a life where you have zero stressors as a leader. You'd have to remove yourself from people, which is antithetical to leadership of any kind. If you are called to be a disciple that makes disciples, you've applied for more stress.

Statistically, 75 percent of pastors report they've had a significant stress-related crisis at least once in their ministry.[4] Half of pastors polled say they've experienced depression or burnout to the extent that they needed to take a leave of absence from ministry.[5] I know, statistics are never really perfect and are more than likely a bit skewed, but if these numbers are skewed, I'd contend they are low. We look at our stress as insignificant, and when those around us keep asking if we're alright, we underrepresent the load we're carrying. We feel miles away from quitting, yet better leaders are doing it every day. Why?

As leaders, especially in the church, our entire calling is a frequent exchange between distress and eustress. As we saw in the last chapter, being switch hitters presses us into days or weeks when we rush from great news to rough news and back to great news. Financial giving at the church has increased, but so has trolling on social media. Attendance has increased, but so has the mess that comes with the extra kiddos. More money. More problems. Good news, bad news. Funerals, weddings. She-bears coming, she-bears going. We experience distress and eustress so much that our body is always cranking, trying to overcome the challenges.

Burnout occurs when we abuse this biological mechanism. We take our creator's architecture that allows us to achieve, build, win, react, respond, and survive, and we slowly destroy it. Think of slowly bleeding our ability to respond rather than abruptly snapping it in half. It's a slow destruction that might take several years to get you to the place of burnout. My journey lasted 15 years, complete with periodic meltdowns, a couple panic attacks, and many long bouts of semi-depression before I truly hit rock bottom. Again, the damage is cumulative and bankable.

That shouldn't shock us since we tend to break many of God's gifts. We are like the kid that jams the batteries into a toy upside down. God gives us gifts, and we break them. He made us a gospel community, and we break it with envy and division. God gives us marriage, and we break it with infidelity and unforgiveness. Spiritual gifts in the church have a legion of abuses. Ultimately, God came as a gift to humankind as our redeeming king, and we abused and broke his body on the cross. As people, we are bad at giving gifts and even worse at receiving and honoring them. Abusing our callings, churches, and bodies is no different. Burning out in leadership is nothing more than our broken bodies telling us, *I cannot go further under these terms because I wasn't created for this. You have abused and broken me.*

Under the Hood

I want you to put yourself in my trail shoes, staring at the 400-pound black bear. See her teeth? Hear your firstborn's fast breathing? Doing the math on how far you are from another human? Looking for big rocks to chuck at the animal? If that is not helpful, imagine sitting there as you hear the news that someone is stealing money from your already thin budget—someone you trusted. Place yourself in the staff meeting where someone confesses to immorality after years of deceitful silence. How about the few minutes before you go out to preach or lead a tough meeting? The moments before a hard confrontation. Does it hit home now?

We all have she-bears. As we move forward, I want you to keep your personal she-bears in mind. Write them in the margin. Be honest. I'd like to show you what's happening under the hood when you have them in mind.

Stage 1: The Alarm Reaction

Once you see the threat, your brain sends your body into a state of alert or what can be called the alarm reaction.[6] That is totally normal and, as we have seen, part of God's brilliance. A cascade of activity, beginning with what you see, leads your brain to churn out hormones, neurotransmitters, and catecholamines that travel incredibly fast from the brain, landing at your adrenal glands. These vital glands produce a few dozen chemicals affecting virtually every part of your body, but in stress response, the kingpin chemicals are adrenaline, noradrenaline,[7] and cortisol.

It all begins with what we perceive. Chris McDougall, a journalist informed in human physiology, explains that when you perceive a threat or danger, your brain does this:

> [It] accesses your long-term memory, scanning whether anything you've done in the past resembles something you're about to attempt in the present. If it hits a match, you're good to go: your muscles will relax, your heart rate will stabilize, your doubts will vanish. But if the amygdala finds no evidence that you've ever, say, climbed down a tall tree, it will lobby your nervous system to shut down the operation."[8]

Then our brain (hypothalamus) communicates with two tiny adrenal glands that are smaller than a golf ball, weigh less than a grape, and sit on top of both your kidneys.[9]

Insignificant in size, they are significantly central in how we fight or flee our way through situations like a she-bear or a traffic accident. It's when we break those glands that our train starts going off the tracks. Health experts refer to the gradual degradation of these glands as adrenal fatigue.[10]

Adrenal fatigue syndrome is when the she-bear won't quit following us. The slide toward sickness is slow and seemingly imperceptible, but when our fire alarm is always pulled, we will eventually get sick.

At Stage 1, there is no deep damage as long as recovery follows soon after the stress response. In my example of the she-bear, my son and I were later able to sit in a stream, soak our feet, and relax. We didn't have to evade more bears or continue running for our lives. For athletes, that would resemble a hard workout followed by a decent level of light work the next day (recovery). Athletic training is virtually stressing out your body because the same chemicals are answering the stressor of physical resistance. As long as an athlete's recovery comes soon after the workout, the body compensates and responds with health, resilience, and growth. Technology is even now at a place where it can prescribe the amount of time before significant stress load can be reapplied. It is no longer anecdotal or by feel.[11]

One of the more at-risk chemicals during prolonged hurry-up sickness is cortisol. It's what I call the executive chemical whose primary function is to help the body dump sugar (glucose) into the bloodstream where it's most needed. It's helpful when you are evading a bear and about to run and climb the nearest tree that is bigger than a sapling.[12] Your body is going to need copious amounts of ATP[13] for the muscles to work, and for that it will need sugar. Cortisol also triggers the body to store fat (in the stomach for men) because it needs a more readily available source of energy, and glucose is more plug-and-play than fat. It's the difference between trying to burn a big fat log or a bunch of oily rags when you need heat quickly. See how brilliant God is? He's giving us fuel to immediately survive. God designed our bodies to store the fuel that is less helpful in a pinch while spending the fuel that helps us the most.

God also knew we wouldn't need our immune system taking up so much bandwidth, so cortisol disables our immune system. Avoiding the sniffles is secondary to basic survival. Pausing immune response frees up even more available energy in order for us to escape or fight it out. Then our blood pressure increases, accompanied by a rise in heart rate. Simply put, our engine is revved up and ready to move quickly with heavy bursts of strength or any other executive action.

In researching for this book, I took a month to measure my blood sugar levels and heart rate before, during, and after a 40-minute sermon. I found that my heart rate rose from a resting heart rate of less than 48 beats per minute to 100 beats during the entire sermon. My body's blood sugar and blood pressure also rose. Even with 20 years of experience in an arena where I felt calm, I found myself in an alarm reaction state. Other public speakers outside of ministry have commented on the same phenomenon. You can see why leading multiple services or meetings and being in the trenches all day on Sunday without a reciprocating rest is not such a brilliant idea. You must accommodate for the load.

The adrenal glands also release adrenaline and noradrenaline, which also have a set of functions to prepare you to engage the bear. Here's what happens with a surge in adrenaline:

- The blood vessels serving your muscles dilate so you can execute that vertical jump you always brag about in order to get away from the bear.
- Your pupils dilate so you can see better. You also go straight to tunnel vision, choking out distractions in the peripheral areas of our view.
- Your body shuts down its ability to make tears because it's a really dumb time to cry, and you need sharp vision.
- Your digestive system stops because you need the blood supply elsewhere. That is why you feel sick to your stomach after the stressful situation has passed.
- You sweat like you're in a Finnish sauna. Some physiologists say that is so you can slip out of someone's grip. I'm not sure I'm buying that, but I will agree that in times of deep stress, I notice the sweat.

- Your hands and feet get cold and clammy as your body shunts the blood supply to the core of your body, serving the primary visceral organs. By the way, that is why mood rings work.

- Your neck and upper back tense up so you can be ready for physical maneuvering in times of danger. We hold tension in key areas during an emergency, which can yield tension headaches.

- Your nails and hair stop growing because it's much more important to survive than have a Tom Brady hair day. Losing your hair in stressful seasons can be partially attributed to this phenomenon.

- Your hands and jaw clench, allegedly so you can absorb blows and grip what is around you—like a club or a stapler, I guess. Again, that is why some people get tension headaches. Clenching your jaw all day long will do that.

- Your brain refuses to think in creative ways, relegated to caveman grunt-level thinking to defeat the danger. No poems or song lyrics during this time. No good sermon prep, either. This innovation assists in survival, not in creating or nurturing ideas.

- Another key chemical worth mentioning is serotonin. It's a neurotransmitter generated in your gut but used all over your body and suppressed in times of high alert. Serotonin has many functions but is key to making you feel happy, proud, satisfied, and relaxed. Serotonin also helps regulate your sleep and maintain your body temperature. It helps you dig deeply into your memory and have a functional appetite, which might be low on your priority list when you are on high alert. You can probably tell that low serotonin doesn't eliminate your ability to be either the bear whisperer or the bear destroyer, but over an extended amount of time, serotonin depletion can get you in a big jam.

When the stressor disappears, your body begins its rebound to return to normal. This interplay between danger and rest is regulated by the body's autonomic nervous system, which has two functions that work together to make sure you respond appropriately. One function, the sympathetic nervous system, aids in fight or flight and helps the progression we just read about. But when the danger subsides, the body employs the parasympathetic nervous system (easy to remember because parachutes bring us back to the ground safely), and the nonessential bodily activities return to normal. That is the rest-and-digest phase of nervous system activity.

Interestingly, you can only have an orgasm or erection in rest-and-digest state, which might help some of you who struggle in sexual intimacy. It's hard to be romantic or even have bedroom eyes when you feel like mortars are going off all around you.

Do you get the picture? Adrenaline, serotonin, cortisol, and more than a dozen other important chemicals do a thousand things in order to streamline your body to react and survive. What is not extremely necessary—your hair and nails growing, digestion, and even immune response—get paused while the things you need—fuel and blood—get shunted quickly to where they're needed. It's fascinatingly intentional and highly engineered. I've heard many scholars describe these systems as having evolved over millennia, but just a cursory glance at it has the mark and signature of how thoughtful God was to build us this way. Scientists are still discovering what some of these chemicals are able to do, yet God knew when he breathed Adam into existence. You are truly fearfully and wonderfully made.

Stage 2: Resistance Response

In my story, the bear only stood there about 15 minutes and then left, but let's say that your she-bear doesn't leave so fast. In fact, most of the stressors I encounter as a leader aren't brief or transient at all. According to health and wellness expert Ben Greenfield, in Stage 2, "stress levels are chronic and constant, and high levels of adrenal hormones have been sustained for weeks, months, and sometimes years. You can still exercise and go about your normal life, but a sense of fatigue (especially at the end of the day) is common."[14]

Greenfield also notes that this happens to be the stage when most folks agree to see a doctor, likely to walk out the door with a prescription for depression medicine. I don't think people are truly convinced they are seriously sick in Stage 2, but they will tolerate a prescription in the name of due diligence. In this stage, remedies are never extreme because the symptoms aren't either. It's in this stage that we refuse to step back and analyze how we're trending.

This stage is also where we start making excuses and false promises. It's where we admit we're not running at full steam but are convinced that small fixes will bring us back to true form. We promise ourselves naps and rest. We threaten to ditch coffee. We might renew our gym membership and get an accountability partner or start being honest with the one we already have. In this stage, our newfound muffin top[15] is blamed on age, and our college sweatpants are fitting a bit snug. Our sleep—mostly our attempt to fall asleep—is starting to feel the wear and tear of the job. We do well until the lunch fade hits between 2:00 p.m. and 3:00 p.m., and then we turn into a foggy-minded donkey. We have 40 percent of our brain capacity yet we are 100 percent jerk.

For those who have already come out of burnout, this stage seems to be the mark or target, like a ground zero of sorts. That's because during most of our lives lived as leaders, we are predominantly rattling around in this stage. It is not healthy, however, and is a stage of adrenal and nervous system dysfunction. We can't always live at DEFCON 3. Stage 2 is not the win we're looking for.

Stage 3: Exhaustion

I'm convinced that Stage 3 is where this book finds many of you. At this stage, we know our small hacks and tweaks aren't producing answers. We're losing hope. At this stage, others outside our household are noticing our bad form and using words like *vacation* and *sabbatical*, but we still think we can right the ship if we just double down on green juice and try harder. Greenfield notes:

> At this point, your body's ability to cope with stress has been depleted. Your adrenal glands are simply unable to produce enough cortisol in response to stress, and because cortisol is necessary for a base level of alertness and awakeness and for your liver to church out sugar-based energy, you begin to suffer from constant exhaustion.[16]

Depleted. That sounds like an awesome place to be. Another perk for those in Stage 3 is that low blood sugar makes you more sensitive to—you guessed it—*stress*. It's like a dog biting its own tail. You become edgy to those around you, regardless of the time of day, and a consistent emotional mess. Every problem is the end of the world. Every difficult personality becomes an enemy. By this stage, you know where all the good hiding spots are to avoid people. You hunger for isolation. You no longer tolerate people; you now officially loathe them. Your sleep is a joke, so you stay up and watch *Golden Girls* or *Transformers* or whatever else requires no brain activity.

In the mornings, you may start the day off in a serviceable place, but by the time 2:00 p.m. comes around, you are winded and just drool on yourself. In fact, the only way you're able to get through a basic day is by hitting Starbucks, and hitting it hard. You also linger too long in front of Panera's bakery case. You are virtually a hunter-gatherer when it comes to pastries, sweet tea, soda, energy drinks, and starchy or carb-rich foods. Especially helpful are the energy drinks in the silvery cans that look like they might be healthy if you squint your eyes when looking at the labels.

You are pursuing starchy and sweet foods because you are looking to get sugar in your blood since cortisol clocked out long ago. In other words, since your body cannot produce free glucose from the stored glycogen due to diminished cortisol, you have to take sugar in exogenously (from the outside). Now you're racking up injuries and inflammations. Fungus, mold, athlete's foot, white tongue, jock itch, gas, indigestion, and other maladies are a new normal for you.

At this stage, the excuses aren't even convincing you, and the promises have stopped because you don't really know what to do except maybe eat more salad and try the latest diet fad roaming around Facebook. You even bought a new CrossFit membership but then pulled a hammy on day two, so now you're limping. You are breaking your system thoroughly by this point. The hurry-up offense has claimed another victim. Get the stretcher out.

Stage 4: Failure

Stage 4 is where I was in 2011. Always the overachiever, I actually made it all the way to Stage 4. Ben Greenfield wrote, "At this point there is a total failure of your adrenal glands to respond to stress—and even trace amounts of cortisol begin to disappear. . . . You basically just want to stay in bed all day."[17] At this stage, we're not just breaking things; we're picking up the broken pieces and shaking them, trying to get one more day out of them. It even feels pathetic.

It's here that going to see a professional is a no-brainer, and even with your flashes of skill and gifting, you're unable to carry out the role you were called and gifted to do. Taking ibuprofen for the pulled hammy and the headaches, Ambien for the sleep issue, Zantac for the reflux, and Zoloft for the depression won't remove your stressors and return you to your baseline proficiency. They may serve you in individual areas, but they never get to the root cause. At Stage 4 of adrenal degradation, a pill in the bottle simply won't cure you. It might give relief in one area for a while, but it can't bring you back to normal—if you remember what normal was.[18]

On a happier note, God displayed his love toward me in allowing me to see the dark side of Stage 4. Had I not, I would have never desired true and lasting change. I would have never looked at the root cause and sin behind the sin that prompted a life of abusing my body. I would have never seen stressors in the context of a great and sovereignly kind God. I would have never repented, worshipped, and processed my motives well. I would have never changed my diet and patterns with furious intention and resolve.

Listen, if you are anywhere close to where I was, God is surely displaying his goodness and greatness to you as well. Leaders are stubborn people. We don't see our finitude. We don't honor the fences around us or rest in our limitations. God loves us too much to let us misrepresent him in this fashion and destroy our lives in the process. If you are in this stage, you are in the worst of places and best of places at the same time.

Basic Stress versus Total Burnout

Total burnout is not the same as basic anxiety. Burnout is accompanied by feeling buckets and buckets of stress. As we saw earlier, being a leader is a one-way ticket to stress no matter how compliant and ironed out all the people and details are. The best way I can describe the relationship is that stress is our body's way of grabbing a problem so tightly that our knuckles turn white, whereas burnout is just letting go altogether out of despair. "As burnout sets in, each dream and relationship that once promised life seems to be an emotional net loss even as it is fulfilled," said counselor Brad Hambrick. "Each accomplishment begins to feel like a mirage in the desert."[19] In basic stress for leaders, there is an anxious fight and urgency, whereas in total burnout, there is a weak little white flag signaling, *I quit*. Dr. Archibald Hart of the Hart Institute comments wisely on this relationship in a comparison list he built to distinguish between burnout and stress:

- Burnout is a defense characterized by disengagement.
- Stress is characterized by over-engagement.
- In burnout, emotions become blunted.
- In stress, emotions become over-reactive.
- In burnout, emotional damage is primary.
- In stress, physical damage is primary.
- The exhaustion of burnout affects motivation and drive.
- The exhaustion of stress affects physical energy.
- Burnout produces demoralization.
- Stress produces disintegration.
- Burnout can best be understood as a loss of ideals and hope.
- Stress can best be understood as a loss of fuel and energy.
- The depression of burnout is caused by the grief engendered by the loss of ideals and hope.
- The depression of stress is produced by the body's need to protect itself and conserve energy.
- Burnout produces a sense of helplessness and hopelessness.
- Stress produces a sense of urgency and hyperactivity.[20]

Dr. Hart is describing the differences between Stage 1 and Stage 4. We truly need help in diagnosing the difference between a hard season of anxiety and stress and encroaching burnout. To be honest, I'm not sure we as individual leaders are the best self-appraisers. I think we need outside help for this. Wives, other leaders, even close family members have a better perspective on how much we change between the stages. Best for this role is someone who will be honest and has nothing to gain or lose by how you answer their questions. The best confidant is the one who allows no possible kickbacks.

It's a slow fade. I would have never admitted I was burned out until it was too late, and even then my pride disallowed me from admitting the weakness. Just a week or two before being incapacitated, I was training for a big race, eating what I thought was healthy, preaching hard, planting hard, and throwing the kids around the yard. I would have laughed at the thought of weeping in my bed until noon just a week later.

However, my wife wouldn't have. She could see the rocky coastline I kept flirting with. The pastors around me were prompting me to rest more and work less. *Delegation* and *sabbath* were words they used often. I was surrounded by people who could see the advancing stages of hurry-up sickness, but I was too proud to listen. It's only basic stress until it's burnout—and you aren't always qualified to make that call. Ask your wife about your temper, your fogginess, your new double-decker love handles, your snoring, your escapism, your sex life. Ask your peers and your kids about your schedule and your insecurity and lack of humility. Friend, there is stress, and then there is approaching burnout.

Hijacked and Hacked

Before you take your propeller hat off, I'd like to address one more key bit of biochemistry. Your body's chemistry has a unique built-in feature for when we are in the later stages of adrenal failure and hurry-up sickness. It will substitute chemicals according to our immediate need. In other words, it will rob Peter to pay Paul.

In the early stages of alert and stress, we still have a decent amount of endorphins. They disappear, however, as degradation marches on. Endorphins are a class of chemicals that bring comfort rather than pain when we are in a painful situation. Have you ever heard of runner's high? It's a real thing because of endorphins. When you belly laugh super hard, endorphins fire off to mask the pain of your rectus abdominus convulsing, which is why you say, "Stop! It hurts to laugh." With endorphins, dopamine, serotonin, and other chemicals diminishing due to overuse, all we have is adrenaline to feast on. Our body then goes about over-producing adrenaline.

We also lose proper production of DHEA (dehydroepiandrosterone) and our sex hormones estrogen and testosterone.[21] Your body uses cholesterol to make a hormone called pregnenolone (*pregna* meaning *mother*), which is basically the mother of a ton of important chemicals. DHEA is one of them, and progesterone is another. Progesterone is what we need to build our sex hormones. All of it is virtually hijacked when we are in pervasive high alert. In high alert moments, the body stops DHEA and progesterone production and sends them to build cortisol to help defeat the danger. Our body hacks itself in order to defend itself. We simply become addicted to our own adrenaline, which leads to our body's demise. In discussing his own burnout, Wayne Cordeiro shared what his doctor told him:

> Serotonin is a chemical like an endorphin. It's a natural, feel-good hormone. It replenishes during times of rest and then fuels you while you're working. If, however, you continue to drive yourself without replenishing, your store of serotonin will be depleted. As a substitute, your body will be forced to replace the serotonin with adrenaline.
>
> The problem is that adrenaline is designed for emergency use only. It's like those doors in a restaurant that when opened cause an alarm to sound. Our problem, though, is that we use these pathways designed for emergency only, but no alarm sounds. Not at first, anyway.
>
> Should you continue to run on adrenaline, it will destroy your system. You will burn out sooner on the inside than you're able to see on the outside. The fuel of adrenaline that keeps your engines running in the beginning will turn on you and destroy you in the end.[22]

You can vividly see that God has provided backup systems to help us in times of increased and longer-term stressors, but if we break the backup system, then we have officially exceeded the limits God has placed within us.

False Positives

I believe in hard assessments. I trust evaluations that don't pull punches and facts devoid of biased opinions. Whether we're assessing a business plan for a new company or a church plant or helping a young couple consider marriage, we are being careful because there is so much on the line. But we can't let the wins of building churches and ministries build a false positive for our health and calling. Our leadership success shouldn't convince us that we're doing everything right as it pertains to self-care.

I would love for you to look past the high-fives and successes that are occurring right now. You may have a great trajectory and see growth points and markers of maturity all around you while you are slowly decaying inside. You have worked tirelessly to get to a place where you now wonder if you can eek out another meeting or meet another deadline. The wicked lie we believe is that because we are seeing health around us, we must be healthy. I'd argue that most of our churches are led by burned out people who have a legion of ripped-off spouses and kiddos. You can't keep up with the hurry-up offense, and you aren't fooling anyone.

Big Rocks First

Although we are looking at your health holistically, it's still helpful to start with the biggest problems. Some of the things I'm covering in this book, like sleep and scalable rest, are more important than others, even though they are all vital. In fact, when I once described the average leader to a researcher and doctor, he said to me, "Luke, if your industry simply fixed their sleep and took sugar out of their diets, they'd probably get 80 percent better immediately. The rest of the changes would be fine tuning."[23] That is why I've curated this material starting with what I believe to be most crucial and ending with what could be considered fine tuning.

MY CRIMES
BURNOUT'S ORIGIN

For this I had deprived myself of rest and health. I had desired it with an ardour that far exceeded moderation; but now that I had finished, the beauty of the dream vanished, and breathless horror and disgust filled my heart.

—Mary Shelley, *Frankenstein*

The smothering anxiety and pace that eventually brought me to ashes had its genesis when I was much younger. Always a high producer, my everyday routine in leadership was five to six hours of sleep, hard-core coffee, hard-core workouts, and hard-core meetings, always ending the day drained. I was too young to know it, but I was burning out before I even got started, already cashing emotional checks I didn't have the budget for.

Most of the innovative material and training on leadership self-care I have come across has been produced in the last couple of decades. Back in the 1990s and early 2000s, not many taught on how ministry leaders should care for themselves. In 1999, my second year in the vocational ministry, I suffered my first anxiety attack. I thought it was a heart attack. Incredibly, I was in my early 20s, an age where I shouldn't have had an anxiety attack, heart attack, or anything attack. I had no category for that kind of pain, so I went to the doctor to get multiple tests. The conclusion: I was overstressed and munching on anxiety so often it had become my new normal. I could no longer differentiate the tough days from the easy days. They all felt hurried and critical. After laughing it off in the car (my wife wasn't laughing), I scheduled a meeting with my boss. Doing the best he could, he gave me a tiny book about stress and told me to take a few days off. The time off came and went, but honestly, my perspective never shifted.

Anxiety, depression, and panic attacks were seen as a bit of a weakness in my circles, kind of like admitting to pornography or something of that nature. Not many guys would confess they were drowning in panic and anxiety. I'm not sure many would have even been able to spot it. Back then, my comprehension of how God views me and his church was warped. I was young, stupid, and invincible, too proud to ask questions and too busy to tap the brakes. And I was surrounded by men doing the best they could but equally without answers.

It would be 15 years later that I would finally peek under the hood of my own heart with a probing intensity, looking for lies I was telling myself. With God showing me how the gospel has saved me and is sustaining me and a newly refreshed awe of God's desire to build his church for his own glory, I saw more clearly where I had veered so far off course.

Leading Lies

When I play poker, I have much more fun playing the people than the cards. I get a kick out of duels that reveal whether someone is bluffing. If it weren't for that, I might as well be playing Go Fish or Spoons. I pride myself on spotting lies, but the irony is that I can't spot the lies I'm telling myself. We all do this. We tell ourselves lies—and then we believe them. It sounds goofy, but in a way, it's like kicking our own butt repeatedly.

An incredible book that should be on every Christian's shelf is *You Can Change* by Tim Chester, who reflected, "Sinful acts always have their origin in some form of unbelief. *Behind every sin is a lie....* People are given over to sinful desires because 'they exchanged the truth about God for a lie' (Romans 1:24–25)."[1] We believe the lie that God isn't good, so we secure what our eyes tell us is good outside of God. We believe the lie that God isn't gracious, so we perform for God. We believe the lie that God isn't in control, so, filled with panic, we wring our hands. Behind every sin is a bent belief about God.

I have personally found great fruit in meditating on the lies I believe about God that have produced sin in my life. I have also seen great profit in the process of taking other leaders through a similar exercise. Much like reverse engineering, we work backward from the ugly result of our unbelief in order to see the source of it. Here is how it has traditionally looked:

First, we begin with the outward and obvious sin and work our way to the lie that provokes the broken behavior.

Second, with this lie in hand, we examine it in light of God's remedy and gospel. We look at how the gospel confronts the lie.

Then, with this new truth in hand, we're able to see what the gospel affords us and how we can change.

In this exercise, we locate a failed behavior pattern that is obvious and write it out in first person as succinctly and honestly as we can. An example of this might be: *I flip out on the wife and kids when I don't get my way.* Often, that is as far as people go in assessing their own flaws. They see the core issue as tantrums, never investigating what is further upstream that causes them to throw a fit. Many times, unfortunately, the outward sin ends up as the target for change through performance adaptation. People don't see heart change, only behavior modification. That alone will never work and is nowhere near enough, so we continue the exercise.

People carry that original honest statement to what they are most hungry for when flipping out or what they feel is being taken from them. They write it down as clearly as possible, taking as much time as needed. An example in this case might be this: *What I really want is control, and the family is preventing that.* At this point, they usually realize they need to repent, not only for breaking blood vessels when yelling at their toddlers but also for the wicked demand to trust in their own God-like control. They begin to see that their tantrums are more complicated and motivated by a base belief. There is a strong moving current under the surface.

From there, they develop what the lie sounds like in the form of a personal accusation against God. They write this out in first person to truly bring it home. Here is an example: *God, I don't believe you're in control, so I'm going to grab the wheel and take control. Even if you are in control, you aren't caring for my current situation. I feel you have dropped me.* Now we're getting somewhere. Not too many people talk like that because they are afraid it will shock God. They feel uncomfortable putting voice to accusations that the heart has already formulated. They need to remind themselves that God's feelings aren't hurt when they admit what he already knows. He is unshockable in that regard. The large body of laments in the Psalms shows us that our brutal honesty is the doorstep to the sanctuary of resolved worship.

From there, people gain insight into how the gentle gospel applies to their jagged and broken edges. God's refreshing news confronts their lies, rendering them empty. When they bring their felt needs to Calvary and a gaping empty tomb, they find satisfaction and answers in Jesus. They learn that God satisfies their deepest felt needs, and they're able to confess that as they spend time applying the good news to their lives. In this case, the gospel might sound like this: *God is in control. In fact, God is so much in control that a tomb couldn't even hold Jesus. When it all seemed out of control and humanity was flipping out, God wasn't flinching, intimidated, on his heels, or behind. My risen hero rescued and changed my heart by his powerful and gracious Spirit. Not only is he in control, but he is very good to me. In the moments where all seems most out of control, God is in control, and his thoughts toward me are good, so I can trust, rest, and be at peace. He is big. He is in control. I am satisfied. I can rest.*

Do you see the difference in how we might handle a lie? It is the difference between this hypothetical guy going home and saying, *Hey, babe, I met with the pastor, and, well, I'm sorry for freaking out. I'll try harder,* as opposed to *Hey, babe, I met with the pastor, and we both discovered I have distrust that God is good and in control, and because I believe that lie, I end up freaking out. Please help me where I don't believe.* One response is very Homer Simpson-ish, and the other smells like freedom and life. One has behavior modification as the goal, and the other has a satisfied heart.

I'm incorporating this exercise into our conversation on burnout because we aren't immune to accusing God in our hearts and sinning. In fact, we're practiced and polished at spiritualizing our sins. As we examine our hearts when orbiting burnout, we must be honest with our motivations. All of us have hidden motivations that aren't in line with our biblical calling. Now, let's walk through the misshapen motivations we carry and the sins they produce as they take us straight to burnout.

Ugly Carrot

Many moons ago at a conference, Mark Driscoll cautioned young men who were planting churches to assuage their daddy issues. I remember laughing and thinking, *Of course, what moron does that?* Then, Jesus very gently showed me that I can be very moronic in my motivations to lead. The only pure pastor and truly qualified shepherd is Jesus. When Jesus leads, there is no rebellious shadow in him, and he doesn't fail under sick motivation. Jesus didn't have a daddy issue, a control problem, security issues, and so on. That is why he never overworked, and this is why he never burned out. We need to be reminded of these basics because I catch myself and others acting like we, too, have a pure heart and there are no sketchy motives for leading God's people. Certainly, we all answered a call to lead and take it seriously with great fear and trembling, but if we're honest, there is always some weirdness mingled in. This weirdness causes us to abuse our roles as we try to secure something for ourselves. This *something* is a very ugly carrot on the end of a long stick.

Whether we have daddy issues,[2] a power trip of sorts, or simply want to make a name for ourselves, there is something that is mixed in with our earnest devotion to be an undershepherd in Jesus's church. Kevin DeYoung noted, "As Christians, especially, we ought to know better because we understand deep down that the problem is not just with our schedules or with the world's complexity—something is not right *with us*. The chaos is at least partly self-created."[3] Because we are not unsullied in our motivations, I feel like it would be helpful to address some of the more common motivations. The key here is to be totally honest with yourself, freely acknowledging that you're a cracked and imperfect jar of clay that God has grace and love for. Health and growth begins there.

I'm burning out because I hunger for control.

Erich Brenn, the famous plate spinner from the 1950s and 1960s on the *Ed Sullivan Show*, paints the well-worn picture of the leader fighting for control. He dashes around the stage spinning plates on tall poles, leaving one to tend to another while the audience simply wonders which one will fall first. In leadership, we can despise chaos, overworking in order to get all the variables balanced. We essentially spin plates. Staying busy and working 70 to 80 hours per week gives us the impression that we are abating chaos and nurturing balance. More hours worked equals more control and balance. That is why for many of us, vacations, sabbath rests, retreats, and even taking a personal day seem heretical. If we aren't spinning plates, then plates are falling. If plates are falling, then we're out of control, and everything is falling apart. If everything falls apart, we are ruined, *and* therefore, we need to clock back in.

With this motivation, we stretch to grab a carrot we'll never get because the more we work, the more mess we see and the less we rest and trust God. The more people we contact, the more mess we see. The more people we hire, the more mess we see. The more people who become Christians and the more weddings we officiate—you guessed it, the more mess we see. If you can't clock out at the end of the day to be fully present with your family because of the pervasive fear that a few plates are falling, then you are overworking due to your intoxication with being in control.

An addiction to being in control also breeds an unhealthy perfectionism. Of course, we want to be excellent since we represent an excellent king, but being perfect is the description of Jesus's role—not ours. Our hunt for perfectionism leads to spending too much time on some tasks and even cutting others out in order to get things just right. Delegation dissolves around us because no one can stop the plates from spinning quite like we can. Here's the truth. There really is no carrot, and we'll never be in control. In fact, the desire to be in control of all of life's spinning plates is a bit of a god complex that deserves deep repentance. If we are motivated by the insatiable desire to control our universe, then we'll either (1) build way too small, taking no risks, or (2) burn out and get sick.

I am burning out because I hunger for value.

I remember getting a name tag for a large conference, and under my name it said, "Legacy Church, Knoxville TN: Lead Planter." It was the first time I had ever been recognized as a lead planter and the first conference with our new church's name on it. I was mesmerized by this name tag, looking at it repeatedly and hoping everyone saw that I wasn't just a conference attender but a lead planter, someone to watch, someone to keep tabs on, someone who will make things happen. Do you see how goofy that is? No one is mesmerized by a name tag. No one even wants to wear those things. What I was fixated on was the recognition that it *might* bring me.

To those burning out, nothing says I'm somebody more than building something successful where everyone likes us and needs our brilliant and irreplaceable skills. Accomplishment brings so much attention that we'll break our bodies in half trying to gain it. That, of course, is another ugly carrot.

As DeYoung wisely shared, "We are busy because we try to do too many things. We do too many things because we say yes to too many people. We say yes to all these people because we want them to like us and we fear their disapproval."[4] We overwork because that is the price tag on being esteemed. When we're not satisfied with our intrinsic gospel-afforded value, we must—we *must*—get it from those around us.

I am burning out because I hunger for security.

When people lead, motivated by security, they may not be the hard-charging personality. They may not be trying to manufacture their celebrity or control their micro-kingdom, but they are still leading from a dangerous posture. Going through the motions in order to ensure safe living is actually a direct route to being claimed by the hurry-up offense. Brad Hambrick fittingly described someone making a bad decision mid-burnout: "Life had become a black-and-white movie with a theme of duty and responsibility. Now anything that introduced color with freedom and excitement was deemed 'good.'"[5] In Hambrick's story, that glimpse of color was an affair. The pedestrian doldrum that is routine comes from a motivation that says, "Don't rock the boat."

Being motivated to lead from this flank also has us constantly watching our backs. Everyone is out to get us and spoil what we have. Distrust and isolation is the norm, and we simply cannot afford to be known. We must be cordoned off, busy at the work that used to excite us, not risking anything in the name of safety and security. Possibly more common in leaders over the age of 35 or so, this motivation is found in leaders who don't know what else they could do to make a living. Making it in the church or ministry is only important because they need to make it and be safe. That, of course, is another ugly carrot that many chase.

I am burning out because I hunger for acceptance.

Martin Luther once suspected that he had permanently ruined his digestive system.

> I was a good monk, and I kept the rule of my order so strictly that I may say that if ever a monk got to heaven by his monkery it was I. All my brothers in the monastery who knew me will bear me out. If I had kept on any longer, I should have killed myself with vigils, prayers, reading, and other work.[6]

Roland Bainton, Luther's biographer, wrote that during this period, "The purpose of his striving was to compensate for his sins, but he could never feel that the ledger was balanced."[7] Trying to clear the ledger sends an army of young leaders to seminary and the mission field. It sounds logical. If I serve God with my vocation and life, then it should erase all the scandalous thoughts and actions of my life.

Like Luther, we all have our monkery. We run our bodies out of resources, proving before God that we really are worth it—worth his patience and love. Leading by this motivation always tries to prove self to the world. That leader proves himself to the middle school basketball coach, the pastor who never gave him a shot, his wife, his dad, and anyone who said it couldn't be done. *See God, look what I have done for you. Certainly this cancels out half of my senior year in college.* We use various monkeries to gain glory and cleanliness before a God who has already provided it for us.

When you are bent on proving yourself, you end up working when others aren't and doing what others won't. It means setting the standards very high and freaking out when they aren't met. It also means everything is mission critical, possibly costing you your glory. Leading from this posture simply drains your body of the fuel it sequesters for emergencies only, because now everything is an emergency. Like the other ugly carrots, this one dangles in front of leaders, motivating them to clean themselves and prove themselves before the world and the one who already provided Jesus.

I'm stopping here on this topic, but entire books have been written on these unhealthy motivations.[8] We all have subconscious undercurrents pulling us toward burnout in the fast lane of leadership. These areas need repetitive repentance. Zack Eswine agrees: "You and I were never meant to repent for not being everywhere for everybody and all at once. You and I are meant to repent because we've tried to be."[9] Be honest and ask yourself what motivates you to lead in a way that is hurried, unsatisfied, and sick.

- Why do you show up too early and stay too late?
- Why must you pick up the phone whenever it rings during dinner?
- Why can't you stop thinking about that meeting when trying to sleep?
- What are you most afraid of? What are you afraid of losing?
- What is your worst nightmare regarding those you lead? Why?

Let's accelerate this exercise and look at the lies we believe and the accusations we form in our hearts. Remember, behind every sin is a lie we nurture regarding God. It may feel awkward to be this blunt and honest, but it will help you be more accurate in your repentance and growth.

God, You Are Insufficient to Build Your Church

God, you aren't getting the job done, so I'm stepping up. This church and city need me, and you're nowhere. I'm rolling up my sleeves and am going to get the job done. Move aside. I'll call you if I need help. We'd never say that out loud, but our burnout reveals that our heart is screaming it. We believe this lie most when we aren't seeing what we want. We begin to think that God isn't interested in building his church. We feel God needs a consultant, a pinch hitter, or even a replacement. Sometimes that manifests in a bloated calendar because we *must* have sovereign control for our good and for our glory.

Very simply, we don't trust that God is (1) strong enough to build his very own church, (2) wise enough to place people in the right churches, and (3) mindful of our dreams. Because we function under this set of accusations, we burn out building our own glory. Ray Ortlund said:

> The temptation of the devil was (and is): "Don't risk yourself on God. Trust your own instincts. Live from within yourself. You need to take control, because you cannot trust God." Adam fell for this temptation. As a result, we are now born bent in on ourselves. It feels normal to rest our hopes on ourselves.[10]

I can believe this lie because it enchants me to trust in self due to God's seemingly absent, unkind, and weak hand. To trust and depend on another feels very vulnerable and odd. It's not immediately comfortable. Ortlund continued:

> At times, admittedly, our hearts still feel that we remain in a precarious position with God. We fear he will let us down. So we fall back into scurrying about to fill our emptiness with our own resources. But God graciously lets us wear ourselves out, and these efforts come to nothing.[11]

God *graciously* lets us burn out. It's hard to believe that burnout can be a gift of grace. As I said in the earlier chapters, having my alarm response system broken was the kindness of God in my life. I thought I was losing my mind, but through all the confusion, tears, pain, and sickness, God was being radically sweet to me. If you are in that place, embrace the moment of God saving you and reminding you how easy his plow is.

Maybe you're not ready to admit vocally that you view God as unsteady, unreliable, unloving, and unwise in the building of the church or ministry, but at least look at your actions and see if they indict you. For the leader defending the hurry-up offense, when God isn't clocked in, *we must be*. When there is no one left to trust, we *must trust in self*. When God isn't brilliant enough to place people in the right church, *we have to compete and steal*. Being a custodian or caretaker in anything significant is already difficult and fraught with obstacles, but trying to build what only God can build is dumb and will land us straight in a coffin. Leaders, we simply cannot be the rescuer and lord of the people we lead. They already have one. Thankfully, Ortlund wisely reminds us:

> Every one of us is always five minutes away from moral and ministry disaster. Let's be realistic about how contrary our desires can be to the ways of God. You and I are not the saviors. There is only one Savior. Therefore, we must hurl ourselves into his arms right now, and never stop doing so, moment by moment, as long as we live.[12]

When we believe that God is an ineffective partner, we will try to pull all the weight. Because we operate in this mode, we get jealous when other churches grow and rude when people leave our church or ministry. We begin peering too long into what we can do with our hands and not long enough into the state of our hearts. You see, if God is insufficient to build, then you *must be* sufficient. Because none of us are sufficient to build in God's stead, we burn out trying. We employ all our strength, not in partnering as an undershepherd but in replacing our kingly Shepherd.

Lord, This Endeavor Is Insufficient without Me

Lord, it's all up to me. No one can do it as well as I can. I would delegate and hand things off, but no one is good enough to take the baton. There's too much on the line. Every day I don't overwork is a day the endeavor doesn't grow. Every day we don't grow is a day we regress. This accusation and lie cuts you out of effective leadership and is motivated by self-importance and a passion to control all the variables. If the quality drops, then people will think you are a failure, so you never let people enter the work with you because they might fumble the ball, making you look bad. You run less *with* those around you and more *in front* of them. Roger Bannister, the first man to crack the four-minute mile back in the mid-twentieth century, once said:

> Every morning in Africa, a gazelle wakes up. It knows it must outrun the fastest lion or it will be killed. Every morning in Africa, a lion wakes up. It knows it must run faster than the slowest gazelle, or it will starve. It doesn't matter whether you're a lion or a gazelle—when the sun comes up, you'd better be running.[13]

And run we do. Every day we wake up in the no-huddle offense with so much on the line and no time to waste by handing opportunities to lesser beings. Our deep-seated fear of others dropping the ball on critical downs has us hogging the ball. We are surrounded by people who can step in and relieve the burden, but as panicked leaders who see ourselves as the only sufficient candidate, we never recruit help. We can't get the job done, yet we won't hand it over to anyone else, either. That obliterates effective leadership.

We ultimately fear the overall quality of our endeavor dropping to the degree that we must do everything ourselves, ensuring a high standard. We fear that if we hand work off to someone else and the quality drops, it will affect our success, and we will fail. So we do it ourselves and view everything as critical, triggering our emergency response systems to go into overdrive. We overwork while perfectly qualified help surrounds us, desiring to help. It's a grandiose crime in leadership.

Here's how I've lived much of my life: If you want it done right, you gotta do it yourself. It has groomed my pride, made me neglect others, and abused my fight-or-flight system. Again, we'd never come out and say we're the only competent people in the church, but our task lists expose us.

It's not just leadership that we get a D- in; we also secede from community because it's hard to be vulnerable and known deeply by those we look down on. Everyone around us becomes a mass of people who fail us and are against us to some degree. We hand people tasks, roles, or responsibilities. When they fail or make mistakes, we turn on them as if they were saboteurs, purposefully ruining what we hold dear. It's difficult to do life on life with those whom we feel are failing us unnecessarily. Because of that, we pull away, which leads to the next accusatory lie.

Lord, Tomorrow Is an Insufficient Time

God, this has to be done now. If I wait to grab this call or fix this issue, it can unwind everything. No, tomorrow won't work. Waiting until tomorrow to win is the same as failing today. The tyranny of the urgent presses us to hurry-up sickness as we're motivated to fix everything immediately. After all, how can we build something bigger, better, and faster if we take the faster out? This is the hurry-up part of the hurry-up offense that is motivated by self-glory and the need to fix all now.

It is more intense for leaders in areas that feel delicate. For example, the inbox might not be zeroed out during dinner, but if there is a discontent staffer or family about to leave, well those things could destroy everything, so we must move immediately no matter what. We reason that if the church suffers, then all could come undone and we could perish. Zack Eswine wrote, "My rushing to defend, to (un)kindly instruct, or to try to immediately fix is likely unwise and will prove unhelpful. A waiting of some kind will be required. Sometimes the waiting will last. No resolution will come until Jesus does."[14] Waiting for Jesus is tough for the burning-out leader, so we try to protect our glory and fix issues immediately.

It might be helpful to note that overworking is not working more than 40 hours; it's working *behind* the hours. You can work 80 hours, and it might just be simple suffering or a difficult season. You can also work 20 hours and overwork by trying to make yourself glorious through that work. I'm not sure where 40 hours became the standard, anyway. Most people I poll on this hover around a comfortable 55 hours. Matt Perman agrees:

> The fact that someone is working a lot does not make that person a workaholic. Some people really enjoy their work

and want to work a lot. This is not in itself workaholism. Sometimes it is the path God has placed before us. Where did we get the idea that we are exempt from suffering in our work lives? If we are suffering from and in our work, it does not necessarily mean we are sinning.... Truth: We will (sometimes) suffer from our work, and it is not sin.[15]

We sin when we are trying to do only what God can do to gain the glory that only God is due. Tomorrow will be fine.

I Am Alone, and My Situation Is Unique

Jesus, no one understands. No one is under this kind of attack, so I am able to get away with a bit more. Seriously, I am entitled to believe and act differently because I am different. As in most lies, there is a tiny shard of truth. I say *tiny* only to honor the fact that some positions—lead church planter, CEO, lead pastor—have loneliness as part of their reality. Of course, our struggles resonate with other lead positions in the city, network, or denomination, so even in these key positions, there really is no such thing as being alone and unique. As alone as I may feel sometimes, all I have to do is pick up the phone and call a church planter or pastor from the long list of names I have. Because we share the same pressures and hardships, we feel less alone.

Elliot Grudem and the Leader's Collective, a peer-based leadership cohort, has very effectively built these types of spaces where peers become allies and then evolve into intimate confidants. It's this last stage of deep friendship that keeps us from burning out due to the jarring loneliness that comes with the job. My experience with Elliot and the Leaders Collective made such a difference in this area that I'm sure it was the difference between my only making it another couple years and my going the distance in my role. In fact, it provoked me to follow through with this book.[16]

The overt lie that we're unique leads to self-fascination and entitlement. Arrogantly withering in self-pity, we consider self *way* too much. "That is why cultivating a gospel culture requires a profound, moment by moment 'unselfing' by every one of us."[17] I absolutely love the term *unselfing.* I feel like I need to unself myself every 20 minutes. Honestly, we really aren't unique at all. The enemy of our souls would love for us to segregate and act entitled because it's the easiest way to be ruined. That's why the *National Geographic* photographer is always focused on the antelope staying a bit too long at the watering hole, segregated and aloof. Every photographer knows that's the one that will get eaten first.

This particular accusation leads us to work in isolation, plowing ahead in silence and not allowing others a voice or a view of our lives. When others take the courageous step of speaking truth to us, it's easy to bellow out, *They don't understand because they aren't in my shoes—no one is.* Reminding ourselves that we are as broken as everyone else and as much in need of community as everyone else is the only way to grow as a leader. If you are alone, pondering your own unique trials deep in self-pity, then you're simply waiting to be taken out. It's disastrous to not let anyone give wisdom or aid. It's also disastrous to lead within a community that you're not even connected to. Burnout visits the solitary and prideful often.

I've Been Forgotten and Will Rot under This Guy

Lord, when I signed up for this, I thought I was going to get to _____, but that was apparently not true. My leader can't lead, and the whole operation is headed in a weird direction. I don't have anywhere to go, and I have no options. You've left me flapping in the wind. I recognize that many leaders reading this aren't in a lead position but rather under one. You may only have semi-control over pace and workload. It may be that you're serving in a not-so-healthy church or maybe a ministry headed in a direction you struggle with. It's possible that the leaders above or around you are doing the best they can but don't empower a culture of balance, rest, and grace. Maybe you should leave—maybe not. Maybe you can do nothing other than just get through the day. All these questions can burn someone out. Hurry-up sickness can find anyone who is losing to anxiety, overreaching, depression, clutter, and frustration. It's not just for leads.[18]

When we find we've been serving in an unhealthy situation, it's easy to believe the lie that God doesn't recognize our plight and is allowing us to waste away. Our enemy wants us to believe we've been dropped and left behind. That lie begets resentment and despair, and we lose even the ability to hope for better. In the last example, we resent those below us; in this one, we resent those above us. We feel unable to captain our lives, with no doors opening for us anywhere.

I'll try to be careful here, but sometimes leaders press those who work alongside them into burnout by placing expectations on them that are impossible without exceeding the parameters God wisely gave us. I'm not saying you might be working with a guy who is busier than you are so he is wrong and you are right. I'm mostly speaking to a workload that demands no sabbath rest, no scheduling etiquette, no grace, no relational health, no honesty, no transparency, and so on. I won't pretend to know what your specific issue is, but if this is you, you'll need to decide how to go further. You'll need to, for the sake of your longevity and health, speak to your overseer and try to come to an understanding. If that doesn't yield results, then again, you'll need to decide what is most important to you—the job or your health.

Lord, If This Ministry Fails, I Fail

Seriously God, I have nothing besides this work. If it grows, people will be fascinated with me, just like I need them to be. If it fails, well, then I'll have shame instead. I know I'm called to build your church, but I am afraid I need your church to build me. Ugh! This exercise isn't much fun, is it? Unsatisfied with God's valuation of us and discontent with God's glory, we look horizontally and exchange the glory of God for the glory of a successful church. By doing that, our identity is no longer tethered to the hero of our gospel but to his bride, so we must overwork and burn out to build ourselves.

Phil Knight, the founder of Nike, once said regarding the more scary early years of his company, "I no longer simply made Nikes; Nikes were making me. If I saw an athlete choose another shoe, if I saw anyone choose another shoe, it wasn't a rejection of the brand alone, but of me."[19] I understand what he is saying, and I bet you do, too. If you can't stand to feel like a failure every time you see another church's sticker on the back of the car in front of you, well, you'll need to overwork—work behind the work—in order to solve that problem.

Lord, You Have Made Me Different Than Others

C'mon. I've heard the statistics, but I'm the leader that is the exception. I don't feel sick, and I don't feel like I'm running on adrenaline all day, so whatever. This lie is the backdoor to burnout. It buries us under the pride of thinking we're above or beyond everyone who has gone before us. Cultural voice Mark Sayers, who experienced an epic burnout and lived to write about it in his book *Facing Leviathan*, understands this person well. "Our understanding of leadership is markedly shaped by the myth of the hero, the idea that through sheer effort and determination we can reshape reality. The myth of the hero tells us that dynamic, charismatic, and glorious individuals can heal cultures through their personal guile, skill, and glory."[20] I think most leaders slamming into burnout entertain this lie. As I mentioned before, it was easier in my earlier days to look with judgment on others who closed up shop because of burnout. I felt that physical fitness, innovation, and eating kale once a month were enough to keep me way ahead of the curve. I felt I was simply more fit for ministry leadership. I've lost count of how many times I have foolishly said to myself, *That won't happen to me.* I find the apostle Paul helpful when he warned us to be careful when we're convinced we're standing firm that we, too, don't fall.[21]

In my short tenure in ministry, I have seen men wiser and more gifted than I burn out as they looked around the room and said, "Not gonna happen to me." Don't buy this lie. You aren't immune to what destroyed that person. You cannot run the no-huddle offense forever and not get flattened.

I remind myself often that I am not more in love with my God than David was, and I am not wiser than Solomon, and they both fell in mission-critical areas. In other words, my brain and brawn aren't enough if they weren't enough for them. Our passion and wisdom are insufficient to avoid hurry-up sickness. I'm done being shocked by the adulteries, suicides, and departures of leaders due to this lie. I am very grieved but no longer shocked. There are many other lies and accusations that pertain to your specific situation, but I simply want to reveal a handful of them so you can see that your burnout is directly linked to the lies you believe about God and yourself.

Look What I Have Done

My hope is that at this point, you've spotted some bent motivations and accusations that lead straight to damaging your body and shipwrecking your leadership of others. I can't overstate how imperative it is that you be honest and truthful with yourself. You've lied to yourself long enough. I know how painful it is to shake hands with yourself and see who you really are, but by the Holy Spirit's love for us, we are able to see the depths of our capacity so the depth of grace's rescue is satisfying to us. I've always appreciated Jerry Bridge's ministry, and he wisely leads us here.

> It is the Holy Spirit's ministry to make us see that we are poverty-stricken because of our sins. He comes to us and says, "You are the man!" Even though such a message may come from the loving, caring lips of a brother in Christ, it is the Holy Spirit who enables us to accept it and to say as David did, "I have sinned against the Lord." The Holy Spirit opens the inner recesses of our hearts and enables us to see the moral cesspools hidden there. This is where He begins His ministry of making us holy.[22]

This is where ministry begins. It is nothing less than the grace of God to us that we see how badly we have messed everything up. It is God's grace that we are able to see that we have tried to build our own kingdom for self-centered and unbelieving reasons. We ought to be shocked and disheartened when our best strategies and attempts fall apart, but even in that moment we can celebrate if it leads us back to God. Let this be a moment of ministry in which you look at what you have done to yourself. Before you look to see what God has done, you must in all earnestness cry out in honesty, "Look what I have done."

YOUR REMEDY

UNPACKING THE TRUTH
THAT LEADS TO HEALTH

The judge upon the rainbow has become the
derelict upon the cross.

—Martin Luther

My babies never slept like a baby, but I understand the adage to mean living without an anxious care. Those who lead hurried and overdrawn lives hunt for that kind of rest like it's a snipe.[1] Leading without the hurry-up pace destroying us can only come as a result of the gospel's work in our lives. God's good news through the life and death of Jesus is the beginning of our renewal. If you read this entire book and miss this chapter, you could return to burnout simply because it shifts at the gospel level first. When our comprehension of the gospel is muddied, everything grows crooked, and we end up sick from overwork, overstress, and deep frustration. I'd love to introduce you to a picture and passage where we see leadership from one who is in a storm yet sleeps like a baby.

> About that time Herod the king laid violent hands on some who belonged to the church. He killed James the brother of John with the sword, and when he saw that it

pleased the Jews, he proceeded to arrest Peter also. This was during the days of Unleavened Bread. And when he had seized him, he put him in prison, delivering him over to four squads of soldiers to guard him, intending after the Passover to bring him out to the people. So Peter was kept in prison, but earnest prayer for him was made to God by the church.

Now when Herod was about to bring him out, on that very night, Peter was sleeping between two soldiers, bound with two chains, and sentries before the door were guarding the prison. And behold, an angel of the Lord stood next to him, and a light shone in the cell. He struck Peter on the side and woke him, saying, "Get up quickly." And the chains fell off his hands. And the angel said to him, "Dress yourself and put on your sandals." And he did so. And he said to him, "Wrap your cloak around you and follow me.[2]

What draws our immediate attention is the sanctified jailbreak, but what is amazing to me isn't the escape—it's the slumber before the escape. I can't believe Peter was actually sleeping.

That's also a miracle. Peter had no obvious reason to be at peace enough to fall asleep. He was facing death by the hand of Herod, who was a black belt at political maneuvering and learned from his daddy and granddaddy. His father was the Herod who murdered John the Baptist for an underage exotic dancer, and his grandpa was the Herod who eliminated the sons of Israel in an attempt to cleanse Jesus from the earth. They both made moves to gain popularity and get their stock values to swell. So, this Herod took advantage of a highly patriotic festival, murdered James, and then threw Peter in jail, likely to be executed the next day. Those are the ingredients to an all-nighter.

Standard operating procedure was to chain a high value prisoner to a guard, but in Peter's case they used two guards. Not only that, they had a couple more trained guards watching by the door. Because the text says there were four squads, most scholars agree that this meant every few hours all the guards changed to stay fresh. No way they were letting

Peter escape to live another day. He was spending his last night on earth. Not only was he about to die, but I'm sure he was mourning his friend James, whom he'd spent pivotal time with. Are you starting to get the feel of the passage?

How on earth was he able to sleep? When traveling, I can't even sleep on a king-sized bed in a hotel with another dude who's sharing the room with me. Forget being chained to two guys I don't even know. How could Peter rest when he'd be publicly shamed and likely killed in several hours? James didn't make it. God didn't rescue him from prison. Stephen didn't make it. God didn't rescue him either. Why would Peter think he'd be rescued?

Lying on a soiled dirt floor while chained between two guards with impending death around the corner and mourning the loss of friends—and Peter is sleeping like a baby. An angel even had to strike Peter on the side in order to rouse him. I think I have a theory.

I believe Peter had already died.

I'm ripping that phrase off from something James Calvert said almost 200 years ago as a missionary to Fiji. Long before it was a vacation spot for celebrities and newlyweds, cannibals killed missionaries there. On Calvert's initial trip, it has been said that the ship's captain tried to turn him and said, "You will lose your life and the lives of those with you if you go among such savages." To that, Calvert replied, "We died before we came here."[3] That's it! Calvary had unselfed Calvert, so peace was plentiful in the midst of terror. Like Calvert, Peter had come to a place where he trusted God and was fine perishing since God was glorified according to his great and brilliant plan. Peter, who watched his Lord sleep in a storm, is now sleeping in his own storm. Amazing!

This isn't only for apostles and old dead missionaries with great beards. It's for you and me. We can yield to the brilliance and safety of the gospel, being unselfed, considering ourselves dead. In this death, we can find true and vibrant life. The truth for sick leaders is that (1) God is very big, and (2) God is very good. That truth has a platform in the gospel story more than any story ever told. Know this, or know no rest. Without a resounding satisfaction in God's generous sovereign love, there is no possibility of avoiding burnout.

He Is Big

Atoms don't spin unless he wills it, and seconds don't pass unless he deems it pleasing to him. Nothing exceeds his carefully measured and brilliant architecture. Nothing causes God to reel backward on his heels and say, "Whoa, I didn't exactly see that happening. I need to conjure up a plan B." In high school fistfights, I witnessed skirmishes that started small only to get out of hand fast, complete with Air Jordans and trapper keepers flying. In the skirmishes we experience against chaos and the enemy, nothing gets out of control. As dirty as the fighting gets, it never is out of God's secure hands. And it gets dirty, doesn't it? The Ultimate Fighting Championship (UFC) used to posture as a no-holds-barred venue. It started when I was in college, and I'd skip classes to see guys go toe-to-toe with no rules. Now, "it's forbidden to bite, spit, curse, claw, pinch, throat-strike, head-butt, flesh-twist, eye-gouge, hair-pull, fish-hook, groin-grab, heel-kick a kidney, head-kick a grounded opponent, or fake an injury. You must wear officially sanctioned shorts and 'be clean and present a tidy appearance.'"[4] As tough as that octagon is, our enemy cares not about a tidy appearance and pulls no punches, yet as heated as it can get, God is in control. All of history is on a tether that is firmly in his grasp.

On God's résumé of being in control, my favorite example is a tomb that couldn't even hold a corpse. Not only did God rein in a black and formless creation for his glory, but he also mocked a grave, commanding it at will to let go. If you ever need a snapshot of God being large and in control when everyone else is spinning anxiously out of control, you won't do better than the vacant tomb.

Psalm 46 is a brilliant description of everything around us coming unstitched, causing anxiety and panic.

> God is our refuge and strength, a very present help in trouble. Therefore we will not fear though the earth gives way, though the mountains be moved into the heart of the sea, though its waters roar and foam, though the mountains tremble at its swelling. *Selah.* There is a river

whose streams make glad the city of God, the holy habitation of the Most High. God is in the midst of her; she shall not be moved; God will help her when morning dawns. The nations rage, the kingdoms totter; he utters his voice, the earth melts. The Lord of hosts is with us; the God of Jacob is our fortress. *Selah.* Come, behold the works of the Lord, how he has brought desolations on the earth. He makes wars cease to the end of the earth; he breaks the bow and shatters the spear; he burns the chariots with fire. "Be still, and know that I am God. I will be exalted among the nations, I will be exalted in the earth!" The Lord of hosts is with us; the God of Jacob is our fortress. *Selah.*[5]

Roaring, foaming, trembling, raging, tottering, melting, desolation, shattering, burning. Not to be dramatic, but sometimes that can feel like Tuesday. I know the scope of this passage has something much larger in mind, but that is what it can feel like when running a hurried pace with inflated problems before me. When leaders burn out, they react as if they were seated in this passage, with everything out of sync and unprotected. But the best part about this passage is that God invites us to "be still, and know" he is sovereign and mighty. The assurance that we can be still and rest in his bigness is amplified later in a small watercraft.

Jesus was fast asleep in the middle of a heavy windstorm that swept across a large lake he and his disciples were crossing. In Mark 4, we read the story of their panic and Jesus's peace. There's something ironic about Jesus asleep inside a small boat on a foaming and writhing lake that was created through him. Out of chaos, it was formed, and now it looks chaotic again. Under the category of feeling out of control, it would be hard to beat a boat being swamped by encroaching waves. I've done serious whitewater rafting on some of the better rivers in the country, and only the recent generations of rafts bail themselves out to stay afloat. Before that, you'd have to bail the raft out between rapids. When you weren't paddling, you were bailing. I'm sure in Mark 4, everyone was doing both—except for Jesus, who was sleeping.

81

"Teacher, do you not care that we are perishing?" is how Jesus was roused (Mark 4:38). That question came from someone in fight-or-flight mode with a tight grip on something. It has a thread of both frustration and petition. Little did they know he not only cared but would later spend his life calming a much more horrific storm, one in which we can't possibly do any bailing.

> And he awoke and rebuked the wind and said to the sea, "Peace! Be still!" And the wind ceased, and there was a great calm.... And they were filled with great fear and said to one another, "Who then is this, that even the wind and the sea obey him?"[6]

Peace and stillness were commanded. Creation responds with great calm. Later in the story of grace, calm comes to the church as not even death itself victimizes us. The firstborn and preeminent hero leaves grave clothes folded and abandons death, shaming it. That action of vanquishing the tomb is our ultimate "be still." God, in his generosity to me, reminds me of this when I am tempted to panic in a phone call, e-mail, bad meeting, bad finance report, bad anything. I am invited to be still. God has calmed creation and won over death. I can rest that he can build his own church. I am free to be the caretaker and custodian he designed me to be.

Being still is more than just not moving. It's having a heart that isn't thrashing with frenetic anxiety or convinced that God is not so big. Being still is being resolved that God cares that water is filling our boats. There is a stillness that can come to the people of God when all around them is coming undone. In the middle of wars and wildfires, cancers and migraines, loneliness and anything that a broken world can throw at you, there is a stillness that sleep cannot even bring. A vacation, a drug, or even a vanishing problem cannot deliver this peace. It is a stillness that comes supernaturally and sinks to the heart. It evades cultural understanding or scientific explanation. It is the stillness we need to define our leadership and last long in leadership. It is the confidence that God is not asleep, so we are free to rest.

He Is Love

Of all the sweet and gentle things I see Jesus telling me in the Gospels, I am most encouraged that he says I belong with him and he is making space for me that will never be removed.

> Let not your hearts be troubled. Believe in God; believe also in me. In my Father's house are many rooms. If it were not so, would I have told you that I go to prepare a place for you? And if I go and prepare a place for you, I will come again and will take you to myself, that where I am you may be also. And you know the way to where I am going.[7]

This is a passage for the panicked, anxious, and overworked. It is a core and primal hunger for humankind to belong and fit and have a space where we are welcomed and not forgotten. Whether we know it or not, we desire permanent dwelling places and permanent acceptance. Without them, we try to build something here to provide a low-calorie version of such a dwelling place. Bob Kellemen once said, "To deal effectively with life's daily fears, we must first deal with life's ultimate fear—to die without a place or Godly acceptance. My ultimate anxiety is my fear that I will never find peace with God, never be accepted by God."[8] J. R. Vassar describes it as our hope to hear God say to us "very good" as he did once in the garden. "What an amazing declaration. The *yes* of God, saying, 'I approve of you! I delight in you! I am thrilled by you! I'm so glad that you are here and that you are mine!' What a verdict."[9]

The unsettled heart that hides behind burnout says, *God is not for us and doesn't care for us. There is no place or room for us. He's not considering us.* In response, we wear our lives thin trying to build something here. Maybe we can even make the church or ministry that place where we belong and are delighted in without ceasing.

You see, God being big is only part of the solution to our problem. It is no therapy to the weary for God to be in control if he is not for us. If God is not for us, then he might as well be against us, regardless of his sovereign reach. The serpent in the garden told this same lie to our long-ago parents, and we still believe it today—the lie that God has long arms and a small heart. We believe that God is *not* for us and is trying to keep us from good things. We believe that we don't belong with him and there is no room for us.

Originally, the garden was a place of belonging for humankind. God fellowshipped with them and spoke "very good" over them. There was no stain on Adam or his work. He took his greatest pleasure not in what he built on earth but in his belonging. That is why Adam didn't overwork or undersleep. He was content in the same satisfaction that produced sleep for Peter on a prison floor. God created a hospitable place, put humans in it, and fellowshipped with them.

Since this place of belonging collapsed under the curse, we've been trying to belong and build this place of *very good* here on earth. It's true that as Christian leaders, we're called to steward the foretaste of this. The church is meant to be a hospitable people, tied together by the gospel and inspired to extend the gospel to broken, inhospitable places. This is not the self-manufacturing of a place on earth I'm referring to. I'm targeting the organization we construct here to replace our close fit with God. If we build an institution for our own glory where people love us and approve of us, where we can be safe and stable, then we can feel *very good* here. When leaders fall to hurry-up sickness, they are often building something that is beautiful but for sick reasons and at a sick pace.

Fortunately, even for sick leaders, Jesus stepped into the "cherubim and a flaming sword"[10] and laid down his life so we can have true life and belonging—not in a garden but in a new kingdom. Jesus remixes *belonging* and *very good* for us. I reflect on this deeply when I'm tempted to engineer a place on earth to make me belong and feel loved. The empty tomb shows that God is massive and in the driver's seat, and the place prepared for me reminds me of how sweet and thoughtful and considerate God is to me.

Save My Seat!

If I were to tie these two mega themes together, I could think of no better picture than the story of Mephibosheth. I am a big believer in preaching the gospel to yourself, and in my favorite sermon to self, this story is my lead passage. To jog your memory, Mephibosheth was the son of Jonathan and the grandson of King Saul. He had royalty in his veins. He outlived both of his ancestors and was alive during the reign of David.

There was something different about Mephibosheth. In the midst of all the royalty and impressive men before him, he was crippled in both feet.[11] Something had happened when he was five years old. There was a panicked stir, and his caretaker felt she needed to grab him. As she did, he fell, and the rest is history. It must have been some fall in order for this to happen, because I have dropped more than a couple of toddlers in my parenting years, and fortunately, all they did was cry. The Bible doesn't give us any more details about his injuries. Suffice it to say that in an age when people were valued by what they brought to the table, he brought nothing. In fact, he very likely had to depend on others for mobility and provision. In addition to being a non-contributor, as an adult, he could have easily been a threat to David. Years later, when Mephibosheth was a man, his name came up again.

> And David said, "Is there still anyone left of the house of Saul, that I may show him kindness for Jonathan's sake?" Now there was a servant of the house of Saul whose name was Ziba, and they called him to David. And the king said to him, "Are you Ziba?" And he said, "I am your servant." And the king said, "Is there not still someone of the house of Saul, that I may show the kindness of God to him?" Ziba said to the king, "There is still a son of Jonathan; he is crippled in his feet." The king said to him, "Where is he?" And Ziba said to the king, "He is in the house of Machir the son of Ammiel, at Lo-debar." Then King David sent and brought him from the house of Machir the son of Ammiel, at Lo-debar. And Mephibosheth the son of Jonathan, son of Saul, came to David and fell on his face and paid homage. And David said, "Mephibosheth!" And he answered, "Behold, I am your servant."[12]

This must have been frightful for Mephibosheth because it was common for new kings to purge the kingdom of the relatives and close relationships of past kings in order to mitigate the chances of a vengeful reprisal. So in this case, it would have been expected for David to find Saul's old bowling buddies and distant cousins and have them executed. Today, all you have to do to see the President of the United States is win a Super Bowl or World Series, and when you get there, you'll get a tour and maybe a group picture. Back then, visiting the king could mean you never came back. That is likely what Mephibosheth pondered on the way to the king's palace. It had to be a dreadful walk. The back story, however, is that David and Jonathan were closer than brothers and had a deeply built bond.[13] Mephibosheth's dad was David's friend, and Mephibosheth was about to benefit greatly from that.

> And David said to him, "Do not fear, for I will show you kindness for the sake of your father Jonathan, and I will restore to you all the land of Saul your father, and you shall eat at my table always." And he paid homage and said, "What is your servant, that you should show regard for a dead dog such as I?"
>
> Then the king called Ziba, Saul's servant, and said to him, "All that belonged to Saul and to all his house I have given to your master's grandson. And you and your sons and your servants shall till the land for him and shall bring in the produce, that your master's grandson may have bread to eat. But Mephibosheth your master's grandson shall always eat at my table." Now Ziba had fifteen sons and twenty servants. Then Ziba said to the king, "According to all that my lord the king commands his servant, so will your servant do." So Mephibosheth ate at David's table, like one of the king's sons.[14]

The unthinkable is happening. Instead of extinguishing Mephibosheth, David vaults him to family status. If you just give this passage a cursory effort, it looks like David is just being nice, but more is occurring. People would have been shocked to see the grandson of an enemy handled with such grace, especially a non-contributor. Even Mephibosheth refers to himself as a dead dog. As interesting as this story is, it has a thread that runs through it and continues all the way to Jesus.

It's typical for readers to carry an imperative from this passage that sounds like *we should love our enemies* or *we should handle the disenfranchised well*. Those wouldn't be false, but they aren't the point, either. This passage is turning our attention to a better king and a better family gathered around a better table. We have a clear view of a king more benevolent than David who is showing non-contributing dead dogs grace, not because of exploits or contributions but because of the king's love for another. This story is about the gospel, and you are in it.

Mephibosheth's name means *destroyer* or *scatterer of shame*, which seems ironic. He didn't scatter shame nearly as much as he lived underneath it. His whole existence was under a cloud of defeated kings and crippled feet. Before Jesus, I, too, was the scatterer and collector of shame. I have the genetics of a vandal like my earliest father Adam. But because God's love for me is greater than David's love for Jonathan, generosity comes to a non-contributor like me. Like Mephibosheth, I'm treated like the king's very own son, sitting at a table I have no business being at in a seat that will never be taken from me among a family into which I've been adopted. I find that refreshing.

You see, this story combines the characteristics of God's love and sovereign strength. As a king, David could have done anything he wanted. All he had to do was say the word, and the dead dog would have been executed, no questions asked. Not only did David represent his strength in forgiving the grandson of his worst enemy, he also showed love by drawing him intimately close. And so it is with us. We bring nothing to the table but our needs and crippled souls. We are as helpless as dead dogs. Our king sees us through the love he has for his own son and grafts us into a place of belonging. We need no longer try to accommodate for our perceived weakness or build our own place of belonging. We are safe, valued, and able to rest.

Courageous Rest

Maybe the idea of resting makes you panic even more. After all, there is a massive amount of work before us. Even leaders who feel secure and healthy in their role as an undershepherd can burn out. Resting when the work is heavy creates more distress for many. That is because we struggle to shift gears between work and rest. The very thought of disengaging from work throws us into fight-or-flight mode. I think there is a paradigm that can serve us well. Oddly enough, it comes through the pre-game speech of a failed war general.

In the story of Joab, King David's secretary of defense, we see some impressive moments—and some blooper reel material. He wasn't always well behaved, to say the least, but I'd like to zoom in on one charge he gave in the heat of battle that has served me well as a recovering leader. In fact, my church uses this passage often when we install new pastors because the leadership principle has proved to bear fruit as we handle hard decisions. A healthy leadership team knows when to fight and when to build, when to dream, and when to discern and wait.

When Israel was at war with Ammon and Syria, they found themselves outflanked and in a dangerous position. You get the drift that this didn't happen often with Joab and the mighty men, yet this had many on edge. Before the arrows flew and swords left the scabbards, Joab and his gang drafted a quick change of plans in how to proceed. With fear and adrenaline in everyone's veins, Joab led them into battle with this charge: "Be of good courage, and let us be courageous for our people, and for the cities of our God, and may the Lord do what seems good to him."[15]

This verse is tattooed on my soul and has guarded me from burning out again. Joab is telling them two major things: (1) Be strong and courageous and wear yourselves out for those around you and those God has entrusted to you, and (2) rest in the fact that God will be God and has a brilliant plan we can all trust.

I know we aren't in a battle like these men, but at the same time, our stakes are very real. We encounter casualties, losses, and great brokenness. As a leader, I have been entrusted with people. I have also been entrusted with the city God has placed me in.

As Charles Spurgeon taught upcoming leaders, "The ministry is a matter which wears the brain and strains the heart, and drains out the life of a man if he attends to it as he should."[16] Leadership drains the life right out of us, and yet we are called to execute it courageously. But as worn down as we can be, our souls can still be at rest. When all the arrows stop, I can rest assured that God is God and will do as God sees fit. That reminds my soul to take a deep breath. I am not called to win; I am only called to fight. I am not called to build the biggest, fastest, and most impressive enterprise in my city; I am only called to build.

Broken Clay

Before we get into the hard application of generating a healthier leadership model, it's important to address the truth that your rest certainly may improve your leadership. But more importantly, it glorifies God. When rest is functionally active in your life, it expresses how you rest contently in God's power. It is, in fact, God's grace to us that we're broken and flawed containers that he fills and pours from. He's an unappraisable treasure in an infinite container. When we lead from this posture, we become more burnout-resistant, but the truth for many of us is that "God honors our finiteness much more than we do."[17] Leading as if we're the treasure rather than carrying the treasure grooms us for leadership sickness. Paul says it best. "But we have this treasure in jars of clay, to show that the surpassing power belongs to God and not to us."[18]

The grand implication of this is that God doesn't need me to be the uber pastor with no boundaries. God exceeds our expectations in how he builds. In year two of our current church plant, I recall lamenting on the phone with my coach and friend. I was whining about how growth was slow and a myriad of other things. He could have put the phone down to go get some coffee, and I would have still been whining when he got back. With his patient counsel, he said something unbelievable to me. *"Luke, has it occurred to you that God is just as interested in building you as he is that church?"* Now, my math is pretty bad, but that made no sense to me. After all, I was one guy trying to reach thousands. He was right, however. God doesn't need me to lead. He wants me to lead, but he doesn't need me to lead. When we're leading from a posture that we are the treasure *and* the vessel, we confuse God's desire for our leadership with his dependence on us. When we feel God *needs* us to lead, we will burn out gloriously because we have convinced ourselves that God cannot work around us, only through us. The healthier posture of being a finite and limited clay vessel honors God's power as the centerpiece of our work. It embodies a trust that God will do as God sees fit, and we are merely called to work hard and rest.

In his book *The Spiritual Life*, Andrew Murray addresses this healthy posture:

> The more conscious we are of the utter valuelessness of the earthen vessel, the more we can rejoice in the glory of the treasure. Here on earth people generally seek to have some proportion between the treasure and the vessel in which it is kept . . . and people think, according to the beauty of the vessel will be the beauty of the treasure. God does the very opposite.[19]

This is valuable insight for sick leaders. When I'm conscious of my lack in view of God's glory and operate within proper boundaries, I find myself working hard but not overreaching. I can deposit myself into difficult leadership but not exceed my finite fences. Murray continues:

> Dear friends, I cannot speak it out plain enough in words. The great reason why our Christian life does not advance more, is: we try to do too much ourselves. We are far too self-active and self-confident. We, perhaps, never learned the simple elementary lesson that the only place for me before God is just to be nothing and God will work in me.[20]

I always use the word *custodian* here, not disparagingly toward vocational custodians but simply to recognize that I am more called to pick up the pieces and bring order than I am to "give the growth."[21]

By now, I hope your soul is able to take a deeper breath knowing these truths:

- God is in control.
- You are deeply loved.
- You have a place with God that will never be withdrawn.
- You are free to work courageously and also rest confidently.
- You are a simple vessel carrying an inestimable treasure.

All these truths helped me hit the reset button. They became the healthy coordinates I needed to respect how I was created and called. You are free to not be the center of the cosmos and free to be a hidden footnote in God's great story. You are free to fail, free to rest, and free to be a healthy leader. Sounds easy, doesn't it? Actually, it's not our factory setting, and we usually have to travel to this place through intentional communion. My flesh doesn't believe all those truths naturally, and I must encourage and strengthen myself in the Lord. That requires sitting at his feet.

Sitting Is Losing

> Now as they went on their way, Jesus entered a village. And a woman named Martha welcomed him into her house. And she had a sister called Mary, who sat at the Lord's feet and listened to his teaching. But Martha was distracted with much serving. And she went up to him and said, "Lord, do you not care that my sister has left me to serve alone? Tell her then to help me." But the Lord answered her, "Martha, Martha, you are anxious and troubled about many things, but one thing is necessary. Mary has chosen the good portion, which will not be taken away from her."[22]

Most leaders tend to be on team Martha. I know, I just used a broad brush, and I have a bunch of friends in leadership who are more Mary in their disposition. But if you're holding this book, you're likely to choose serving in lieu of sitting. Growing up as a leader, I never felt like

Martha got a fair shake in this passage. Serving, laboring, and doing the stuff no one else wants to do felt more responsible and admirable. If I had reimagined this story, Mary would been rebuked and shamed, and Martha would have gotten some ice cream or something.

This thinking was like a program operating in the background pre-burnout. Sitting and intentionally creating space to hear God speak is critical and truly the good portion. I know, you just nodded your head in agreement, but consider what your version of laboring versus sitting looks like. What are you doing instead of sitting? What has made you "anxious and troubled about many things" to the point where sitting feels more like losing?

Many leaders say they're sitting at Jesus's feet during sermon or Bible study preparation. Their loophole is this: "It's the Bible, so what's the big deal?" The big deal is that when you are preparing, you are listening for what Jesus is saying to someone else, not what he's saying to you. You're imagining how good the passage is for the troublemaker in your midst or the person who is discouraged. We have already seen how fatigued leaders are known for bringing health to others when they themselves are flaming out. I'd argue that only those who can hear and savor what God is saying to them are qualified and effective to lead others. In other words, if you cannot be fed, you are ineffective at feeding.

Paul Tripp in his book *Dangerous Calling* is also convinced of this.

> I am more and more convinced that what gives a ministry its motivations, perseverance, humility, joy, tenderness, passion, and grace is the devotional life of the one doing ministry. When I daily admit how needy I am, daily meditate on the grace of the Lord Jesus Christ, and daily feed on the restorative wisdom of his Word, I am propelled to share with others the grace that I am daily receiving at the hands of my Savior.[23]

Soul-care is key to self-care. I'm a professional at burning out, and I hang everything on the tired leader's ability to sit with Jesus as the first step out of burnout. Skip this and know no healthy leadership.

When the prologue of our hard workdays is spent being refreshed by the gospel, it reorders all our strategies, problems, and tasks. Abiding restfully—not for others but for ourselves—drives us to look more like Jesus. Paul reminds us that this moment at our hero's feet brings durability to our hearts, and even though we get saggy skin and cataracts, our inner person is being refined and refreshed.[24] As a result of this sacred time when our affections are nurtured for Jesus, we finally become useful to others. I know this is incredibly basic and the thought of a frequent time of retreat into Jesus is assumed, but I've never met a pastor who is about to tap out of the up-tempo cadence of ministry who did a superb job here.

For team Martha, there is always a great excuse dressed in noble words. We know how valuable time with God is, but not really. It's one of the first blocks of time jettisoned from a bloated calendar. One day becomes two, and that turns into a couple months very quickly. If this is you, reconsider why you approach the feet of Jesus and what is happening in that time. God not only speaks to us through his word; he confronts our idols and brings fresh mercy to us. We answer by saying no to what's on fire and yes to his timeless wisdom, insight, and encouragement. It's during this time that God reminds us that he is big and loving and that everything is going to be okay. Even when everything is out of control and doomed, God reminds us that there will always be trouble here and that he is coming soon to defeat it forever. He enchants us with the truth that we'll have all we need for that day, and He will be with us. It seems dumb to skip this time, but in our minds, sitting is for losers, especially when the world needs us to be a hero.

Exhibit A in what this time looks like for the leader surrounded by need is David in 1 Samuel 30. The scene is riveting. David returns from a business trip with his mighty men only to find their village burned and all their wives, kiddos, and stuff gone. The scriptures describe this painful event that brought them all to so many tears that they had no more strength to weep. These are warriors who ran dry of the energy to even mourn. This smothering anxiety and despair led the mighty companions of David to walk around the burned remains and size up stones to throw at David. The passage says they were bitter in soul. They were going to kill their friend and leader.

I don't want to make light of this moment or strip it of its unique context by using a weaker comparison, but being bitter in soul in the face of loss and destruction is the very thing that convinces us that we have no time to pursue the feet of Jesus. As leaders, we are sure to find the camp on fire because of cowardly enemies. We are sure to see great loss. As leaders, we'll always be surrounded by people who aren't sure we're the person for the job and are looking to cause trouble. In all seriousness, this seems like a foolish time to stop and create space for God to commune with us. The very scene screams, *Get going! Act! Execute! Take charge!* I can be so easily convinced that choosing Mary's better portion is something that can always happen *after* the action is done, when the people and possessions are recovered and the camp has been rebuilt. Then, in times of peace, we can freely sit and fellowship with our kind God. It's funny how that time never really comes.

David, with his leadership capital deflating, shows us where he turned when he needed to lead others. He didn't panic himself into the hero everyone needed; he turned to his hero.

> And David was greatly distressed, for the people spoke of stoning him, because all the people were bitter in soul, each for his sons and daughters. But David strengthened himself in the LORD his God.[25]

I'm not sure *how* David did this, and I appreciate how that is left open. I've heard everything from David spoke in tongues to David sang a song to David preached the gospel to himself and everything in between. I think this joins the ranks of Paul's thorn in the flesh. *What* David did is less important to me than the fact that He *did* something to draw close to God for his own bitter soul. In deep loss and discouragement, he found a reservoir of strength. You're watching soul-care while the camp is still smoldering and everything screams, *Be heroic!*

Then David successfully leads the charge to recover everyone and everything. Nothing was missing. It reminds me of another hero— Jesus—who loses nothing or no one God gives him. It's a great story, and it begs the question of what you're doing to find strength in the Lord. What does that look like, and is it prioritized and guarded? Most importantly, how does it hold up when the camp—or the people around you—is smoldering?

Andrew Murray wisely said, "Let every foreboding anxiety drive you to God."[26] The typical anxiety instead drives me to build a task list when I am smoldering and overdrawn. That's because Martha seems more responsible and helpful than Mary. If you're called to lead and make disciples, know that the camp is *always* smoldering. You must fight to sit at Jesus's feet and hear the voice of the one who is not freaked out. Commune and share your heart with him. Join David as he prays, "Search me, O God, and know my heart; test me and know my anxious thoughts. See if there is any offensive way in me, and lead me in the way everlasting."[27]

Swap Meet

A roomful of burned-out leaders are burning out for a roomful of different reasons. I often hear leaders discuss idols in terms of being both near and far (or source and surface), which is a good way to look at idols. The near, or more surface, idols are what we normally attribute to our hurry-up sickness. Achievement, social media, attendance, image, work, and more are easier to spot and easier to put down. There are more camouflaged and sinister idols—comfort, security, glory, approval—that are also causing damage. You'll need to do the hard work of finding the far, or source, idols that remain deeply covered. If you get these mixed up, you'll simply exchange surface idols to feed the deeper ones.

A race is a good example. On the morning of a race, the runners who have been training for several focused months show up early. There's a similarity among many of them. Although no one really knows each other, they always engage in small talk before the race. I've heard a lot of stories before the races I've run, stories that reveal surface idols in their past that they have exchanged for running. Many used to be meth, work, or alcohol addicts. They self-medicated often in their previous lives. Swapping a 50-mile trail race or an Ironman triathlon for prescription meds is socially tolerable, but for our discussion, it's just trading idols. By accomplishing great feats in a race, they are able to take control of their lives and experience the comforting admiration of others. It's just a different drug, but society applauds it. But they still have no freedom because the source idol remains untouched, fed now by training and racing.

Substance abuse is another example. No one gets hooked on a substance because they are flush with comfort and peace in their life. They are using a substance because they're in a living hell and just want out. To just take the substance away may be applauded by society, yet it leaves the deeper hungers untouched. It doesn't profit anyone to declare war on worshipping a surface idol of work or achievement and not seek to put down the more source idols of approval and glory. Leaving the idols untouched will have you trading a bloated 70-hour workweek and an inflated social media presence for substitutes that will still feed the remaining hunger.

Leaders who get sick because of their work are often soft in dealing with the source idols in their lives and need to pull a page from William Gurnall's dramatic playbook regarding source idols.

> Soul, take the lust, which is the child dearest to your heart, your Isaac, the sin from which you intend to gain the greatest pleasure. Lay hands on it and offer it up; pour out it's blood before Me; run the sacrificing knife into the very heart of it—and do it joyfully! This is more than the human spirit can bear to hear. Our lust will not lie so patiently on the altar . . . our flesh will roar and shriek, rending the heart with its hideous cries.[28]

Collect and practice questions to keep an eye on where your idols are trafficking. Be cognizant and own what is attempting to "roar and shriek" on the altar.

- Am I able to enjoy anonymity and being unnoticed?
- What does the idea of being overlooked do to me?
- Am I exhausting myself to be impressive? Before whom? Why?
- What am I trying to control? Why?

- Am I fixated on winning right now? Can I enjoy coming in last place?
- Am I okay disappearing in this moment?"

Not only do I have a list of questions like this, but so do my wife and confidants—and they ask me those questions. That's why creating a protected space to frequently commune with our God must become nonnegotiable. This work is impossible for the occasional Mary, the one who only sits when it's convenient. The gospel of God for humankind is perfect for idol worshippers and best when reapplied often. Yes, everything is smoldering, and the notifications are blowing up our phones. We can't get our minds out of the weeds of the day, but we must fight for this time and celebrate it often. Like David, we must strengthen ourselves in God. Like Mephibosheth, we must celebrate our seat at a table reserved for family. Like Mary, we must sit even though there is much to be done.

Moving On

As we move forward to exit strategies for burnout, be warned that nothing will happen quickly. When I was a personal trainer during college, I told my clients to not expect any measurable changes for about six weeks. I could get rid of their water weight in less than a week, but for the more substantial alterations like fat content, dress size, and all the other stuff people care about when they hire a trainer, I needed a month and a half. My intent wasn't to discourage them but also to encourage them that on day 22, when they weren't noticing too much difference, they weren't failing. I'll say the same to you.

My journey is still in transit, but it has taken a few years of high intentionality. Most of my leadership health's improvement came in the first year, but I am still noticing big gains in key areas. My hope for you is to unpack your big boxes first to speed up your return to leadership health as fast as possible. But you likely won't notice a ton of improvement overnight. In fact, you may even feel a bit worse for a season.[29]

THE WALKING DEAD
UNCOMPLICATING SLEEP

The only time I have problems is when I sleep.

—Tupac Shakur

Everything feels different at 2:36 a.m. The house makes sounds that aren't drowned out by the noise of the day, and everything is paused mid-thought from the day before. I hate being awake while the rest of the world is snoozing. I hate seeing the newspaper guy awkwardly drive down the street trying to hit the front lawn and watching sprinkler systems turn on when I shouldn't be seeing any of that. I should be sound asleep, but instead, I am a card-carrying member of the 2:36 a.m. club. In fact, I think I may be the club's president.

I've even tried to repurpose those hours. I've tried to be thankful, joyful, and prayerful. I've tried reading, singing, and even journaling. I've tried everything I can think of to leverage that misplaced time. It's amazing that anything done in those early hours is hardly even remembered by dinner that same day. It feels like a faint memory. As the sun begins to peek over the housetops, the rest of the world gets up and doesn't really care that I have put in 10 hours of work before lunch that day. Whether it's falling asleep or staying asleep, sleep is a problem for way too many people. For most of us who struggle in the hurry-up offense, sleep is no fun.

In church plant number one, I struggled to stay asleep, always thinking about how I could maneuver and fix all that was broken. I would churn, imagining what people thought of me, and wring my hands over stuff that was insignificant. Insomnia was my constant partner. In church plant number two, insomnia left, but I had a dump truck full of night terrors. I'd get two or three crazy dreams a week, and my wife would have to shake me awake to get the screaming and thrashing to stop. I felt like I was in the old freaky movie *Flatliners*. In church plant number three, it was back to my old friend insomnia with the fresh addition of finding it hard to get to sleep in the first place. I'd just lay there and stare at the ceiling, frustrated because the next day was huge, and I knew I was going to be worthless. How do you try harder to go to sleep when trying harder just makes it harder to go to sleep? Sleep expert Dr. Peter Hauri agrees. "And nothing retards sleep like panic. Trying to force yourself to sleep is the surest way of preventing somnolence."[1] I'd bet a paycheck that for 20 years I've experienced more insufferable nights than the average leader. To this day, I have to focus on sleep strategies because 2:36 a.m. is just a mistake or two away for me.

It wasn't until my flame-out that I focused attention and experimentation on sleep. I stopped allowing sleep to become an accidental or presumed reality. I learned what does and doesn't work. I've explored free, cheap, and even expensive sleep aids. I hope to help you develop a routine that works for you because not every person is the same. I hope to give you enough to recognize your sleep issues and build a functional routine. Even if you lock in the perfect diet, fitness, and consistent recovery routines, if you screw up with your sleep, you'll be the walking dead joining the 2:36 a.m. club on the way to burning out.

Cultural Garbage and Bad Advice

It must have been tough for my wife and the men around me to counsel or pastor me in sleep health. Sleep technology, specifically accurate and affordable metrics, weren't as accessible or trendy back in the late 1990s and early 2000s. No smartphones or wearable technologies monitored anything. Back then, having a pager was the far edge of the tech wave. As pastors, all we had were anecdotal bits of advice doled out with the best of intentions yet with little to no scientific backbone. Even with all the current advancements in sleep technology, I still see some of the residual and boringly predictable bad advice regarding sleep being handed down.

Much of the advice we give and receive is borrowed from the idea that sleep is, at best, an insignificant part of healthy leadership and, at worst, a symbol of weakness. That isn't a new construct, either, but something that leaders have fumbled for centuries. Martin Luther, upon becoming a professor at his university and a preacher in the local village church, also found himself as the director of 11 monasteries. He was so busy and behind that he stacked up his prayers for a few weeks and then got caught up in a day or two of nothing but fasting and praying. "After such an orgy in 1520 his head reeled. For five days he could get no sleep, and lay on his bed as one dead, until the doctor gave him a sedative…. The permanent residue of the experience was insomnia."[2] So even Luther found 2:36 a.m. not much fun.

Even today I hear influential leaders endorse a five-hour sleep regimen because they heard that some brilliant theologian or effective pastor was doing it. *Look what that guy is doing for God. If he can do it, then I can, too.* Before Jesus rescued me, I saw long, deep sleep as weak. Sleep was what losers did while I was getting ahead in life. After Jesus rescued me, I naturally carried over that brilliant sleep philosophy. There were no wise voices telling me otherwise. I hate to say it, but there still isn't much about sleep health for the ministry leader.

Maybe we shouldn't take our sleep hygiene cues from our favorite action heroes or the famous pastor or leader we've never even met. I'm suggesting that we take a more informed look at sleep through the lens of how we're created. What if it's not masculine, tough, spiritual, or entrepreneurial to get very little sleep? What if it's just sin dressed up? What if we're shipwrecking our slumber due to diet or routine? What if it can be changed to serve us and reflect God's glory in a much healthier fashion? Let's look at this scientifically, because you were called to lead, not to be a vampire.

Sleeping Beauty

If you were to see a cross section of sleep, maybe you wouldn't be so convinced that it's wasted time in which only wimps and sluggards indulge. Sleep is where all the action is. It's where God repairs and reconstructs us from the foundation up, and it's in his brilliance that we greet each day with new grace and new biology. Sure, our bodies are busy during the day, but when we pass out at night, the body resets and reformats us in the most incredible and glorious ways. Here's what happens when we sleep.

- Our immune system kicks into high gear, producing what it needs to fight off infection, sickness, and disease. That is why you sleep like a Hobbit when you're sick.
- Testosterone and pituitary growth hormones increase. We need them to regenerate muscle, tissue, and bone. Growth hormone + sleep = better toenails and bench presses.
- Adrenal glands recharge, making them able to churn out cortisol, epinephrine, norepinephrine, and more than 40 other vital chemicals.
- We get new skin cells, so we're actually getting beauty sleep. That is also why the average mattress gains weight over time due to old skin cells being sloughed off. Nasty.
- As opposed to daytime when we're catabolic, churning through oxygen and fuel to make energy, at night we see hormonal changes that place us in an anabolic stage where repair and growth occur.
- Our brain administrates our memories, unpacking them and handling the emotional and cognitive details in order to help us produce new insights and ideas.[3]
- Our brain sweeps up and disposes cellular garbage (autophagy) and reorganizes neural networks. When we sleep, our brain takes trash to the curb and incorporates new things learned and integrates them with things we already knew.[4]
- Our ability to utilize language, maintain attention, and excel in comprehension is bolstered. Reading Puritan literature or even forming complete sentences is just horrible when we've only slept a few hours, right?

- Our nervous system finds the most balance while we sleep, helping us recognize better when it's time to fight or flee or rest or digest.

This is a micro-snapshot of the activity in our bodies when we're doing the hard work of sleep. It's not wasted time after all. Author and fitness expert Ben Greenfield wrote, "because of the crucial role that sleep plays in the health of your nervous system, getting adequate sleep is the single most important strategy you can employ to fix your brain and enhance your mental function."[5]

This is also why sleep deprivation is credited with pervasive health issues. When the elves cannot come out and rebuild the treehouse, it all starts to fall apart. Current figures reveal that only 15 percent of teenagers get the recommended eight hours of sleep.[6] And before we say, *Well, that's because they're teenagers*, you should know that only 16 percent of ministry leaders polled get the recommended eight hours. You likely have the sleep IQ of a squeaky 13-year-old. Congratulations.

If you want another snapshot of what happens to your body when you miss quality sleep, just take the earlier bullet list and reverse it. It's sobering and pretty much describes high school and college for many of us. It also describes last Tuesday. Here are some of the results of sleep deprivation:

- Your stunted immune system fails to fight sickness. Try no sleep for a few days and lick a doorknob. You'll catch the cold and maybe Ebola. Just try it.
- The stress hormones you learned about earlier are in beast mode, which makes it harder to nap or sleep, which in turn churns out more fight-or-flight chemicals. It's a broken loop.
- The hormones telling you to eat (ghrelin) accelerate, and the ones telling you to quit (leptin) are repressed. Essentially, we stay snacky.
- Inflammatory response is in high gear, which is why you may have sprained ankles, snot, and rashes that won't go away.

Boringly Predictable

Before we go deeper, it's vital that you understand the master clock God gave us and how he programmed us to operate within his cosmos. Science calls this clock a circadian rhythm, and we all have one, whether you consider yourself a night owl or a morning lark. The circadian rhythm is mediated by the sun but can be slightly altered by fitness, sleep, and diet.

God gifted us all with a group of nerve cells in the brain that creates a chemical called melatonin, which is effectively a magic potion God provides to make us sleepy and yawny. Our eyes tell these neighboring nerves in the brain whether it's daytime or nighttime, and this simple bit of intel is enough to slow or speed up melatonin production. Like your thermostat on a feedback loop, light in the eyes (especially the blue light wavelength) signals a slowing of melatonin production. Melatonin levels climb as we sleep, because, well it's typically dark. That is why casinos in Las Vegas keep a ton of lights on 24/7. They aim to influence this chemical's production to keep you shoveling hard-earned money into a slot machine or folding repeatedly at the poker table. It's not a conspiracy as much as biology.

We break biology when we ignore that God built bookends for our day. We get up long before the sun, and we go to bed long after the sun. Long ago, we didn't struggle with this as much; that is, until we invented the clock. It wasn't until the 1200s that we saw clocks, which might have dinged every now and then but nothing like what we see today. Later, minute and second hands were added to clocks. Historian Daniel Boorstin remarked, "Here was man's declaration of independence from the sun, new proof of his mastery over himself and his surroundings. Only later would it be revealed that he had accomplished this mastery by putting himself under the dominion of a machine with imperious demands all its own."[7] We began to trade the sun for the watch.

In 1879, Thomas Edison produced the first electric light. "If the clock broke up the day, the light bulb broke up the night. Humanity was flushed with its presumed victory over yet another of nature's limitations. Yet all victories have their associated costs. The clock and the light— they gifted us with time, then they stole it away."[8] Now, we can flick all the lights on and drink some coffee, and voilà, we've manufactured daytime. No longer must we step to the beat of the creator's drum.

Author Charlie Wardle gives insight here by relaying the story of the Copiapó mining accident in Chile in 2010. It reveals the importance of light for circadian rhythms.

> NASA consultants advised the miners to segregate their space into working, sleeping and recreation areas. They used the lights on their helmets and the headlights on the mining trucks to create a communal 'light' area. The sleeping area was kept dark, meaning that the miners could regulate the daylight cycle artificially and maintain a regular pattern of sleep.[9]

Humans weren't engineered to sleep during the day and party all night. If you've ever had a night shift or experienced severe jet lag, you know exactly what I'm talking about. Usurping God's intended rhythm for us long term tends to wreck our bodies. Folks who have pattern night shifts are at greater risk of cancer and heart disease.[10] The same has shown to be true with international flight crews who experience a disruption in circadian rhythm as a part of their normal routines.[11]

I would be willing to wager that if we could fire up the flux capacitor and go back in time before there was electricity, you wouldn't find so much in the way of health problems generated by sleep deprivation. People would have naturally gone to bed when the sun went down and gotten up once the sun came up. You can only do so much by the light of a candle, and you're only stubbing your toes when you're up when you shouldn't be. Today, however, we can make nighttime look exactly like day and biohack our fatigued brains. Even if we turn the lights down to low, we're still flanked by a series of bright screens that emit a blue light telling our bodies to stop melatonin production. If the miners in Chile could alter this rhythm with headlamps and a couple of truck lights, then what chance do we have in our technologically-bright worlds?

Sleep Debt

I can't think of a conversation where the word *debt* is welcome. The word *sleep* is no different. Sleep, like stress, is a bankable commodity and can traffic as both debit and credit. We all have a magic number of hours we should target and build for sleep. We'll call it a baseline. Every evening that we neglect that number (in both quantity and quality), we accrue sleep debt. Getting cruddy sleep every now and then is simply human, but accruing debt continually with no intent on *crediting* the sleep account is a formula for disaster. That is why napping at key times and replacing lost hours is so key to a healthy leader's mind, body, and calling.

Sleep is bankable, and accruing debt is dangerous. Wardle warns:

> If the pattern continues and your sleep debt increases, then the likelihood is that the effects will start to shift from short-term sleep deprivation symptoms to more concerning and dangerous longer-term sleep deprivation symptoms. These will potentially have quite a negative impact on your life in many ways as they affect you physically, mentally and emotionally.[12]

We all go through seasons of horrible sleep for very benign and unavoidable reasons, but a decline in sleep hours has been shown to contribute to modern disease. In 1950, the average American slept 8.5 hours per night. Sounds crazy, right? We struggle doing that on vacation. In 1970, it dropped to 7.5 hours, which would still have most of us high-fiving each other. In 2000, the same doctors found that the average American sleeps 6.25 hours per night.[13] Not. Very. Impressive.

Think about that number—6.25 hours—for a moment. That is very close to the average I hear from those I poll regarding sleep. My magic number currently happens to be 7 hours and 50 minutes. I'll tell you exactly how I came to that number shortly. It doesn't seem a long way from six hours and change, but when you do the math, there is a developing delta. If I were to suddenly get only 6.25 hours, then after only a month, I would have accrued a sleep debt of almost 48 hours. For every month of sleeping like that, I would have been behind six nights of sleep. There is no way a person loses six nights for every 30 and comes out of that equation feeling like dynamite. After a year of this, you could have potentially lost 10 weeks of sleep. Kevin DeYoung commented on this accruing debt:

> Very few of us can survive, let alone thrive, on four or five hours a night.... According to the Center for Disease Control and Prevention, more than 40 million Americans get fewer than six hours of sleep per night. Though we often brag about how little sleep we get, studies show sleep deprivation is a trigger for problems like diabetes and obesity.[14]

That explains why you slip into a coma on days one through three of any vacation. You're actually catching up on that precious commodity of sleep. Because you accrued a cumulative sleep debt, you've got to pay back the piper. Remember, sleep deprivation is used as a form of interrogation or torture in some shady places. It doesn't really reveal us at our best. I do the worst impersonation of myself when I am off a few hours of sleep.

Asleep during Worship

Sleep is trust in the most basic form. When we sleep, we're in a required biological sabbath, trusting God to work *in* us and *around* us as we drool on the pillow. We passively practice one of the most basic forms of trust in which we cease producing and instead simply lay fallow. We go from spending a tremendous amount of calories during the day to burning around 50 calories per hour in our sleep when our bodies focus on rebuilding the baseline. That invites worship, where we gladly declare inadequacy and helplessness and are satisfied as God works around us.

As a young man, I wasn't able to see sleep as an act of trusting worship. I viewed sleep as something to escape so (1) productivity could occur or (2) recreation could happen on my terms. In other words, I wanted to work or reward myself with leisure instead of sleep. Both errors would land me in the same place. In fact, it got me less than the average 6.25 hours we looked at earlier.

I have lost count of how many evenings I sat hunched over a keyboard or on the phone, fixing some crucial problem. Ironically, I'd sell out my own health to maneuver others toward health. I don't think we do this solely because we love people, but because we feel that if we don't fix it right then, it will never get fixed, as if God weren't in the equation. Waking too early and staying up way too late in order to overwork became my badge of honor. I think many are like me, giving ourselves the purple heart of martyrdom and proving we're effective by neglecting self-care so others may live.

I have also lost count of how many evenings I've sat up watching Netflix from episode to episode, feeling entitled to stay up and self-medicate with leisure. Desperate for the comfort I got in watching others fight battles and winning over evil, I'd sit and stare at the TV while the rest of the family was fast asleep. I'm not a gamer, but I know a few, and the song sounds the same. They burn into the early morning hours shooting, passing, and winning.

Overworking and capturing leisure in lieu of sleep are both ways of saying that sleep is not good. It says sleep must be bypassed, escaped, and hacked. We may never say out loud that we don't trust God to bring us comfort or grow his church, but by wiggling out of a normal sleep pattern, that is exactly what we are saying. What if we looked at sleep as another opportunity to honor God's design and intent in creation? What if sleep were a way we worshipped him by trusting him alone for true comfort and gospel progress around us while we lay unproductive? What if sleeping was the most worshipful thing we could do when the sun set?

Let's assume for a moment that you understand it—that God created you to be in dependence every night (sleep) and that he created a rhythm for all creation to honor (circadian rhythm). Let's further assume that you're able to see sleep as a trusting act of worship to be embraced rather than escaped. What now? How do you discern whether your current sleep is adequate? How do you find out what a good base number of hours is for you? How can you capture better quality of sleep?

I'd like to look at that in detail, because without a good sleep pattern, you'll never really come out of a burned-out biology, and you'll never be able to keep your health from spiraling.

You're Not Fine

Several years ago, I spoke at a conference for pastors on the topic of neglecting self-care and burning out. Because I only had 45 minutes, I chose the subject of sleep. I knew if I declared war on their fast-food diets, the room would clear out. I gave the facts, preached the gospel, and pushed hard into their sleep hygiene. I knew ahead of time that this wasn't the kind of subject that gets a ton of applause, but I certainly didn't expect what came after. Immediately, a couple of pastors approached me to lovingly say that although they were convicted by the message, there is no way they were going to change their broken routines. They didn't think the five-hour-per-night plan was bad for them and that something closer to the recommended eight hours was grossly unnecessary. They also name-dropped a list of reputable ministry leaders who endorsed a minimal sleep regimen. I was stunned, not that they came up and told me that (although that was a bit awkward) but that with all the facts and science of sleep, their current routines were still attractive to them.

I tell you this because you may have a similar viewpoint. You may hear but not see where sleep deprivation affects you. You might not feel sleepy, cranky, or cloudy most of the time, so why alter your schedule? In fact, who says that eight hours a night is the gold standard? If God made everybody different, why wouldn't sleep be reflected in those differences? These are good questions, and I'd like to look a bit more deeply at what science has learned about sleep.

Drunk at the Pulpit

Current sleep science has exposed sleep deprivation in a way that's very disturbing to me. It's not disturbing because it's provocative but because it's common. The U.S. Army spent 12 years and around $18 million developing a biomathematical fatigue model known as SAFTE, which stands for sleep, activity, fatigue, task, effectiveness. It predicts in a highly accurate way how sleep quantity, quality, and location of sleep affects cognitive proficiency. This brain speed versus sleep variables model is the working one today for the entire Department of Defense.

What they found represented my college lifestyle when sleep is perpetually deprived. "Once a user reaches only 70% effectiveness, that value is the rough equivalent of a 0.08 blood alcohol level. This essentially means that if you're driving, you'll be 40% slower to respond if you have reached that 70% effectiveness level – and so as tired as you are, you might as well be drunk."[15] In other words, if your sleep stinks and you can't get out of sleep debt, you might as well be drunk—or nearly 40 percent slower at best. These should forever recast in your mind that a solid six is not so solid after all.

When I heard of this model, I didn't even argue with the findings. Of course, it makes sense. We've all felt the lag in the space-time continuum when someone asks us an easy question. We've all forgotten to take our Slurpee off the hood of the car before driving off. We've all felt slaphappy, laughing at dumb things for no reason except that we're underslept or, as the U.S. Army would say, virtually drunk.

To borrow the same illustration, Charles Czeisler, Professor of Sleep Medicine at Harvard, pretty much describes an unhealthy leader's existence. "We now know that 24 hours without sleep or a week of sleeping four or five hours a night induces an impairment equivalent to a blood alcohol level of 0.1%."[16] We keep hearing the word *drunk* used by people who know what they are talking about, and it makes me wonder how many times I've stepped up to preach, led a high-value meeting, or even connected with my neighbors as if I were cognitively drunk. Again, acknowledging episodic sleep deprivation due to life in general where we have no control, many of us can make changes to live and lead in a more sober way as a whole.

Sleeping Like LeBron

One reason sleep science has advanced exponentially is athletics. Teams of all sports are embracing sleep, which is becoming the new performance-enhancing drug. Watch your favorite team as they exit the team bus or plane, and you'll notice that they all have wearable technology that relays their heart rate, heart rate variability, and various sleep metrics to a strength coach or team doctor. It's fascinating to see how the lucrative sports industry has churned out some of the best data on sleep's effect on performance. And we get to borrow from it for free.

For example, let's say a wide receiver from the East Coast boards a plane bound for the West Coast for a game. The athlete is crossing multiple time zones, collecting jet lag, and sitting for long periods in what feels like a toddler's booster seat. When he exits the plane, his circadian rhythm notices that the sun's in the wrong place. Then he attempts to sleep in a hotel bed that someone else was snoring in 18 hours earlier. The room isn't comfortable because the air conditioner is wheezing and coughing a suspicious bouquet of mold. He doesn't have his favorite pillow and can still smell the bathroom cleaner from housekeeping. Oh yeah, and someone keeps letting the door slam down the hall. To add to the tossing and turning, he knows he has a major game coming up that will be watched by millions. Quality sleep isn't going to happen.

That's the main reason that teams of just about every sport prefer to play on their home turf. The anecdotal three-point handicap for playing at home isn't just about a rabid fan base as much as it is about science. After talking to Dr. Richard Cohen about the effects of a night of sleep like this, he shared that the deprivation effect can be measured in cognitive speed, or what we may call reflex. This poor wide receiver could be 10 percent to 20 percent slower cognitively after a bad night's sleep. That's not good. That's a dropped pass, an incorrect route, and millions of dollars down the drain.

Good sleep improves split-second decision-making by an average of 4.3 percent. After four days of bad sleep, an average athlete's bench press drops 20 pounds. Tennis players have found that after adequate sleep was introduced into their training, their accuracy jumped 42 percent.[17] Do you see a pattern? That is why Lebron James gets 12 hours of sleep per night, barely outdoing Roger Federer who gets 11 to 12 hours per night. Sleep has become a secret weapon. Grant Hill says, "I think sleep is just as important as diet or exercise."[18] Steve Nash agrees, saying, "For me sleeping well could mean the difference between putting up 30 points and living with 15."[19]

Now, I know what you're thinking—*Luke, c'mon. Lebron James? Of course he gets 12 hours. What else is he going to do? Besides, he abuses his body much more than a person like me. He also makes more money than some small countries.* I agree. He abuses his body and has time to sleep. Most pro athletes do, but as we've already seen, science has shown physical stress to be less catastrophic than emotional stress. It's much easier on the body's stress response system to play high stakes basketball than it is to lead a church or business.

But Luke, is 12 hours what we're supposed to shoot for? I doubt it, but can we agree that the number isn't less than six? We've always heard that eight hours is the gold standard, and I have to admit, anecdotal or not, that number is very close to being what science has found to be true.

But here's my point. These athletes are willing to do what they need to do because they see value in it. I'm not playing for a ring anytime soon, but I have cities I want to see Jesus change. I have churches I want to plant. I have marriages I'd love to see bend under the glory and weight of the gospel. I have drunkards I want to see baptized. I have universities I'm resolved to see awakened. There is so much I'd like to be part of, and for me, that's more valuable than making it on a hall of fame ballot. I have a calling from my king to reflect his glory by enjoying him before the world, and if it means getting an extra couple hours of sleep per night as a sign of trust and worship, then why would I balk at that?

Step 1: Determine Your Ideal Sleep Quantity

How many hours should I sleep? More important than quantity is quality, but we still need to know how much we need, right? Because we're all different in every physiological way, we need to discern our unique optimum sleeping range. As I said earlier, my magic number happens to be between 7 hours and 45 minutes and 8 hours. The number goes up when I'm carrying a heavy load physically or emotionally. In times of a very heavy load, I have no problem sleeping in by adding hours to the front end of my sleep. How did I find that magic number? To answer that and help you go further, I want to introduce Free Form Sleeping.

Free Form Sleeping is sleeping with no set wake-up time, like when you go camping. You sort of wake up whenever you feel like it, not because you have to get ready for anything. In fact, many people literally go camping when they work this number out in order to avoid all man-made blue light and anything else that can interfere. You'll need two to three weeks where nothing beckons you to wake at any specific time. It might be a vacation or down time of the year when you have a more fluid schedule. Free Form Sleeping only requires a journal or an app to log when you fall asleep and wake within reasonable accuracy. It's also not wise to be grabbing naps here and there because we're looking to lock in a range for your nighttime sleep, and a nap can alter that.

In the first week, you'll likely find sleep to be inconsistent and sporadic. That's your body catching up from the sleep debt accrued over time. Your body is simply stabilizing. After the first week or so, you'll begin to notice a pattern and discern an amount that can become a good starting point for you. Simply (1) write down the time you fell asleep and (2) the time you woke up, and then do the math. Develop an average by knocking out the highest and lowest two nights of sleep and do the best you can to figure a realistic average. I did this exercise and found I needed 7 hours and 50 minutes, which has held true to this day. For me, there is no need to get less than that. When I get far less or far more than that, I end up a half a step behind everyone else all day.

But where do you get those hours? Just like in real estate, sleep is a matter of location, location, location.

Step 2: Turn the Clock Back

As we get into the details of what it takes to sleep like a teenager, we have to decide where we get the extra hours of sleep we'll be adding. That is where quantity translates to quality yet happens to be where most people go wrong. If your Free Form Sleeping revealed that you do well naturally with 8.25 hours, it won't do you any good to go to bed at 1:00 a.m. and wake up at 9:15 a.m. To explain why that is so, we need to go back to our friend the circadian rhythm, God's master clock.

Like it or hate it, we all have a master clock inside of us that functions well when it's in rhythm with God's creation. There's slight variation from person to person (chronotype), which is why some claim to be night owls while others say they're morning people. Preference, however, does not negate this master circadian rhythm. In other words, the following times may adjust slightly, but not so much that the circadian rhythm isn't true for someone. Below is a basic layout of our body's response to this rhythm.

00:00	Midnight
02:00	Deepest sleep is occurring
04:30	Lowest body temperature
06:00	Natural cortisol surge designed to rouse you[20]
06:45	Sharpest rise in blood pressure
07:30	Melatonin production ends
09:00	Highest testosterone secretion
10:00	Very high alertness
12:00	Noon
14:30	Best coordination
15:30	Fastest reaction times
17:00	Greatest cardio and muscle strength
18:30	Highest blood pressure
19:00	Highest body temperature
21:00	Melatonin production begins
23:00	Deep sleep begins

Do you see why it's important to locate your sleep in a wise place? If you begin sleeping at 1:00 a.m. (a favorite time for creatives), you miss over half of your deepest sleep, scheduled for autophagy, cognitive refreshing, and idea assimilation. You also miss melatonin's effect in your later hours of sleep due to decreased secretion in the early morning. It's also been observed by doctors such as James Wilson and Jonathan Wright that encroaching on the later hours of the evening fires your adrenal glands into a sort of second wind. "It is important to be in bed and asleep before your second wind hits at about 11:00 p.m. Riding your second wind and staying up until 1:00 or 2:00 in the morning will further exhaust your adrenals."[21] Going to bed too late throws everything out of sync, and you will cumulatively reap the rewards of junky sleep until you get sick. Quality is as valuable as quantity.

When adding time, learn to add on to the *front* side of the clock, not the back side. Your deepest sleep is when your REM[22] cycles happen most frequently, getting longer as they proceed, and that typically takes place between 11:00 p.m. and 2:00 a.m. That high value block of sleep is the deepest. Hitting a foul ball here may get you quantity but never quality.

It's All about REM

Sleep has phases and progressions. It's not all one continuous bout of slobbering and dreaming but has cyclical stages we must honor. All these stages have a purpose, and when we subtract and interrupt those stages, it has a gross effect on the body. Just ask new parents.

In the course of any given full night's sleep, you will pass through four or five cycles of REM sleep, which can be considered active sleep. Everything else is NREM (non-REM) sleep or quiet sleep. As much press as REM gets, NREM sleep makes up 75 to 80 percent of our total sleep and is still crucial for leadership health. Our first REM cycle occurs an hour or so after falling asleep and after a bout of very deep sleep. It's also when we experience dreams.[23]

I know this can all be overwhelming, so just remember, when you need extra sleep, locate it on the front end. That ensures you'll get the correct amount of sleep, affording your body the ability to wake up at the proper time. Currently, no matter when I make it to sleep, I wake up at the same time without the use of an alarm. If I need to grab an extra hour here or there, I have to work backward. I find that true for other leaders and athletes as well.

Step 3: Get a Plan

Build a smart routine that progressively calms you down and readies you for the highest shot at quality sleep. You need to have an intentional plan, not just go to bed accidentally. It might take a while to develop something that works for you, but routines are powerful, and if you follow one repetitively, it will help throttle you back. That's a key step to leaving burnout. In fact, these routines become even more helpful when you're traveling and are significantly out of your normal routine. Here's a rough skeleton of my routine:

- On average, I need to be up by 5:30 a.m., which means I need to be in bed by 9:00 p.m. or 9:15 p.m. the night before, which means I need to begin my routine earlier than 9:15 p.m.
- After dinner and clean-up, I sit with my wife and rub her feet as we talk about the day or watch a show. Foot rubbing is her love language, and I have very strong hands.
- During that time, I drink a magnesium-calcium drink that aids my depleted electrolyte balance and calms me. If I put in a hard training session that day, I'll include valerian root or other adaptogenic herb.
- After 45 minutes or so, I patrol the house and make sure everything is as it ought to be—I call it sweeping the perimeter so it at least sounds cool. Here's the thing. I'm doing everything very, very slowly. I walk slowly, breathe slowly, move slowly, brush my teeth and floss slowly, flip lights off slowly—everything at sloth speed. It sounds easy, but it's not. Just try it. Practice your lowest gear. If you're advanced, do all your breathing through your nose.[24]
- After the doors are locked, the air conditioner is dialed in, the dishwasher is started, and so on, I take time to read a real book with real pages.[25]
- I also use a sound machine that has either brown noise or something very similar with a bass range. Any light I am using is very low and does not have the blue wavelength.
- For about 15 to 30 minutes, I read something unprovoking so I'm not up until 1:00 a.m. highlighting quotes. I began with old science fiction and am now reading sports biographies. You can only read so much about running and robots from the early 1900s before you pass out.

- I lie in bed any way except on my stomach, diaphragmatically breathing through my nose while slowing my rate. I inhale for four counts, hold for four counts, exhale for four counts, and hold for four counts. It's called box breathing and is widely used by special forces and Olympic athletes. I also find myself doing this before I preach or race. It is very calming but requires practice.

Your routine will look a bit different. I know some who journal, stretch, or even sing, but you get the picture. Begin early, move slowly, process the day, add supplements when needed, read what pulls your mind from the day's activity, and breathe methodically and calmly. It took me a while to get the hang of it, but through repetition and discipline, I carved out a very helpful routine that has served me well, even in fast-paced seasons or in hotels.

Bedroom Hygiene

Now is as good a time as any to address sleep hygiene, or how you keep the bedroom sacrosanct. It's important to keep the bedroom set for just two things: sleep and sex. In other words, move your office out of the bedroom and quit watching hours of TV in the same bed you're about to try to sleep in. Keeping that environment as holy ground regarding sleep and sex will help you change gears and focus on what needs to happen in that room. If you are flanked by work and leisure and the bedroom is where you spend a bunch of time *not* sleeping or being sexy, then it will absolutely alter your sleep. In my routine, I haven't really seen my bedroom all day, so when I walk in, I know it's time to read, breathe, make out, and count sheep.

Sleep hygiene also improves by getting away from the dirty electric cloud some call an EMF cloud.[26] Science shows that those who struggle with sleep aren't helped much by the cell phone searching for a signal or updating Facebook Messenger nine inches from your skull. If you must have your phone on, turn it to airplane mode so your sleep tracker and alarm work fine, but make sure it is the only thing anywhere close to you that's plugged in. I know, I sound like *Star Trek* right now, and I've even heard some health and wellness experts talk of shutting the electricity to their room off at the breaker box. They also disable the Wi-Fi router, which is ironically becoming an option on newer routers. I can tell a small difference between days I forget to turn my phone to airplane mode and days I don't. No, you don't need to wear a foil hat, but if you're having maddening sleep issues, I'd suggest not ruling it out. The research for EMF interruption is growing.

Experts also agree that the ideal sleeping temperature is between 66 and 68 degrees. I have played around with temperature in my own research, experimenting from 30 degrees all the way up to 90 degrees. As you might expect, 30 degrees was not much fun, but I'm a nerd who wanted to be thorough. I have found that when I dial the temperature to about 68 degrees, I am out quick, and I don't turn or toss all night. If your spouse cannot do 66 to 68 degrees without hating you, there are many hacks that can, at the minimum, make the room *feel* cooler. Wool mattress pads, bamboo sheets, and directional fans have also helped us make a room feel cooler than the ambient air temperature.

Finally, the darker the room, the better. You want to create a virtual cave. Even the flickering light on your cell phone makes a difference. Look around the next time you're in your bedroom or hotel room and make note of all the little LED or indicator lights. They are everywhere, and they have an effect on how your body processes and produces melatonin. I know it seems unlikely due to the insignificant size of the little lights, but there are growing reports and studies that show evidence of their slight effect on our bodies.

Step 4: Stop These Things Now

So with a better hygiene and good routine telling you when to be intentional with a better amount and quality of sleep, here are some immediate fixes. Remember, you'll have poor nights from time to time, but we're trying to set ourselves up for success.

Stop drinking coffee. Seriously, coffee is throwing gasoline on the fire of adrenal fatigue and burnout anyway, but it will also absolutely obliterate your sleep. That goes for decaf coffee and black tea as well, which still have caffeine in them. Every time I bring this up in coaching or conferences, I hear groans, but we all know it is true. Even dark chocolate (the healthier chocolate) contains stimulants, setting you back.

Stop eating after 7:00 p.m. When we eat, our blood sugar spikes, and so do other chemicals that delay our ability to go to sleep as quickly as we want. So don't snack, especially on foods with a high carbohydrate or glycemic load or index.

Stop working out late. There are differing opinions on this, but as a good rule of thumb, you shouldn't be working out after dinner unless it's light mobility work or the less strenuous flavors of stretching or yoga. Working out elevates the heart rate deep into the night, making it difficult for adrenaline to subside. My resting heart rate is in the mid-40s, but when I work out in the evening, it's in the 70s and 80s even when I lie down. Trying to sleep when your heart is racing is pretty ridiculous.

Stop drinking alcohol. Alcohol dehydrates, which is why you often feel like you've eaten a bag of sand the next morning. Even the healthier red wine will cause you to wake up around 2:36 a.m. due to metabolizing sugars from the grapes. A nightcap is an oxymoron. There is nothing nighty-night about alcohol except that it makes you feel tired. So you may have little trouble falling asleep, but you will wake up or have poor quality sleep afterward.

Stop watching things blow up. Stop watching TV at night unless you have a blue light filter on it. You can use a blue light filter on phones and tablets and even some of the newer TVs, but I know of health advocates and athletes who use glasses for blocking blue light. They make you look like you're shooting clay targets, but at least you're producing melatonin. However you decide to filter out the waking wavelength of light, be careful with the content of what you watch, too. Make sure it isn't something that will elicit an excited adrenaline response. I noticed a big difference when I switched from watching Jack Bauer hit people to *Downton Abbey*. Don't judge me.

Stop taking bad naps. Naps aren't bad but can be used unwisely. Anything under 40 minutes in the mid-morning or early afternoon is sufficient and can be a great way to gain back sleep deficit. Anything longer or later and you're possibly entering sleep cycles that will disrupt your circadian rhythm. Wardle comments on late long naps, "The problem with napping like this is that the person only sleeps for short periods of time. This means that they are likely to get lots of light sleep without ever passing through all the sleep stages; in particular, they fail to achieve the essential deep sleep necessary for restoration of mind and body, and fail to recover their sleep debt."[27] He is effectively saying that you'd be sleeping too light in the middle of the day and throwing off your sleep at night. Be careful here.

Step 5: Do These Things Now

Just as there are things you need to stop doing, there are things you ought to be adding. Some are free and could be applied immediately; others might take some money and time.

Start taking supplements. I'm not talking about fruit-punch-flavored creatine. I'm talking about herbal supplements that aid in displacing residual adrenaline. Many call these adaptogenic *herbs.* I use valerian root as an adrenaline sink, and it helps tremendously. I also drink a magnesium-calcium drink that shuttles me down a gear, hydrates me, and adds magnesium, which is largely lacking in the American diet.

However, be cautious using melatonin long term. Melatonin is a popular sleep aid and can be found in various dosages just about anywhere. It's only supposed to be used for eight to 10 weeks consistently, and studies haven't been done on prolonged use. The jury is out on using it long term. Our bodies produce melatonin, and you should always be careful taking something exogenously that your body already produces. If you do experiment with melatonin, aim for 3-milligram doses. I see some manufacturers build up to 10–15 milligram doses, but more is not better. In fact, if you take too much, you'll likely wake up in the middle of the night. If your body senses an abundance of melatonin, it will refuse to make any. So when the 10–15 milligrams run out, you are roused as if it were morning. I think the manufacturers know this, but they also know we buy according to the idea that more must be better.

Begin praying or journaling. I enjoy journaling at night as much as I enjoy listening to bell choirs, but as I slow down my routine in the moments before going to bed, I take time to process where God has shown me grace and revealed himself to me in obvious ways. Journaling achieves that for many. Whether you pray, listen, journal, or sing, find something that helps you defragment the day and submit it to God thankfully.

Work out during the day. I have a whole chapter devoted to this, but it's important to note here that a good morning or afternoon routine will go a long way to cement a more rigid master clock rhythm. Ben Greenfield, the wellness coach mentioned earlier, favors light cardio in the morning and harder weights or glycolytic training in the early to mid-afternoon. That has proved helpful by matching the body's natural spike in muscular and vascular readiness. It's best to cooperate with your body's biology when locating your workout.

Begin rethinking your bed. Some of your problem is that you may be sleeping on the equivalent of a garage sale futon. You need to save for a better long-term solution. Yes, up front it feels like you're paying for a semester of college, but when parsed out, it amounts to less than a buck a day for the life of the mattress. If you had it in high school, you may need to upgrade your bed. In today's mattress industry, you can even have mattresses dropped off and picked up after trying them for a few months, no questions asked. Experimenting with different mattresses in your own home is more realistic than laying on them for 19 seconds at the mall. It also allows you to see if you are allergic or prefer a certain material.

Get accountable. Begin using a sleep tracker, which is available on just about any phone platform and wearable technology. As of this writing, some bed manufacturers are building it into the beds themselves. Watch for trends in your sleep (time and quality) and see how much sleep debt you're accruing. That has been very helpful for me, serving as a sort of rumble strip on the way to the ditch of burnout. I diagnose where my sleep health is going sideways and make changes. You don't even have to spend money on this. The accelerometers in watches and phones are sensitive enough to track specific REM cycles and give advice on how to alter your numbers. That technology wasn't available a decade ago, so although not perfect, it beats repeat visits to a sleep professional.

Experiment with scents. I am going full *Star Trek* again, but certain smells such as lavender, geranium, chamomile, and ylang ylang help activate alpha-wave activity in your brain that speeds up relaxation and therefore sounder sleep.[28] We use essential oil diffusers to crop dust the room, but again, be careful to not use something that has a light on it. There is now indoor paint for your room embedded with lavender scent. Whatever you try, you no longer have to burn incense like you did in college.

Start breathing . . . well. Yes, there is a better way to breathe. When we breathe through our nose, it stimulates the parasympathetic nervous system, which activates our rest and digest pathway, which is the yang to the fight-or-flight ying. Take long deep breaths through your nose. It requires a bit of focus at first.

The first hose you spray on the raging bonfire of burnout and over-fatigue is fixing sleep. I can't overstate the importance of that part of the recovery from your hurry-up pace. Most of what I've given you is free and can be administered in steps. And yes, it will take time to get a solid routine down. After a few weeks or so, you'll notice a slight difference, but when you forget and go old school one night, you will definitely notice how bad your sleep is. That's how most of the change will occur in your life. It's very gradual and nearly imperceptible, but when you fall off the wagon, you'll see how far you've come. I quit nodding off at 2:00 p.m. many years ago, and I'm never going back. It's a big part of my reformed health, and I hope you can start recovering by implementing some of these steps toward better sleep. Even more importantly, I hope you're able to be thankful and joyful that God is rebuilding you as you trust in him.

SANDER FLOOR
RHYTHMS OF RECOVERY

The ministry is a matter which wears the brain and strains the heart, and drains out the life of a man if he attends to it as he should.

—C. H. Spurgeon

My favorite movie of all time is the original *Karate Kid* from 1984—not the sequels, remakes, or spin-offs, but the original. There are no flaws in that movie; it is movie-making at its finest with all the elements of a great movie. It has a kid without a dad meeting a father figure with no son. It has a struggling single mom, the obligatory teenage romance, and the necessary high school bullies.[1] It had 1980s music, the hair, the crane kick, and, best of all, Daniel Larusso beating a Cobra Kai warlord by doing nothing more than sticking to rehearsed basics. Not only did he practice basic patterns, but he did so in times of peace when it seemed unnecessary. Whenever it gets to that part—Daniel realizing he hasn't been doing chores as much as burning in new patterns and rhythms for times of fighting—I want to jump out of the chair and start high-fiving everyone. Turns out he wasn't just washing cars; he was blocking punches. He wasn't painting fences; he was perfecting his defensive skills. It's in that moment that the master reveals that the new rhythmic movements are going to save him from getting thumped in his next fight. The best part is the look on Daniel's face and the shock that *it's working!* If you haven't seen this masterpiece of American film, stop reading and immediately buy it so you can watch it repeatedly.

Sensei Larusso can teach all of us a valuable lesson: Stick to the basic rhythms and patterns that will save your butt. In the movie, Daniel didn't earn points in the All-Valley Tournament by acting like Jackie Chan; he stayed very basic and walked away with a big trophy, a dad, a girlfriend, and a sweet yellow car. It all came down to sanding floors and painting fences. Protecting those rhythms actually protected him.

Pastors and leaders neglect the rhythms meant to protect them, and once they get into a serious fight, they have no ability to defend themselves well. When added to a broken theology of work and rest, the net result is flameout. I'd even put rhythm protection above diet and fitness. When our routine rhythms are healthy, we won't gas out so quickly in the hurry-up offense of our callings.

When I coach and serve other leaders, I refer to this concept as rhythms of recovery. I'm a big believer in working incredibly hard and then recovering just as intensely. Toggling back and forth between focused work and focused rest increases our longevity and resilience. If we aren't wise about how we rest, we end up resting accidentally, cramming rest into awkward moments, which never really works. We might not be working in certain blocks of time, but we're definitely not resting, either. We're in between, feeling either guilty or ripped off.

No one can design our work-rest moments perfectly, but by being intentional, we at least hedge our bets in the right direction. I'll wager on a broken week that was intentionally scheduled over a week lived accidentally. Very simply, a broken plan is better than no plan at all.

You aren't going to hear me suggest exterminating all stressors, as I mentioned earlier. When I hear various experts try to help people by sending them on a journey to eradicate all stressors, I realize it's not a viable option for you or me. I'm not a Tibetan monk raking sand but a leader forming other disciple leaders and starting new works. Stressors and clamor abound. Setting out to rid our lives of all stress is simply sanitizing our life from people and mission, which is antithetical to our calling as leaders. In fact, I'll contend that incorporating purposeful moments of rest enables us to work much harder than we would otherwise. Truth be told, you may not be working hard enough.

The goal of self-care isn't to build an army of hypochondriacs but to create boundaries and rhythms that allow us to bear more fruit longer. Just because you're busy doesn't mean you're working hard. It definitely doesn't mean you're productive. I know, this all sounds odd in a book about burnout, but your lack of recovery is crippling your work's quality.

Recovery Is for Winners

Recovering after an intense load is actually something we already understand. We see it displayed in the world of fitness. For instance, when you crush it at the bench press or jumping jacks, you aren't likely to do the exact same thing again the next day because you're tight, you're sore, and you can barely open a door. When you run a marathon as fast as you can, you aren't likely to turn around and do it the very next day because your legs and core are trashed. Your muscles are damaged and in need of a break to repair from the stress you put them through. It's during this break that you rebuild and recover from the load applied, so the body can regroup. This resilience, or ability to spring back to proper form after tension, occurs in times of rest. Quality expenditure demands quality rest.

As a running coach for about a decade, I had to be highly intentional about programming recovery days into the architecture of my athletes. Those days aren't wasted days but rather high-value days when we help the body compensate. Skipping recovery can be just as bad as skipping high-quality speed work and could even beckon a hairy injury. As we saw earlier, it's not going to be any different for leaders. The mechanics in athletes attempting to avoid overtraining apply to those who are avoiding leadership sickness.

We're borrowing again from advanced sports science. Research has been done ad nauseum on athletes who overtrain or fail to recover. Science observed in detail what occurs in an athlete's blood, hormones, organs, sleep, and a host of other markers. Because training is virtually stressing out the body, many of the biomarkers are so similar between athletes and stressed out leaders that we would be wise to pay attention.

Entering God's rest is honoring and stewarding God's gift of a body to us and setting ourselves up for better work in the future. It builds resilience for the work we're called to carry out. In his helpful work *Crazy Busy*, Kevin DeYoung gives us some insight on this.

> The land won't produce a harvest if it never lies fallow. We can't be "all in" all the time. Just think of the Israelite calendar. It had times for feasting and times for fasting. It was for their piety and their productivity that God put them on a predictable pattern filled with daily, weekly, monthly, seasonal, annual, and multiyear rhythms. Which is why it's so concerning that our lives are getting more and more rhythm-less. We don't have healthy routines. We can't keep our feasting and fasting apart. Evening and morning have lost their feel. Sunday has lost its significance. Everything is blurred together. The faucet is a constant drip. Life becomes a malaise, until we can't take any more and spiral into illness, burnout, or depression.[2]

Oscillation and Linearity

DeYoung is describing two rhythmic phenomena. We are either in oscillation or linearity. Oscillation is a basic balanced wave, like cosine (or sine) wave, those things you've worked so hard to forget from high school. You'll notice that when balanced, the wave above the axis is the same as below. That is a commensurate rhythm. It's what we're looking for in our expenditures and rests. When rest is proportional to work in intensity, we have balance and even overcompensation, which is what happens when your bench press increases after work and rest. The same concept describes your ability to read longer now than when you were younger. When rest is adequately compensating the workload, we see healthy future work and even opportunities to increase our workload.

oscillation

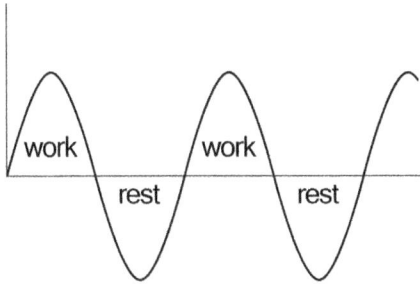

When rest is reduced and not adequate, however, the workload can only respond by reducing in intensity. That drags the wave out of balance and to what we call burnout. This digression is called linearity. An example of linearity is resting for half a day after a two-week intensive mission trip. Yes, there was rest, but no, it was not at all proportional. Notice I am saying that the intensity and quality of the rest—not the time—needs to be proportional.

linearity

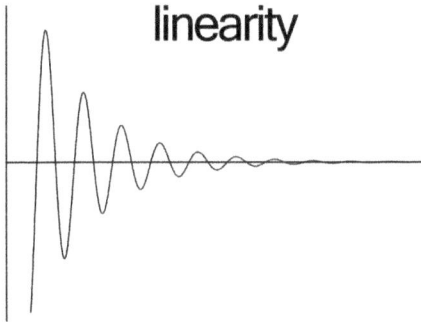

Here's our key concept: *Rest is more than not working*.

Rest is not losing or slacking. Rest is nothing to feel guilty or panicked about. In their helpful book *The Power of Full Engagement*, James Loehr and Tony Schwartz wrote, "Increase the intensity of the training or the performance demand, and it is necessary to commensurately increase the amount of energy renewal.... We need energy to perform, and recovery is more than the absence of work. It serves not just health and happiness, but also performance."[3] As leaders, we have an inner drive to run a rabid two-minute drill but never feel the need to rest in depth or quality.[4] Our rest and work must cooperate. We simply cannot always be working any more than we can always be resting. The amplitude of rest must match the work. Bruce Miller, who wrote *Your Church in Rhythm*, instructs, "We can't sit at Jesus' feet all the time nor can we feed the five thousand all the time, so we often try to solve the dilemma by finding a balance between the two."[5]

Burned out, fatigued leaders are living in simple linearity and aren't able to execute their leadership roles with quality output. When you honor oscillation, you can enjoy focused and intense leadership performance and enjoy rest without guilt. By building oscillation in your work-rest rhythms, you can be free of all the oppressive expectations and the sneaking guilt that you should be doing something else.

Honoring this rhythmic display of work-rest also provokes growth. Remember that the stressors in our world are not the enemy; they're normal. Resting properly like we would after a heavy workout takes the stressors and assimilates them or, as some physiologists say, realizes them into our constitution, allowing us to be much stronger the next bout. If your workweek is hard, you should be resting hard. Doing anything else invites linearity, which for our purposes is the path to leadership burnout.

Drive-Through Eating

Jesus often modeled leadership oscillation. No one said nerdy words like that back then, but the idea of engaging and disengaging came through Jesus before it did through the myriad of books and TED talks.

> The apostles returned to Jesus and told him all that they had done and taught. And he said to them, "Come away by yourselves to a desolate place and rest a while." For many were coming and going, and they had no leisure even to eat. And they went away in the boat to a desolate place by themselves. Now many saw them going and recognized them, and they ran there on foot from all the towns and

got there ahead of them. When he went ashore he saw a great crowd, and he had compassion on them, because they were like sheep without a shepherd. And he began to teach them many things.[6]

Right after this seemingly insignificant trip across the water, Jesus fed at least 5,000 from a posture of compassion. Before this trip across the water, there was also immense output. John the Baptist's murder was still trending news, persecution from the elite was escalating, needy people were swarming in larger numbers, active ministry was taking place, and celebration was occurring. Just before that, the disciples returned from their work to report all the exciting news to Jesus. So much happened before and after the boat trip that there was no time to even eat. Ever run through a drive-through? Ever eat as you drive, as you talk on the phone, as you speed to the next thing? You understand this if you have run the up-tempo scheme.

I'm going to take some license here and pretend I was in that boat shoving out into remoter waters, not to fish or work but to rest a while. I'd guess that if team Jesus is anything like us, their durability was waning. Their compassion was likely up for grabs. I'm imagining this to be the case because as leaders, we leak in durability and compassion as well.

Back in the 1950s, nurses started exhibiting signs similar to combat stress reaction (shell shock) seen in battle-exposed soldiers. Nurses and other first responders were experiencing what is now called secondary traumatic stress, or compassion fatigue. Since it began being charted, it has appeared in other professions involved in the care of people, including lawyers, firefighters, and, you guessed it, ministry leaders. As we deeply care for others for extended amounts of time with no rest, we also experience a very real compassion fatigue. There must be a time to be fed before we return to feed others.

I'll also cover how we leak compassion differently. Because I'm increasingly becoming more introverted, I'm finding that I leak faster in smaller high-value meetings. I can do one or two within a few hours, but a third? Not so much. I'm also more inclined to minister compassionately before the Sunday morning doubleheader than after.

We see oscillation in the passage from Mark. The disciples left work and were headed for more work. Compassion was the heavy expenditure both times. I appreciate that Jesus honors our finiteness more than we do. The boat ride brought them away from work so they could replenish what they lost, but it also readied them for work that was before them. We need rest and solitude not only to defragment and process what just happened but also to be ready for compassionate leadership before us.

Failing to build amplitudes of rest in our routines is a failure to be useful long term. It's also a failure to understand that God produces when we don't. The gospel states we are a sabbath people free to rest. Our sabbath is a person now, not a specific day, yet we can rest on a day to honor what this person has done. We're free from neglecting self-care in order to produce more work. Neglecting rest and growing into decreasing linearity is the symptom of a deeper conversation we're having internally. *I don't have time to rest, because if I rest, I'm not working. If I'm not working, nothing is happening. If nothing is happening, I'm not winning. If I'm not winning, the ministry will not grow. If the ministry won't grow, I'm a failing nobody.*

Leaders in linearity remind me of the movies where a hero has to hold his breath and go underwater to do something heroic, like free someone from wreckage. The hero is only able to commit expenditure equal to the breath. Linearity is where the hero dies underwater for lack of air. Jesus told his leaders in training to take a breath, because there is much work to be done. We must accommodate for the life of entering and retreating from a toxic and broken world where we lay our lives down and sacrifice deeply for others. Jesus is our retreat, and we honor him as we leave the trenches after hard work to find a desolate place and pause a while. Our rest honors him and his passionate work for us. Our rest is also trust that he carries on without us, or despite us. So we're called to preach the gospel with our mouths, and I think there is room for us to depict it with our daily planner and calendar.

I know we weren't in that boat, but listen to Jesus as he speaks to you along the same lines.

Are you tired? Worn out? Burned out on religion? Come to me. Get away with me and you'll recover your life. I'll show you how to take a real rest. Walk with me and work with me—watch how I do it. Learn the unforced rhythms of grace. I won't lay anything heavy or ill-fitting on you. Keep company with me and you'll learn to live freely and lightly.[7]

Tank Warfare

Before we get into deeper practicality, it's important to admit that we don't have boundless energy. Resting and retreating into God isn't what we do when we're all out of work to do either. You would have heard me in the past contending that resting is what slackers do when they should be working, reading, praying, scheduling, talking, preparing, strategizing, answering, e-mailing, and fixing. I think if we were honest, we would all admit that we have a little bit of that person in us. We don't like to admit that we are finite and have edges and borders to our capacity, because it feels too much like we are weak. We have fences that limit what we can do, but embracing them is an act of trust in what God is doing around us when we aren't doing anything. It's a gospel-framed portrait of us resting in another's work. Failing to trust God by resting in his care, we press our bodies beyond capacity and drain the tank until there is nothing left.

To carry the tank analogy further, it's helpful to acknowledge that our capacity changes, depending on what day of the week it is and the nature of the work. Even on the same day, our tank dwindles to its reserves as the day progresses. Richard Swenson, Wayne Cordeiro, and other doctors, pastors, and coaches have recognized that some activities fill this tank, and others drain it.[8] Knowing the difference between the two is crucial in how we program our calendars and daily rhythms. I say *program* because if rest isn't intentionally built, it will get replaced by something that seems nobler at the moment.

For instance, I know meeting with people in smaller pastoral settings can drain my tank quickly. It doesn't mean I don't like it or avoid it; I simply notice a bunch of energy gone when I finish a kneecap-to-kneecap moment with someone. I'm also aware that I get a bunch of life from the operational or entrepreneurial responsibilities of my role, like budgets, staff meetings, and big-picture leadership. Because I'm cognizant of which blocks of time hit me hard and which ones refresh, I'm able to program the order it all falls in. Of course, there's no perfect arrangement, and we'll always be subject to a certain level of urgent matters, but we can at least hedge our rhythms to protect us from chronic fatigue. When I look under the hood of sick leaders' calendars, I typically see a bunch of tank-draining activities all in a row with no recovery programmed wisely. It becomes obvious why the leaders are struggling to operate in a healthy manner. They've simply not taken the time to be honest and aware of how their energy moves back and forth.

With this knowledge, you also can determine what gets punted into the next day. If you're like me, you can get more jerky and your edges more frayed as hard days move forward. When emotionally circling the drain at the end of a hard day, it may not be a good time to meet with the bleeding, non-giving, rebellious person who requires your best and immediate attention. Schedule that time when you have a full tank. Better yet, hand it off to someone who gets their tank filled by those types of meetings. Bill Hybels said, "To engage in a cycle of working incredibly hard and then resting up is to rejuvenate only partially. There must also be consideration given to what you're reading, who you're surrounding yourself with, and what recreational activities you're pursuing that will genuinely refill your tanks."[9]

Currently, one of our bi-vocational pastors excels in difficult meetings where surgical gospel coaching and skilled priestly care is needed. Nurturing pastoral care is his passion. I can do those meetings adequately, but he can do 20 of those meetings in a row with a smile on his face. As much as I'm mystified by his endurance and skill, he says the same thing of my capacity for kingly leadership, ordering chaos, and arranging structure. Those activities drain his tank, and his eyes glaze within 82 seconds. We've helped guide each other on what fills and drains us. Sometimes, it's not so obvious.

I think that as leaders, we have problems in two areas regarding how we handle our bandwidth in work. We either (1) stack a bunch of blocks of upstream work together without giving much thought to recovery, or (2) don't resource those around us to do what gasses us out. What is upstream work for us is downstream work for many around us. These two failures come simply from a lack of self-awareness and honesty. Commenting on developing this awareness, Dr. Swenson said this:

> No matter how large or small the quantum of emotional energy is at the start of the day, and no matter how fast or slow it is exchanging with the environment, one thing is certain: The amount within us is finite. No one has an infinite capacity for emotional discharge. When our reserves are depleted, they are depleted. . . . It is important to learn what our limits are, and not to make further withdrawals if we are already maximally depleted.[10]

Most of us already know this, but our dumbest decisions are made with depleted reserves. That is why many leaders are told to make heavy career decisions *after* a sabbatical, not before. Depleted reserves cause many to go straight to www.ireallyshouldntbehere.com. It's when we fritz out on the kids. It's when careers in the ministry end, and churches are smashed by a leader's weak moment. It's when we say things we regret. We're never rested, full, and inspired when that stuff happens. I've always heard that most pastors who cheat on their brides do so on Mondays. If that's true, I'm not sure that's a coincidence. Their tanks are dry.

When your tank runs dry—and it will—stop draining it more. The best way to do that is not just better scheduling but also retreating into God's rest. We aren't empty and burned up because we're bad schedulers as much as bad retreaters. Just because we've scheduled rest doesn't mean we're resting well.

Bad Retreating

So why does our soul struggle so violently to take a deep breath? Why don't we rest well? It seems so basic that even having a chapter on it seems like overkill. A couple key reasons we stink at enjoying God's rest is because we want to be the hero and can't figure out how to honor a calendar. It's a 1:1 ratio many times, part pride and part undisciplined self-leadership.

There's no lofty reputation gained when it comes to resting. There is no glory in resting. No one headlines a conference for resting well. There is so much work to be done, and it isn't going to do it itself. We crave to be in control. Even if you aren't in the office, you're still likely working in your mind because it gives you the sense of control over circumstances. Even to anxiously fret gives the illusion that we are at least attempting to control a big mess, if even just strategizing in our minds. To rest—truly rest—and let it all go feels eerily similar to giving up.

We also don't guard the calendar well. Even when we're able to rest in our hearts, we're more Labradoodle than Doberman when it comes to guarding our recuperation. DeYoung wrote, "We all know we need rest from work, but we don't realize we have to work hard just to rest. We have to plan for breaks. We have to schedule time to be unscheduled. That's the way life is for most of us. Scattered, frantic, boundary-less busyness comes naturally. The rhythms of work and rest require planning."[11] In other words, we may be working poorly because we do a C- job of etching rest into our bloated calendars.

Simple Sabbath

Whether it's a day, hour, or week, sabbath rest requires an easy and helpful definition in the face of all the counterfeits our culture suggests. Sabbath rest is stopping, surrendering, remembering, rejoicing, resting, and refreshing. I'm risking over simplicity, but this kind of rest is over-thought and made unnecessarily complex. Sabbath rest is finding the tail end of work and not stepping back over the line to do more work. It's laying a bookmark down, whether it is for a minute or a month. It's lying fallow and not plowing or producing. Sabbath rest isn't simply retreating to a cave to be alone for the sake of being alone, nor is it the flurry of leisure activity we do on the weekends. It's being still in the radiance of what God has done, remembering where he is taking us. This place of reflection is where we surrender to God's gaze and grace. It's where we memorialize the gospel's active work for us.

It doesn't have to be all about reading and praying, either. Resting in the Lord is enjoying and celebrating his grace. I'm able to celebrate and enjoy this grace by throwing my kids up in the air, making out with my wife, standing around a fire pit, thinking, dreaming, praying, singing, reading, running, sleeping, creating, and anything else that refreshes and energizes me in the Lord. My diagnostic in sabbath rest is simple: *Am I trying to produce something right now—secretly getting work done but dressing it in things that look restful? Is my mind at rest, or just the keyboard?*

I think you know what I mean here. It's easy to lie in a hammock after a hard week and still be clocked in. You can spend inordinate amounts of energy without lifting a finger. You'll know when you are experiencing a sabbath moment by how you feel when you're done. If you feel unchanged, you most likely were working or needed more time. An anxious heart exhausts us even if we never leave the bed. Anxiety, as we've already learned, is incredibly taxing, and when we stay hyper-vigilant, our bodies are busy, churning even if we aren't. If you're always exhausted, even after an off-day, you may be missing rest by a country mile. As an anxiety addict, I'd try to preempt countless problems in my head on days or weeks my family thought I was resting. The psalmist tells us, "It is in vain that you rise up early and go late to rest, eating the bread of anxious toil, for he gives to his beloved sleep."[12] This verse is hard for me, because I have both risen early and retired late in place of resting far too many days.

Is your wick short? Are you acting like a donkey after resting in the Lord? Something might have gone wrong in your attempt at sabbath rest. "If we violate the Sabbath rest, something morphs in our soul. We start to get proud, edgy, anxious."[13] I think the proof of our consistency isn't shown as much in our calendar or work quality as in our hearts. Sabbath rest knocks the edges off by reminding us that we are God's prized children, he has won, and we are safe. In sabbath rest, we enjoy the overwhelming truth that God is excited about us and desires to engage us intimately.

Sabbath rest is not what we do when we are tired. It's what we do because we are cherished. We're a sabbath people because we need not work for our acceptance. Our hero has worked for us and created space for us to rest. We don't push away from the workstation and laptop because everything is finally finished but so we can trust and remember that God has it all under control and is working powerfully as we lean into his might and brilliance. We are the sabbath people of God, created to rest in him.

Counterfeit: Leisure

Spurgeon once said, "Quietude, which some men cannot abide because it reveals their inward poverty, is as a palace of cedar to the wise, for along its hallowed courts the King in His beauty deigns to walk."[14] Inward poverty is less fun to meditate on than putting a lifejacket on before we crawl onto a jet ski. One of the counterfeits we buy into instead of sabbath rest is leisure activity. Leisure can be very healthy and is typically defined as free time spent away from necessary activities. It looks a lot like binging through episodes of whatever show is trending, or tailgating with your best friends. Leisure, however, can also exhaust you. "Leisure might be the name we give our time away from work, but it is not a synonym for rest."[15] Dr. Swenson makes sense here. Many times on a sabbath day, I mess up by spending the majority of time in leisure. Exhausted, broke, and sunburned, I'll be edgy the following day or week. This should also explain the vacation syndrome, which I call the need we all have for a vacation *after* our vacation. Nothing says, "I need a vacation" like a vacation at Disney World or snow skiing.

I'm not saying we should avoid leisure activities in our sabbath moments, days, or weeks, but we should be careful to not conflate the two. Remember that eustress and distress are interpreted the same by your body. The adrenaline coursing through your pipes when you're zip-lining looks the same to your internal parts as the adrenaline that comes when your social media account is hacked. Some kinds of leisure activities require a respite as much as any work we do.

Counterfeit: Isolation

Isolation and solitude also aren't the same thing. *Solitude is a chosen separation for the refining of the soul. Isolation is what you crave when you neglect the first.* Jesus shows us vividly what solitude looks like, but he never indulged in isolation. These wires get crossed often and I trip over many leaders who speak of solitude when what they're describing is pure isolation.

When we were babies, we'd cry when our senses overloaded at the end of the day. I remember hearing that a newborn assimilates up to seven new scents or colors a day. I don't know how scientific that is, but it at least holds a ribbon of truth. As babies, we'd implement so many new colors, sounds, and smells, that eventually we'd go atomic from being so overstimulated. This is why if you're a parent you can probably tell the "I'm hungry" cry from the "I need my crib" cry. As an evolving introvert, I can only take so much stimulation, and then I need a crib to make it all stop. At that moment, it's not solitude I crave as much as isolation. I want to be separate for the sake of being separate. I think this is a mistake for me and others like me.

Don't misunderstand me. I'm not suggesting we don't get alone ever. Jesus leads us well in being alone, yet we ought to pursue aloneness not as much to escape people and feed our flesh, but to escape frenetic life and feed our soul. The difference here is so subtle. After Sunday at 2:00 p.m., my flesh desires isolation, yet I won't find what I'm looking for there. I can only find satisfying contentment in solitude and in sabbath rest. So, how do we leverage solitude, remembrance, tank-filling, and rest into our cramped schedules? Next, I hope to set you up with practical guidance that has helped me walk away from a burned-out shadow of myself into someone far more rested, healthy, and productive.

STOP START
WORK AND REST COOPERATING

Don't think of it as a 26-mile race. Consider it 26 one-mile races.

S tanding still at race aid stations while others whiz by seems like a poor race strategy—after all, I'm standing there while others aren't. I've learned the hard way, however, that by strategically planning respites, I stand a much better chance of placing well. My best races have been the ones in which I was disciplined in stopping. *As it turns out, slow is fast.*

Retreating into key moments located at strategic times is the point to this chapter. Practicing this will keep your leadership both productive and healthy. Productivity isn't the main concern of this material—health is—but locating rest wisely increases both work quality and margin. And for a sick leader, creating and guarding margin should be a primary focus. Increasing margin in our schedules must also mean better work, because we'll simply be working less. There are many well-written books on how to produce more work in less time, but the chassis I hope to build with you is to work key aid stations into your busy workload. Now, this new motion of resting where we previously worked will be a newly awkward one for most leaders. "When we withdraw, we learn new movements. We move from striving to abiding, from competing to communing, from broadcasting to being. We make a break with the anxiety that drives so much of modern life and, sadly, so much of contemporary leadership."[1] Leading resiliently means increasing your IQ when it comes to *where* and *how* you place your "aid stations."

Not only does rest guard our health and celebrate the gospel, it also promotes more creative and efficient workflow. Resting better means leading better. Leonardo da Vinci was known to upset benefactors and investors when they'd check in on his progress. They would expect him to be working hard sketching or painting, only to find him practicing his cornhole toss. He once was reported to say, "It's a very good plan now and then to go away and have a little relaxation. . . . When you come back to the work your judgment will be surer, since to remain constantly at work will cause you to lose the power of judgment."[2] I think his words are something we all know intuitively. He's speaking to the fresh start we *feel* when re-approaching the pile of work after an appropriate rest.

Schwartz and Loehr, in their previously mentioned work on energy management, noticed that professional tennis players would take around 15 to 20 seconds between serves to build a routine of "micro-resting." You'll notice something similar with MLB pitchers and batters. They aren't trying to make the game longer, but attempting to lower their heart rate, "get their head straight," relax, and focus on the next 1.2 seconds of intense work. Army gunnery crews were even found to be more accurate with their mortar rounds when they too napped and found rest.[3] Again, intuitively this all makes sense. Adding "aid stations" logically improves accuracy and quality of work, yet when it comes to leadership in our respective arenas, we think we're unable to *afford* the rest. In your normal flow of leadership, learning *how* to retreat and re-engage is crucial. In fact, *where* we place respites is almost as important as taking them to begin with. Location, location, location.

Stewarding Energy

As I type this, I have half a cord of wood that still needs to be split. If you don't know what that means, you're missing a great exercise. Splitting wood was CrossFit before spandex and bad lifting form. It means swinging heavy mauls, axes, and sledges to master giant sections of wood down until it is useful. Normally, men get a teenage boy to do the work, or they rent a machine, but I've made a habit of splitting a little bit every day. My current home office is so close to that woodpile, that every couple hours or so on heavy office days, I'll just step outside, put on my gloves, and chop wood for 10 to 15 minutes in the sun. It's a sabbath moment for me. I'm not working, only working up a sweat. I'm stopping to stare at a tree or a bug and thank God for his graces. I then put the tool down and go back to work. It looks like loafing, but I'm actually cycling in such a way as to get more quality work done while staying healthy. Splitting wood isn't just rest, it's rest that's strategically located. I don't think about the last phone call or the sermon ahead of me. I just swing the big heavy sharp tool and enjoy Jesus. I'm not thinking about working "on" or "in" the church, but thanking God that he rescued me "into" his church. It's really too simple to write much more on. Every once in a while, I catch my teenage son out there chopping wood and I have to stop him, because he's so young he'll split the whole load in an hour or two, and I'll have to buy more wood. It's been a valuable help for me coming out of a no-huddle paced career.

You might not have wood to chop or a home office, but the brief moment of retreat I'm focusing on here is more about how we handle *energy* than *time*. When working with sick or recovering leaders, the common chorus I hear is, "I need more time!" I definitely know what they're feeling. It can be so convincing that to add just a few hours to the week could be the difference between burning out and being the best version of ourselves. With no margin, it feels like time would be the panacea. It's not time we need more of, however, *but energy*. It's energy that we're going to learn to leverage. We want both margin *and* reprieve in our productivity rhythms. Without these two crucial ingredients, the calendar will always break, or break the person trying to follow it.

Chronobiology 101

There's a branch of biology that is concerned with periodic behaviors and rhythms in our bodies, particularly as it pertains to the sun and natural movement of nature. To be a healthy leader, not only is honoring natural rhythms (like circadian) important for our sleep and eating, we also need to leverage what is called an *ultradian rhythm*. I know that's a new word, but I promise you don't need a propeller hat for this. We typically have around seven of these ultradian rhythms per day. You likely refer to them as "*bursts*" of energy. As it turns out, our body only delivers so much focused attention without coming up for air.

These bursts, or ultradian rhythms, are roughly 90 to 120 minutes. Between them, we need to come up for air. Of course, it depends on whether the work is tank-filling or draining, how you slept, time of day, blood sugar, stress level, and other factors, but generally speaking, you have a limited amount of time in this ultradian burst. This too is likely something you intuitively already knew. Whenever an ultradian rhythm or burst of energy has run its course, you'll catch yourself mentally wandering, yawning, looking around, feeling snacky, and ready for a break. You'll begin to crave the end point, which is when you know you've run that rhythm to its end.

Again, you can't really set a clock to how long this burst is, but there are definitely ways you can develop and stretch it. This allows you to accomplish more deep work, and for our purposes build more rest and margin into your schedule. Consider a bell curve, where the body of the curve represents 80 percent of your working moment with a 10 percent fringe on either side of the curve. We all know that the first 10 percent of a working cycle of time is spent pushing through distractions like how cold the room is, flopping a few last-minute items onto a running to-do list, wondering why the coffee smells weird, and other small specks of orphan thoughts that are outside your target focus. After that small amount of time though, you find yourself in deep work (the 80 percent portion of the curve). This is where the majority of your innovation, creativity, and productivity lie. After about 90 or 120 minutes, you'll feel like you need to break, and the distractions come flowing back. *What you just experienced was an ultradian burst of deep work.*

Recognizing these rhythms means you can leverage and nurture them to serve you better. After my burnout and implementation of this rhythmic engage/disengage process, I simply got more done in less time and was able to steward rest far better. Again, our goal isn't to burn

ultradian rhythm

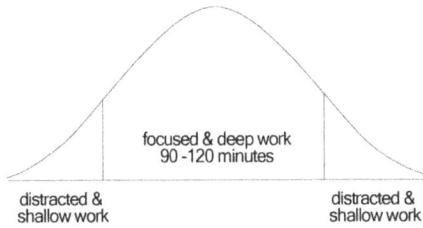

focused & deep work
90 -120 minutes

distracted &
shallow work

distracted &
shallow work

out faster by getting more done in our current work philosophy, but to build margin to intelligently retreat. This single adaptation brought improvement to both my work and rest, which is why I consider it vital for the sick leader hunting for time. "It is my contention that bad approaches and productivity systems (and having no system is itself a system!) are one of the chief causes of our frustration," says productivity expert Matt Perman. "With a bad system, it's hard to get things done with a sense of confidence, relaxed control, and purpose."[4] For you, leadership health might mean your productivity system getting an oil change.

Habitually Linear

By introducing oscillation versus linearity in the last chapter, we have a great opportunity to bring it back on a more micro scale. Inviting oscillation into our daily grind is going to help us much like it does in big picture rhythmic movements like rest days or weeks. We crave oscillation in our days like we do in our months and years. Rest answering work and work answering rest. This daily oscillation will vary in depth (amplitude) and length (wavelength) depending on the work, how you feel, and other key factors such as diet and sleep. Focused work simply needs a focused reprieve and vice versa. Without this cooperation, the quality of your work gets increasingly worse, and the time to produce something takes much longer. We simply expire mentally and emotionally without sufficient recovery.

This degrading motion into cruddy, uncreative work is what we have already referred to as linearity. By treating our day as a marathon, our quality and speed diminish until about 3:00 to 4:00 p.m., when our bodies reach their lowest potential for deep work and are ready for a cinnamon roll and entertainment. Dr. James Wilson attributes this accelerating quality drop to adrenal dysfunction. "These people may appear to friends and family to . . . have lost their ambition, when in reality quite the opposite is true; they are forced to drive themselves much harder than people with healthy adrenal function merely to accomplish life's everyday tasks."[5] When sick, I remember working hard but never feeling creative, thoughtful, compassionate, or productive. Unmotivated, grumpy, and sad would have been descriptions my wife would have used. As Solomon says in Ecclesiastes, "If the iron is blunt, and one does not sharpen the edge, he must use more strength, but wisdom helps one to succeed."[6] Linearity is preventable. We just need to sharpen the axe.

So if this engage/disengage rhythm is so helpful, why isn't everyone doing it? Well, part nature, and part nurture. Culture doesn't really subscribe to a healthy, productive work scheme containing restful pauses. Physiologist Martin Moore-Ede, the president of Circadian Technologies and author of *The Twenty-Four Hour Society*, states it even more bluntly: "At the heart of the problem is a fundamental conflict between the demands of our man-made civilization and the very design of the human brain and body."[7] In other words, we work against our biology. Current leadership culture places a premium on high productivity, so we've attempted to hack our body's natural limits and construct new ones. This has obviously failed greatly. Schwartz and Loehr further comment, "We must learn to establish stopping points in our days, inviolable times when we step off the track, cease processing information and shift our attention from achievement to restoration."[8] So, what does it look like for us to "step off the track" in the middle of a busy workday? What can it look like between these deep work ultradian cycles?

Between Gears

The space between our ultradian rhythms can be filled with moments of rest that looks like smiling, laughing, defragmenting, taking a breath, racing the kids once in Mario Kart (just once), joking with the staff, throwing a dart, singing, doing a set of push-ups, breathing deeply, watching parkour fails, racing the dog, and thanking Jesus. We all have things we can do to retreat for a moment, only to re-approach our day with a renewed vigor. Just like an MLB batter who steps away from the plate between pitches only to readjust his glove straps, touch his helmet, spit, and take a couple practice swings, routines can really help here.

What are some specific ways you can recharge? Dr. Swenson describes this as a time to "catch up, take a deep breath, close your eyes, pray, call your spouse, reorient your priorities, and diffuse your tension."[9] One of my great friends plays the trombone, guitar, and piano when he can—right there in his office. Another friend literally goes out and chops trees down on his land to burn the next winter. Here are a few more examples of "stepping off the track" for a minute:

- *Wandering.* Walk around the block or neighborhood without your phone. Very basic, but highly therapeutic. Defragmenting and reorienting yourself toward what really matters. Currently, I have a dog, who helps me switch mental rails when I walk him. Congratulating the dog on his poop is much more helpful to the work awaiting me than you may think.

- *Turning pages.* I reserve most of my reading and thinking time for the morning when I am cognitively sharpest, but I also leave reading to interact with throughout the day. Not emails, but pages of a book that is easy to pick up *and* put down.

- *Singing.* Okay, not me, because I'm not that guy, but I know some leaders who every two to three hours will grab a guitar and sing to Jesus for a few minutes. They swear by its therapy. If you like singing or reciting a poem out loud, it will help you leverage more restful moments into your hectic pace.

- *Stretching.* I'll get into this in more detail when we discuss fitness, but a great stretch routine can be a huge additive to your rest, especially if paired with controlled nasal and diaphragmatic breathing. In layman's terms, this action communicates to the body that it's "okay to relax." Focus on stretching your lower back, neck, and legs.

- *Taking the long way.* When I drive across town sometimes, I'll go whatever way allows me to roll the windows down and reflect.

I do this most often if I am moving from one appointment to another. Just try going the long way five miles below the speed limit and see how antsy you get. It's proof that our normal is unsettled and hurried.

- *Slow dancing.* Not square dancing, but slow dancing. No kidding. Stop reading right now, grab your spouse for a slow dance, and see if you're thanking God for the work on your desk, or the beloved in your arms. It works. You won't be thinking about work at all.

- *Bar games.* I think every church office ought to have a dartboard or ping-pong table, or something that requires no high-level thinking—just trash talk and memories. Show this chapter to the finance committee so you can make room in the next budget. More darts = more productivity = healthy leadership.

- *Raise your heartrate.* We'll get into this in detail with our work on fitness, but I'll dice my more sedentary days with bouts of *active resistance work.* A few pull-ups, air squats, push-ups, wall sits, stretched poses, or anything else that is less "burst" oriented and more iso/plyometric.[10]

- *"Loling".* Laughter injects a restful moment even in tough seasons, and is unarguably and physiologically good for us.[11] It's true that too much entertainment in a workday is counterproductive, but sometimes watching people scare each other on YouTube for seven minutes is the best medicine for my adrenal health, productivity, and energy.

- *Breathing.* Don't tune me out, but focused and rhythmic breathing through the nose will elicit parasympathetic firing and within minutes place you in less of a fight/flight posture and into more of a rest/digest one. Close your eyes and try box breathing[12] for five minutes, and see if you feel even a little different.[13]

You get the picture—there are lots of options, and they all look a little bit like loafing, which is why we instead put our heads down and keep grinding into sad linearity. But these are prized times when we aren't fixing anything or being productive, but zooming out and taking a big breath. Without panning out for a moment, it's inevitable we'll get bogged down in the weeds.

As long as I'm explaining sports analogies, getting "stuck in the weeds" is a golf phrase. It's when you're so deep in the rough (where 90 percent of golfers frequent), you can't even see the hole anymore, just the 49 trees between you and where the green is likely to be. Rather than drill the ball through more weeds and trees, you "punch" the ball laterally into the safe fairway. A lateral shot feels wasted because the ball is being pitched sideways and not forward, yet the shot sideways saves you a half dozen more bad shots through the impervious forest in front of you. When I get stuck in the weeds of ministry and work, just "punching out" and getting perspective on the goal is enough to resettle me for healthier work. The point I'm making is that placing moments where we push away from the desk and do something not on the task list is healthy, not slothful.

Side-Thinking, Overcompensating Plasticity

So, we've seen that our biology has a natural set of cycles within the day, and when we cooperate with these cycles, we'll see healthier work. When we ignore these cycles, we grind into linearity. Something interesting occurs when we practice stepping off and then back on the track. *We find our rhythms getting longer and deeper, especially if we change into another body of work.* You'll remember this being called overcompensation in previous chapters. You'll simply be able to focus longer with more creative clarity. When sick, I noticed my ultradian bursts were relatively short and needed an inordinate amount of rest in between. We'll call this low productivity endurance. After a few years of practicing this method of working, I've noticed my bursts getting longer and more creative. This is particularly noticeable when I change tasks for every ultradian burst of work.

Coming out of a restful moment only to re-approach the *same* work waiting for you where you left it will make your next cycle of productivity and creativity slightly shorter. You might recognize this phenomenon when returning to a frustrating problem you left unsolved. When this happens, like in sermon preparation for instance, we "loop" through all of what's easy and finished, never approaching the hard problem with full vigor or creativity. Looping is virtually avoiding what is hard or draining. You see people loop in conversations where something hard needs to be said. We call it "beating around the bush." Instead of saying the difficult words, they loop through what is more agreeable. Likewise, when you re-engage the same work subject you left pre-break, you're much more prone to unproductively loop.

Better to define a stop point, locating where you will begin when you return to it later that day or the next day. By stating (or even writing) what you have achieved and where you're stopping, you'll be putting a hard edge to that work so that no residual carry-over occurs. The phenomenon where tasks without defined edges or bookmarks linger in our loose attention is called the Zeigarnik effect. The Zeigarnik effect describes our remembering *unfinished* business more than we do *finished* business. By placing a hard stop at the end of a work cycle, we are, in a way, *putting a period after the moment, not an ellipsis.* By putting one subject away to pick up another, you can mitigate this residual carry-over.

As an example, when I'm preparing for a pastor's meeting and I'm at the end of a work cycle, I give it coordinates that let me get it off the brain. These brain coordinates might sound like, "I'm *finished* posting all the updates and devotional direction for this meeting. The next time I work on this I will *begin* with strategic items for next year's budget." This is different than just dropping everything. Without coordinates and a plan for that work cycle, the unfinished project will undoubtedly carry over into my attention throughout future work cycles. I know it sounds cumbersome, but I feel less residual distraction and more focused work by doing this.

Shifting into something different after a rest will also spark more vigor and creativity due to another phenomenon called "side-thinking." Side-thinking is essentially thinking without thinking. It's where your brain runs in the background, completing an unbalanced formula you struggled with earlier. It's why we remember where we put our keys when we're not frantically looking all over for them. I can be in the middle of intense work, only to stop and scribble something random on the whiteboard for later. That random note on the whiteboard is a result of side-thinking. At first glance, this might look counter to what we just saw as the Zeigarnik effect, but side-thinking happens at a more subconscious level, not with great focus or intentionality. I've learned that my best creativity has come through side-thinking. No one gets their best ideas at work. So much of our leadership's load is bound in how we innovate, problem solve, render new thoughts, and communicate for effectiveness. For this type of leader, side-thinking will always happen, but that doesn't mean you're using it or leveraging it to its maximum potential. By resting and resetting in a *different* direction, you can employ this helpful way of thinking.

Creative work occurs in great degree at the unconscious and subconscious level, when the rational and logical left hemisphere of the brain has been exhausted. Again, this is why, right when you wake or just before you fall asleep, you remember things that evaded you all day. Schwartz and Loehr comment, "In short, the highest form of creativity depends on a rhythmic movement between engagement and disengagement, thinking and letting go, activity and rest. Both sides of the equation are necessary, but neither is sufficient by itself."[14] The brain, just like your legs or arms, requires recovery from heavy exertion. Schwartz and Loehr continue, "After we have learned new information or had new experiences, it takes time for the brain to consolidate and encode what it has learned. In the absence of downtime, or recovery, this learning cannot take place as efficiently."[15] In short, our brains have plasticity (neuroplasticity), forming and reforming to accommodate new ideas and different ways of thinking. What throttles this neuroplasticity into high gear? Rest and recovery at key times. If you want to accomplish more in a healthier way—*you simply need to work less.*

An example of engaging and disengaging in this fashion could be a work rhythm spent reading and taking notes, breaking, and then returning to a different task such as a meeting or even creative work. If you have four or five good cycles in a workday, spend them in four or five different directions. In other words, chop multiple trees throughout the day with renewed vigor and collective side-thinking at your disposal, not the same tree repeatedly.

This is most mishandled with teaching/preaching pastors readying for a sermon. Sunday is a fixed deadline, so putting the work down before the sermon's ready seems like a bad move in the middle to late part of the week. We feel like we need to work until the job is completed. The truth is that returning to the same flavor of work (same sermon) will yield only a tiny increase in productivity compared to the amount seen when moving in a different direction. For instance, let's say you work on a sermon for two hours and then come up for air to rest. Returning to the same sermon prep will only help you complete a smaller percentage of work than previously seen. You'd have much higher gains if you changed tasks and developed a budget outline, prepped for a staff meeting, etc. *The point is, I'd rather make big gains in five different directions than have shrinking gains in a single direction.* The net gain is much less when we chop the same tree all day long.

I know what you're thinking. "But Luke, that limits how many hours I can spend on one item per week! I need more." In the example of sermon preparation, you should probably be more than four or five days ahead. Begin two to three weeks ahead on certain aspects of your sermon preparation, and you'll experience more creative side-thinking for longer. You'll gain creativity and meditation time. Second, you'll need *less* time to prepare a sermon compared to what you normally spend. I noticed my sermon preparation decreasing, while the creative quality and thoughtfulness increased. This is why I feel working in this manner to be healthier for the leader. It's not just that they get more done faster, but that they also create more margin. This might be new to you, but you have to admit that anything—anything—beats cramming eight hours of linear work into a Friday or Saturday. That just produces uncreative work and sick leaders.

Peripatetic Thinking

Of all the ways in which I rest from deep cycles of work and side-thinking, I thought it might be helpful to elaborate on one that stands out: peripatetic thinking. It simply means traveling from place to place. The idea of working in this fashion can likely be traced back to Aristotle. Ultrarunner and author Dean Karnazes found some of the same benefit in peripatetic thought, noting how Aristotle would split his work between the academy and gymnasium with other thinkers and students by simply walking with them. "Aristotle would move outside the walls of the gymnasium and conduct his classes while walking around. His pupils became known as Peripatetics (wanderers)."[16] Friedrich Nietzsche would later say, "Only those thoughts that come by walking have any value."[17] The list is deep when it comes to thinkers who combined wandering with deep thought. Science is beginning to get underneath the mechanics of this thinking format, but anecdotally people have favored this for quite a while. "Jean-Jacques Rousseau found in his solitary walks the inspiration for a new Romantic sensitivity, alien to his salon obsessed contemporaries," says philosopher Jean-Marc Pascal. "Unlike Socrates for whom walking was a way of letting his mind wander and hit upon the right train of thought, Rousseau strove to lose his 'civilised' self and let his 'natural' side enjoy the basic sensations of being at one with his surroundings."[18]

You're even beginning to hear of industry leaders and high-level thinkers moving their collaborative meetings to a peripatetic format. They're talking, participating, and combining ideas all while they are walking—just as influential thinkers have in times past. I interviewed Allen Taha, the Lead Pastor of Trinity Church in Boerne, Texas, about his PhD dissertation research titled, "Physical Self-Care Practices for Sustainable Pastoral Leadership in Local Church Ministry." Taha is a big fan of this restorative and rejuvenating walking, and when asked what was one of the biggest innovations he personally made to drive his leadership health in a better direction, he said, "I make sure to walk around during the workday. Walking meetings in the parking lot and getting up during the day to walk around the church and read, think, or pray keeps me active."[19] His research and personal experience stretch far back to Aristotle.

One caveat. This level of rest/side-think is less valuable if the environment you're traveling requires navigation. Burning up RAM by trying to decide whether you have time to make it across the crosswalk or have to navigate slower walkers in front of you will devalue the moment a bit. Science shows us rather that walking in less distracting natural environments increases peripatetic and restful thinking. I assume it's due to the combination of low distraction, vitamin D, and all the other benefits of being outdoors. I have also found this to be true for me.

Increasing Margin

So why get more done more quickly? Is it to do more work? For the leader who's prone to burnout, the newly created margin is a tempting invitation to tackle new projects, but that newly created margin is far more valuable than more work. Much like a savings account, margin creates space and resource to confront challenges not even seen yet. The traditional leadership model is to pack the week with as much work as possible in order to produce more results. If we aim to work 55 hours per week, we will literally lodge 55 hours of work into our weekly planner without any thought to margin. This is similar to a budget where every dollar coming in is spoken for, what we always call living "paycheck-to-paycheck." When hidden challenges present themselves, however, we end up panicked—*mostly due to the lack of time we have to deal with it.* This is why "margin" finds itself in our conversation. No margin means more stress, and more stress means sick leadership. Dr. Swenson speaks directly to the need for free-floating margin. "Margin is the space between our load and our limits. It is the amount allowed beyond that which is needed. It is something held in reserve for contingencies or unanticipated situations. Margin is the gap between rest and exhaustion, the space between breathing freely and suffocating."[20]

When sick, if someone I knew ended up in the hospital with something critical, I'd drop whatever I was doing in order to get there. The unforeseen challenge would then (1) move all of my workload in my planner forward, (2) cram it all into smaller spaces, or (3) shuttle the seemingly less important items off the planner. Because my energy and time were spent living paycheck-to-paycheck, I had no room for emergencies, adding several new emergencies created by the initial one. I might have spent important time at the hospital per my role, but now I would have to operate in fight or flight mechanics in order to get the rest of my workload finished. Preparing a sermon on date night, ditching fitness, or truncating devotionals—everything got jostled. This jostling was because I was irresponsible in not building margin into my life. You've likely experienced what I'm describing.

I'm not suggesting we bubble-wrap our lives from contingencies, but rather prepare ahead of time for them. Leaders who run without margin are leading hypocritically. When we lead others with zero financial savings or surplus, we likely talk to them about stewarding God's money. We tell them that they're managers of what God owns. We speak to them about saying no to things. Yet, when it comes to our own energy and time, we spiritualize our mismanagement, blaming it on emergencies. *If you're in leadership, you can go ahead and plan on having a dump truck full of emergencies every week, so building margin for contingencies needs to be a fixture for you.* If you aren't programming margin into your calendar, you are programming burnout instead.

I highly recommend Dr. Richard Swenson's book *Margin: Restoring Emotional, Physical, Financial, and Time Reserves to Overloaded Lives.* Although I might not share the totality of his conclusions, his diagnosis couldn't be more helpful or accurate. "The formula for margin is straightforward: Power – Load = Margin. . . . When our load is greater than our power, we enter into negative margin status, that is, we are overloaded. Endured long-term, this is not a healthy state. Severe negative margin for an extended period of time is another name for burnout."[21] Negative margin was my factory setting when sick and is common with almost all sick leaders. Your temptation may be to stuff 65 or even 70 hours of work into 55 hours. But as Swenson noted, this places you in margin *debt.*

Most of the hard work in creating this breathing room will be in growing comfortable with a slower pace, learning how to delegate and equip leaders around you, and simply adding a new word to your vocabulary: *no.* In order to be a more resilient leader, you must tend the broken garden you're in with better planning and stewardship. Responsible and healthy leaders design their schedule with free floating margin.

Before I leave this aspect of energy management, *I'd suggest tithing toward your margin as a general rule.* When I design my calendar ahead of time, I'll take 10 percent of the hours I am called to work and leave it fallow. Friday afternoon is where I put those hours. If there is an emergency, I have room to shove things around. If there isn't, I have room to work on a future project, or even rest if needed. Either way, I don't feel suffocated and enslaved to the calendar—it's now serving me.

Multi-failing and Shallow Work

While we're in the subject matter of healthier energy management and creative production, it's probably appropriate we discuss multitasking. *No, you're not good at it.* You may find that performing multiple tasks is normal for you, but that only means you're normally executing what Cal Newport calls shallow work. Shallow work describes a kind of work that is not demanding, is logistical in nature, and can be done while heavily distracted.[22] This work doesn't create much value in the world, however, and others can do it just as well as you. Checking emails, scheduling social media posts, and multitasking give the impression that much is getting done, yet nothing significant is really getting done, not deeply anyway. In his book *Deep Work*, Newport addresses multitasking and notes that when we switch from one task to another, our attention lags a bit behind and carries residue from the previous task into the next one. We're buried underneath the Zeigarnik effect. When we switch from one task to another, our attention doesn't follow suit, but is still stuck a bit on the last task, so we carry its residue into the next task, fragmenting our attention. Newport adds, "This residue gets especially thick if your work on Task A was unbounded and of low intensity before you switched, but even if you finish Task A before moving on, your attention remains divided for a while."[23] *Unbounded* is what we discussed earlier as stopping a work cycle without a mental bookmark or coordinate placed on it for the next time we pick it back up. Multitasking clogs the brain up with orphan particles of thought, fragmenting our attention in the next task. This accumulates and accrues shallow thought like a lint roller picking up lint.

Because we are knowledge workers needing deep and productive innovation, creation, and problem solving, moving back and forth between different applications means we might be finishing shallow tasks, but not ones significant to our responsibilities. For instance, I can wash dishes, listen to the football game, and goof off with my nine-year-old with no problem because it's shallow. There may be a lag, or residual carry-over, but it's no big deal if I missed a play of the game or it took me three minutes longer to clean the dishes. But I cannot write this book or have a hard conversation while checking my inbox every few minutes. If I try, then every time I go back to refocus on deep work, it takes between seven and 20 minutes to regain focus and depth.[24] You've noticed this yourself as you're on the phone with someone, yet read an email or text at the same time. You'll go back to talking to that person, but there is residual carry-over and attention fragmentation.

Newport notes a study performed by Gloria Mark, professor of informatics at University of California, Irvine, who happens to be an expert in the science of attention fragmentation. Mark observed knowledge workers in real offices and found that even short interruptions delay the total time required to complete a task by a significant amount.[25] If you continue to keep many applications open at the same time, your work grows shallow, and you fall behind in the deep work you're called to do. There is deep work those around you need you to be occupied with, and multitasking erodes that. There is a time for shallow work, but not when attempting more significant work. So, it's settled by science. Pick something and work hard on it, switching only when you're ready to switch tasks. This is called "switchtasking," which is a healthier way to manage your energy and focus.

Switchtasking pulls many of the above threads together. It's what experts like Mark, Perman, and Newport refer to as picking up a different task or work direction when they're finished with the previous one. *We've been referring to it as an ultradian rhythm.* When the work rhythm has run its course and you have taken a restful moment, switch and be devoted to another task. Switchtasking is not mixing tasks, but lining them up sequentially. With renewed vigor coming from restful moments in between tasks, you'll get far more done than pretending to multitask. Rather than keeping your inbox or social media account open and floating back and forth from different applications with different goals, devote yourself deeply to one for an ultradian burst, break, pick up the next, break, pick up the next, and so on. This requires discipline and practice, but you'll end up getting better quality work done and creating the margin you so desperately need to be healthier.

Declaring War on Distractions

Because we don't live in a perfect world carved into neat 90- to 120-minute cycles where we're undistracted, we have to navigate distractions so they don't rip us out of our endeavor to be healthy leaders. It seems odd to consider an interruption harmful to leadership health, *but an interruption accrues interest as it pushes us from the deep work we need.* It's like a line of dominoes that start a reaction. When we trip over a needless distraction, it fragments our attention so we don't get work done in the time we have. This collapses our margin and places us in debt. Without that margin, we're overworking into sickness. If you're clumsy with distractions, you'll eventually find yourself running an up-tempo cadence until you become sick. So what do you do when a distraction comes while you're in the zone?

I think Matt Perman provides the most intuitive advice here. "If an interruption comes, quickly assess whether the value of the interruption will be greater than the time and focus you will lose on your current task. If it's significantly greater, go ahead."[26] I find that helpful advice because if you're like me, *all distractions* feel either urgent, or too easily answered to be pushed aside for later. Both the tyranny of the urgent and the allure of "getting it off our plate" quickly can entice us to abandon our deeper rhythm of work for work much more shallow in nature. So, what do we do with the distractions dressed up as easy or urgent? We assess whether it's significant enough to shift gears. If so, we end that particular work rhythm that was interrupted. If not, we get it on a list and off the mind so we can move forward. Productivity consultant David Allen and others since him have referred to this fluid state of focus as *"mind like water,"*[27] or "flow," which refers to a state where the mind is clear, creative, and able to work deeply sans distraction.

Perman follows this logic by noting our conscious mind is intended as a focusing tool, not a storage place for random items begging for the spotlight of your attention. *"When we seek to keep all the things we have to do in our head, they constantly pull at our attention and become a large source of our stress. . . . If we are able to off-load these tasks into a trusted system we review regularly, we get rid of the unconscious stress of having to track and remember so many things."*[28] Just to remind you, the reason

I'm taking the time to address productivity to this degree is for *health*. When I coach or consult suffering leaders, they task me to help them with their sleep, fitness, and nutrition, but what inevitably happens when I dig around is that although those obvious areas could use adjustments, their energy management requires a total overhaul. My goal isn't to get you to do *more* better and faster or to do what's best next—there are several volumes addressing that brilliantly. My goal is to show that your failure to manage your energy is directly affecting your leadership health.

There's no honest treatment of distractions and shallow work without at least taking a jab at social media and other forms of instant notifications. As you disinfect your work from distractions, you'll need to disable notifications to all the various applications you use and audit which ones you even need. Notifications are the obvious low hanging fruit of interruptions. Not only can they rob you of valuable energy, but they rarely carry significant value. You have total control over how your devices alert you, so this is preventable. You're the one defining how wide the gate is. Watches, phones, laptops, tablets—turn all notifications off, and just watch the world (1) not explode or (2) care that you turned it all off. If you need to use those applications, reserve a time block for them. It's shallow work that might be important, but not at the price tag of your deep work diminishing. Once I went to zero notifications and zeroing out the inbox once a day (yep, just once), I noticed immediately how much more I was able to think and work meaningfully. I became healthier simply because I was able to master my devices instead of the other way around. I also saw improvement in residual carry-over and fragmented attention.

Interruptions also come via your work environment, flushing you from the deep ultradian work rhythms we're looking to build. If you're relegated to pubs, coffee shops, and other public places, and your goal isn't to meet new people but to get some solid, deep work done, you'd do well to get some noise cancellation headphones and use a noise application on one of your devices. Widely known to facilitate focus and sleep, noise applications will let you customize frequencies to build variations of white, pink, and brown "noise." This is one of the more utilized work hacks I employ and has helped stretch and deepen the ultradian rhythms

I find myself in. I'll even use brown noise in my church office or home office so I am not distracted by staffers fighting the coffee machine or my kiddos playing the violin. The different colors represent frequencies and many wellness experts contend they are efficacious in different ways. The goal for our purposes here, however, is to simply flood the ears with a constant level of fluid sound so that intermittent ambient noise doesn't permeate your devoted attention. I can be in a noisy coffee shop using brown noise, my chosen frequency, and never hear the mug dropped 30 feet away or the kid breathing back and forth through his toy harmonica. It's all lost in the low rumble of the noise I'm being fed. It's almost womblike, focused and yet relaxed. Although it might take some getting used to, adding this to a no-notification-world sets you up for success in building deeper ultradian bursts.

Clocking Out

Restructuring our daily rhythm with rest in mind also means looking at how we navigate our evenings. I've found 5:00 p.m. to 10:00 p.m. to be one of the key sticking places for ministry leaders unable to shift gears from leading the church to leading the family. Partitioning the day helps us so that the hurry-up pace of the church isn't carried into the evening, when we should be investing in our families. Your evening has to be more than just an epilogue to your "real" day. Craig Groeschel, lead pastor of LifeChurch.tv, helps us by showing us the fence he built around his evenings. *"I don't do evening meetings, don't schedule dinner meetings, and don't have the elders meeting in the evening. . . . I get home around 5:15 every night, and that is practically set in stone."*[29] When we build fences like this in our day, it's not a confession that we're not willing to help or serve others, but that we're committed to focusing on what God has before us. If God is sovereign, and has given me responsibility and influence in my family, then I am free to say no to whatever tries its demands upon those key moments of the day.

I have a very similar routine to Groeschel. The only evenings I have on the books where I'm not with my entire family at home is (1) a weekly date night with my bride and (2) gathering with our missional community a couple of times per month. We don't allow repetitive meetings to encroach on this routine. Occasionally, we'll have a crisis requiring an evening meeting, but this is very rare because we make sure it's rare. Not everything is a crisis, and most situations can be handled the next day. If you struggle with this concept and make everyone's crisis your crisis, you'll destroy all semblance of a healthy evening routine. Not only will your health pay the steep price, but so will your family's.

Another practical step taken to protect the evening is what our staff and leadership know as "airplane mode." My phone goes into airplane mode as soon as I walk in the door. It's not the most convenient thing for the leaders at our church, but they've gotten used to contacting me before 5:30 p.m. because of this rule.[30] It's also teaching the young up-and-coming planters and leaders the example of how to value their time in their first church: the family. This one adjustment was overwhelming, and I cheated several times before becoming comfortable with it. I already know what you're thinking: "*But Luke, what if there's a serious tragedy or accident?*" Answer: You'll miss it! If it's that big of a deal, someone will get in touch with my wife or come by the house. It's a matter of cold hard math—you might miss one tragedy every 600 days, but you will also miss 5,000 needless calls, social media notifications, and text messages that start your brain toward thinking about and fixing tomorrow's issues. Let the calls, emails, text messages, and status updates stack like a cord of wood, and then handle them the next day.

Just like rebooting a machine helps it run cleaner when it starts back up, the leader running a hurry-up pace needs to formally shut down their hectic day for the sake of the *following* one. Remember the oscillation we've been referencing? When we shift broken gardens from the average daily workflow to our family and home, we're also resting by changing our environment and goals. Cal Newport remarks, "Only [with] the confidence that you're done with work until the next day can you convince your brain to downshift to the level where it can begin to recharge for the next day to follow."[31] A structured shutdown habit builds this confidence by acknowledging (1) work is done and (2) restoration can begin. To cheat this process and let the edges of work and home overlap in the evenings potentially robs the family's and leader's health. Trying to squeeze just a little bit more out of a workday can certainly jeopardize your effectiveness the next day to the point you actually get *less* done. It's wiser to respect a deliberate shutdown habit.[32]

Stepping away from the dinner table for a minute to return a text or taking 19 minutes to go to the bathroom in order to finish a "quick" call are actually robbing your family and your rest. You may be putting out a quick fire, but you're setting several more. If you think that leaving the problem overnight will make it much worse and you're needed to save the day, go back to Chapters 4 and 5 and determine whether you truly believe God is sovereign, or if he really needs you to be Superman and clock back in.

Margin is hard to build and guard without taking strategic steps. My goal has been to help you understand energy management, navigating distractions, deep work cycles, side-thinking, and other realities that can help you shape better work and afford more rest. Fixing your sleep and fitness will reap big benefits for the sick leader, but fail to manage your energy and you'll always trend toward leading as a sick person.

FRENCH RESTING
WHEN THE SABBATH IS BIOHACKED

God gave me the gospel and a horse. I've killed the horse,
so I can no longer preach the gospel.

—Robert Murray McCheyne

In the 1700s, the French developed a different calendar in a futile attempt to scrub any residue of God from how we divide time. During the French Revolution when sanitizing culture from God, they cooked up what is called the French Revolutionary Calendar. The main things we'd all notice immediately is the months have different names. The new month also had 10 days in the week instead of seven. They were fascinated with the number 10, which is why this is the period from which we inherited the metric system. This only lasted around 12 years, however, because Napoleon thought it was dumb and quashed it, returning to our current calendar. One of the primary aversions to the new calendar was the number of days *off* work. They went from no less than 52 days of recovery a year to around 35. That's over a 40 percent reduction in recovery time, and workers were getting burned out, overworked, over-fatigued, and grumpy. They revolted, and things went back to normal. (Unfortunately for us all, the metric system stayed.)

The moral to this history lesson is that God knew best what we'd need regarding rest. When we try to biohack this, we burn out. This French calendar lasted only 12 short years, but for sick leaders, it's still hanging on the wall. We are tempted to operate on the French's busted up and cobwebbed calendar. Only 56 percent of polled pastors regularly take off one day each week. Twenty-one percent confessed they take zero days off.[1] Even if you aren't uber-disciplined in reserving a day of sabbath rest every week, I hope you can at least admit working every day with no retreat isn't helping your health.

So far, we've been focused on how the body's rhythms work during the day when under load. We've seen that God created particular rhythms, like circadian and ultradian rhythms, to govern our activity and rest. Cooperating and trusting in these God-designed rhythms with gospel motivations leads us to resilient leadership. Now, I'd like to pan out and look at our macro-rhythms. How we rest weekly, seasonally, annually, and even beyond speaks to how we see our finiteness and how our rest honors God's capability. It's time to put the broken calendar away.

Weekly Rest

It's not really the goal of this book to lay down a lengthy apologetic on what and where the sabbath ought to be in our lives, but I will submit that it's a biblical imperative that ought to be honored. I hear too often that we're liberated from the bondage of a sabbath rule in our life, but the cross and vacant grave do not nullify the gift of the sabbath to us— they *focus and recalibrate it*. If you differ in how you perceive the sabbath day, I still challenge you to look into what I'm saying before you exit. Even if your theology differs from mine, thanks to science, and the car wreck that was the French calendar, I hope to change your mind.

I'm totally convinced that leaders don't take a day of rest because the work isn't done yet. But can we all be honest for a minute? The work will never be done. Not if you're doing it right. If you finally get to the bottom of your to-do list, then you have missed the mark somewhere. Broken people and broken cities will always keep our lists flush. We don't rest because we run out of things to do and get bored, but because we'll never run out of things to do. We need God to replenish, remind, and recalibrate our hearts as we employ our effort for his glory.

Consider the context of the sabbath when the Jewish nation received it as a gift. Not only did they work six days and rest on the seventh, but they even rested the land. There was certainly work that could have been done, but a picture was being illustrated of God's people resting in the arms of a sufficiently active God. Later, this would come into full focus as Jesus worked and plowed for us so that we'd enjoy an eternal sabbath in him. Jesus is our sabbath rest. DeYoung relates it similarly: "The observance of this mandate is a day of commemoration of God's creative rest, a celebration that Christ has entered that rest, that believers have begun to enter such rest, and a pointing forward to believers completely entering that rest."[2] Simply, we're a sabbath people who have a gift of sabbath rest we get to celebrate.

Again, I'm not going to get into a slap fight over whether this ought to be on Sunday or Saturday, but I hope you see that the creational mandate of the sabbath agrees with what the French found out the hard way: We need rest and we need it *often*. He made the sabbath for people, not people for the sabbath.[3] He did this because people need it. We will burn out if we place industriousness ahead of honoring God's wiring in us. If I'm more fascinated in my work than God's, then I'm aiming for a rocky coastline in my health. With an eroding trust in Jesus's peace, I will shipwreck my leadership health. If I am fascinated with God's work, however, then it will require acknowledging I'm carved out of dust and require recovery.

Additionally, consider that your "day off" is not always a very good sabbath. Sometimes, a day off is just another day of work in a different garden. Trading staff meetings for broken toilet plumbing. Replacing the mouse and keyboard for the water pump on the family van. Even off days spent on the lake may be more tiring than the workday you left the day before. Recall in past chapters how leisure isn't work, but it also isn't always rest. I personally long for the off days when I can sit and rest and watch at least one half of a good college football game, run a trail where I won't see anyone, pray, catch up on some reading, destroy my kids in whatever game still works on the Wii, etc. Those days are full of rest mingled with a bit of leisure. I'm not fixing, solving, or being taxed. I'm simply day off-ing. I've also had off days where I've hiked in the sun for over six or seven miles with grumpy girls or spent the day at Dollywood.[4] Those days have me coming home more wiped out than any workday. That was a day off, *but not a suitable rest day.*

I'm drawing a distinction between resting and day off-ing because too many will take a day off that exhausts them, yet consider it a sabbath rest day. Wrong. If you enter the next day still emotionally wonky from the day off, it may have been a day off, but it most certainly wasn't a restful day. On weeks like that, you'd be wise to take an *extra* day, or a couple half days. Predictably, I get push back here due to the reduction in scheduled work time, but remember, *rest is more than not working.* Rest resets us for better and more creative work. It's multiplication by subtraction. You'll get more done in less time as you cooperate with how God has engineered your biology.

Be especially discerning on heavy weeks where the day off is also abnormally intense. On those weeks, be diligent to create space to rest in God. For example, my rest day is Monday, and my day off is typically Saturday. If my Saturday is very restful and I have a lot of flex where I can steer it, then I may choose to work a bit on Monday afternoon. Right now, however, we're in a home remodel, so Saturdays are full of flooring, demolition, installation, and a billion trips to Lowe's because I got the wrong thing. Those days aren't restful at all, but wear me down. I'll be needing that Monday after all. Too many leaders congratulate themselves on working six days and checking the "rest" box because they take Saturday off. Maybe, maybe not. It depends on how taxing that Saturday is.

If my Saturday wasn't too taxing, I'll *still* be careful as to what *kind* of work I'm doing on Monday. After all, Sunday was just yesterday, and I still have the residue from it. If you lead or preach on Sundays and enjoy it like I do, you are unarguably still in need of rest. It's useless to try to convince yourself that Sunday is your sabbath rest if you are a preacher/ teacher. You might as well be a Dallas Cowboy and try to convince people that game day is restful. Your body is being taxed emotionally and cognitively as much as any athlete and more than most.[5] You may remember from an earlier chapter my self-experimentation while preaching. The goal was to analyze the effects and emotional load on the nervous and endocrine system of a common Sunday preacher, measuring heart rate; heart rate variability; cortisol response; and blood pressure before, during, and after the service. I was certainly able to see a "fight or flight" signature.[6] Even though I enjoyed the work, the eustress and distress cocktail from Sunday required a commensurate rest. Sabbath rest isn't archaic and optional to leaders hunting resilience. Not only do we see biblical wisdom and care in this recalibrating celebration, we see that our work—*even the work that energizes us*—is stretching our biochemistry to the point it requires recovery.

I've tried many different variations of rest/work when it comes to the weekend, and I keep finding fruit in a restful family day on Saturday (where I'm predominantly day off-ing), working hard on Sunday, and taking Monday at whatever pace makes sense given the preceding Saturday. If Saturday was taxing, I'm going to rest totally on Monday. If Saturday was mostly restful, I'll enter work on Monday at some point, typically around the middle of the day. Even then, the type of work is radically lighter. I bubble wrap myself on Mondays because I'm still not quite ready to be spread thin. Dr. Archibald Hart, an expert in the effects of stress on the leader, explains, "I advise pastors to work on Mondays, but to use that day to do low-energy or routine activities. It's the time to tidy your desk, throw out the trash or do some filing. . . . It's not a time to pick a fight, go hassle those who annoy you, make a critical decision or deal with difficult budget problems. If you get your adrenaline up again, you may feel all right, but you'll rob your body of rest and recuperation."[7] Mondays will be the day I get caught up on my lighter entrepreneurial work, reading, studying, and other tasks I can do with low emotional deposit. My assistant and other leaders, however, know that I am not accessible on that day, and my phone is either off or in a mode where only particular calls can get through. This allows me to holistically process Sunday and yield better leadership Tuesday through Friday.

When we act French and try to hack the work/rest rhythm, we are recruiting damage and sickness. No one burns out for skipping a rest day, but everyone burns out if they skip a big bucket of rest days. If you're not building these wisely into your calendar and guarding them, you'll see linearity and health that's deteriorating. When you think about it, you're preaching with your calendar, and your message is, "God's work wasn't enough and he isn't strong or good enough, so I need to stay clocked in." Even Martin Luther struggled here. Biographer Roland Bainton notes Luther's struggle to retreat from work: "I did not want to come here," Luther wrote, "I wanted to be in the fray." And again regarding rest, "I had rather burn on live coals than rot here."[8] Bainton goes on to list out Luther's medical report to include gems like constipation, anxiety, poor nutrition, and insomnia. Most would agree that he accomplished volumes in his life, and we'd further agree that God worked greatly through him, and yet even this giant among men struggled with resting.

Monthly Rest

Toward the end of King George V's reign, he was asked what he would do if he could do anything. He quickly answered that he'd "take his biggest car and drive and drive as far as it would take him. There, he would find a little farmhouse, and in the farmhouse there would be a small, clean, whitewashed room, furnished only with a bed and an open fire. He would lie down on the bed, and lying so, alone in the small, clean room, he would look at the glowing coals of the fire, and the flames playing blue about them—and so he would rest. For once in a royal lifetime he would rest."[9] I think we all get George. He's describing an unhurried place that is different and inaccessible. My kingdom is much smaller than George's, but I need to take a day or two every so often and create space to move slowly, be inaccessible, and move outside of my typical context.

As mentioned earlier, I keep a hammock in my truck next to my trail shoes. I also have a sort of "go box" full of what I'd need to camp for a couple days and nights if I needed to leave quickly. Once every five to six weeks or so, I make use of the mountains and streams around me. I even named my hammock King George because staring at a campfire ends up being one of the more spiritual and therapeutic things I get to do. Of all the changes I kicked against, this wasn't one of them. I've simply profited too much from it. I leave behind all media, hanging to-do list items, and unreturned phone calls. Retreating to the mountains where I can square my shoulders with the beauty of God, I rest. This has been such a game changer for me that my wife makes sure these days are put in my calendar a year in advance.

During the spring, summer, and early fall, I camp. In the late fall, winter, and early spring months, I find a cabin. I bring as little as possible and may even fast during most of these retreats, which makes them easier to slip in and out of. The whole goal is to get alone—gain perspective; be unhurried; be untouchable—and rest. Sometimes, I read a book that happens to be timely; sometimes I journal. Often, I use a personal assessment that is designed for my temperament and weaknesses. This spiritual discipline has radically shifted my leadership health, and I cannot recommend it enough.

I've personalized my self-assessment to specifications, knowing where I can skid off track and where my personal danger zones are. This means I'm innovating the assessment often, adding or taking away prompts as I change over time. It's purposefully a work in progress, like a living document. I also handwrite everything because I'm often in places where a laptop would just ruin it all. When going through this assessment, I always take my time. I'm never in a hurry and may not even finish. There have been times when I never make it past the halfway mark. The goal for me is to take a deep breath, defragment, and get my swing back.[10] I'll list some of my prompts, but suggest you make your own to reflect you.

A *hotspot* is what distance runners call the discomfort that comes just before a blister. Pre-blister, the skin gets pretty hot, but can be easy to miss. Hotspots develop in key areas of friction, and if you don't address them by tying your shoes differently, changing socks, or applying a lubricant (yes, there is lubricant for feet), they bloom into impressive blisters. As I retreat into these deep moments, I'm hoping to keep hotspots from becoming blisters. Both my wife and leadership team can tell when I've had these times. I'm rested and leading with a full tank.

Here are some examples of my assessment prompts. After answering the initial question, I always follow with "*why?*" and then end with (1) what I can do to see change and (2) how I can pray right now. As you drive your life into healthy resiliency, I hope you enjoy this exercise as I have.

- What have been some recent examples of God's grace in my life?
- How accurately have I seen God recently? Where have I perceived him wrongly?
- How has my confidence been lately before God in prayer and worship?
- How's my dominion over electronics and media?
- Where is my eye line, and what am I allowing myself to look at?
- How has my connection with my wife been?
- How has my discipling of my individual kids been?
- How have I handled my mouth?
- How has my discipline been regarding my schedule and time?
- Has my energy been spent in the proper places?
- How has my delegation been?
- What's filling my tank? What's draining it?
- How have my personal study, sabbath, and times of solitude been?
- How have my sermon and teaching prep/delivery been?
- What sins have been the hardest for me?
- How have my health and energy levels been?
- How has my sleep been?
- How has my stewardship of wealth been?
- Who has sinned against me, and how am I responding to them?
- Where should I currently be seeking wisdom?
- Are there any early warning signs of burnout?
- How honest have I been lately with myself, and is there any self-deception I am accommodating for?
- How has my writing been (journaling, blogging, personal study)?
- Where am I currently being a coward?
- What is currently my biggest fear?
- How have I been in preaching the gospel to myself? Kids? Wife?
- What opportunities are overwhelming me?
- What am I currently expecting that only God can do?
- What decisions am I avoiding because of the "fear of failure?"

This isn't time spent escaping hard work, but time you invest into the future of your leadership fitness. London and Wiseman speak to this in their book *Pastors at Greater Risk,* and they happen to agree with the leadership hygiene that these monthly pauses produce. After their research, they comment, "We think a pastor should establish a practice of getting away for a whole day once a month to a quiet place where he does nothing but read the Bible and think about personal spiritual growth. This isn't time away from ministry but time that feeds ministry."[11] I understand "personal spiritual growth" is a wide category, but times like these are best spent examining our emotional awareness (EQ) and how we're currently interacting with God and others. When it comes to emotions, we don't really set the agenda. You need uninterrupted time to consider deeply what you're unable to consider during the frenetic pace of leadership. If you neglect this valuable time, the emotions don't really pass by, but dig in deep. They stack in layers and erupt later. Developing emotional intelligence escapes the scope of this book, but make no mistake, exploring your cluttered emotional self in times of retreat is far better than seeing it all reveal itself improperly later during burnout.

I can already hear your push-back and see your smirk. "Soooo I'm supposed to leave my wife with the kids?" "How can I afford that?" "Not everyone lives in the mountains." Sabbath moments? Sure. Sabbath days? Okay. Even sabbaticals get a pass, but for too many, this periodic retreat seems unnecessary. I felt the same way at first, but when I returned from my first two-dayer, my wife immediately noticed the shift in me. In fact, she became the biggest supporter of these trips. *"I'd much rather have you gone one or two days per month if I get this upgraded version of you when you're here!"* The leaders around me agree, which leads me to the next point. The expenses for this are firmly in our church's budget. Right under "Pastoral Retreat," everything from the gas to the firewood and cabin rental. It seemed odd to our team to fund my books and conference travels to help me lead better, but not endorse this crucial aspect of leadership health. They know a chunk of my health depends on it.

Not only my health, but my ability to carry vision, creativity, and inspiration is fueled by these periodic trips. Bubba Jennings spoke with Matt Perman about this in Perman's work *What's Best Next* and also designs these days not just for physical or emotional health, but for the ability to be refreshed and inspired. "If you don't take time to get outside of your regular rhythms and dream, you'll never innovate. You need to reinvent your rhythms every so often and block out a day, like a dream day. Look at all the things weighing you down, look at how you can actually get them done or who you can delegate them to. Look at what rhythms are working and which aren't working. If you don't give yourself the flexibility and freedom to do that as needed, you'll burn yourself out."[12] Jennings is right: Remember that one of the key symptoms of burnout is feeling distant, unmotivated, and uninspired. The raw truth is the longer you remain in the same place doing the same basic thing, the more you'll have to *work* at staying inspired and engaged. Gallup found that after six months doing the same task, only 38 percent of employees were able to stay engaged. After three years, the figure drops to an unimpressive 22 percent.[13] You need to retreat for health, but you also need to retreat for a refreshed heart and mind to continue faithful leadership. This is what it means to be resilient.

I know that not everyone has paradise in their backyard. I grew up in dusty West Texas, so I know how much of a pilgrimage it can be to get somewhere impressive. Let me repeat: The goal isn't to go somewhere *exotic*, but to get somewhere *else*. Even if it is the Holiday Inn in a neighboring town, or a friend's house when they're gone. Recalibrate your surroundings away from familiarity. When you skip this step, you end up opening jars and killing bugs for the girls, picking up the phone, and slipping into your everyday routine. Stay put and you'll be too easily reclaimed by the average environment.

On a practical note, I typically leave for these one- to two-day retreats *right after I preach.* I take off the mic, slip out the back door, and am in the mountains within 45 minutes. This allows me to leverage my Sunday afternoons, gives me a full Monday, and allows me to return on Tuesday. I have found that this spread of time creates enough space for me. Another day feels too long and eats up too much of the week, but any shorter and I end up feeling rushed. You may need a different format, but beware of locating them so that you're tempted to prepare a sermon while away. Or even worse, turn your retreat *into* a sermon—don't do that. Whatever the format, *unrushed time elsewhere* is the essential ingredient. Brennan Manning says it best: "It takes time for the water to settle. Coming to interior stillness requires waiting. Any attempt to hasten the process only stirs up the water anew."[14]

Annual Resting

Scaling outward toward longer moments and days of rest, you'll immediately notice the rise in the need to intentionally plan and invest. Don't be overly concerned about the increase in investment. A leader who isn't getting away annually is a pastor who may save money and time short term, but pays a heavier long-term price tag in unrelenting fatigue and dreams of quitting. I'm specifically talking about taking *vacations* and annual spiritual *retreats* here.

It's unfortunate that I have to comment on ministry leaders scheduling a vacation, but almost two out of three ministry leaders reveal they don't take adequate vacations each year. Many grab a quick "day or two here or there," or plop an extra day on the back of a work trip and call it a vacation day to little effect. Although I'm a big fan of making use of conveniently placed days of rest around trips or holidays, it can't add up to the time you really need. Taking two or three weeks off at a time is more valuable than taking equivalent time broken up over the span of a year. Just as Manning explained earlier, water takes a while to settle down, and there is no good way to rush it.

It takes a few days of vacation to even realize you're on vacation, and the last couple days are spent thinking about what's waiting upon return. In other words, a two-week vacation is really closer to nine or ten days. I cannot recommend too highly taking as much vacation as your ministry or church allows and placing it *all in a row*. If you're a teaching and preaching pastor, I'd also suggest you take a month off of your preaching roster. I've done this for the last several years, and it's been powerfully refreshing. Not the same thing as a sabbatical or retreat, but it still frees up an inordinate amount of time and removes the deadline of Sunday morning. It's amazing how much RAM is freed up to rest, get caught up on reading, leave town, or work on things that fill your tank and bring refreshment to you. Access the bullpen around you (or build one) and give those leaders opportunities to serve. When I do this in the deep summer, I'm able to stay at a 30,000 feet cruising altitude where I can examine who we are and where we're going.

I'm starting to see younger pastors leverage their sermon load in summers, which is refreshing and makes sense. July, especially in college towns or larger metro areas, is a great time to do this. I've even noticed how some leaders will attend other congregations on Sundays during that month to be encouraged without the temptation to clock back in. This is especially helpful for those preachers and teachers who are unable to afford a true sabbatical. In church plants or young ministries, a sabbatical may be a bit tougher to come by as it requires so much in the way of expense and leadership capital. Sabbaticals aren't impossible in church plants, just more difficult. A month of no preaching every year until the church can carry a sabbatical is an innovative answer.

Sabbaticals

We currently have a new president in the White House, which means we also have an ex-president on vacation. A long one. Seeing pictures of him relaxing after a long, hard job reminded me of another president, Teddy Roosevelt. I've read a few of his biographies, and it's often recorded that after every tough campaign or presidential term, you'd find Theodore hunting elephants in Africa or exploring jungles in South America. It was his thing. It'd take him forever to get over there and forever to get back, and he'd spend copious time tromping through God's country or stalking large game. I'm going to call that his *sabbatical* in a certain sense. He wasn't quitting public service, but knew he'd need a moment to collect himself so he could return with durability and vision. As we zoom out even further, we come to the rest we should find every several years.

As a young church, we're presently looking to build out my first sabbatical. I have to admit; the thought of it frightens me. Everyone I know who has traveled through a true sabbatical considers it both the greatest and hardest thing they've done. Some even exit these long rests deciding not to enter the same position or role again. I understand that isn't the best endorsement to those already unsure of their future.

For many, the sabbatical is equal parts frightening and enchanting. For the burned-out leader or one who has already wrestled burnout, the sabbatical must be a serious consideration, not a mythological artifact.

Wayne Cordeiro handles this last part of scalable rest well, and if you're considering one, I highly recommend reading his thoughts on taking sabbaticals. He wisely suggests a third of a sabbatical to be spent reinforcing education through extra reading, conferences, maybe even a college class. "Congregational life, technology, and societal norms change rapidly, and the educational opportunities a sabbatical provides ensure that the leadership and the congregation do not end up in a slow, downward spiral to obsolescence."[15] This allows the leader to fly at the entrepreneurial level by "futuring" and expanding their breadth of knowledge. Education can be both exciting and refreshing and carries no obligations to implement it on the spot.

Also, according to Cordeiro, the remainder of a sabbatical is wisely spent in rest and recreation. I've witnessed friends employ something similar. They'll traffic in continuing education for things they happen to be interested in, and the rest of the time they do whatever they want that isn't work. I have one friend who revisited his Greek and did an exhaustive work through the book of John—when he wasn't sailing a small boat. I heard of another leader on sabbatical who spent time learning how to make guitars. Another hiked a chunk of the Appalachian Trail. You get the picture.

What makes a sabbatical efficacious isn't just doing what you want, or brushing up on a class or two, but it's the copious time allowed to do those things. In fact, most who go on a true sabbatical talk of how uncomfortable the amount of time was, which is indicative of a workaholic in deep need of retreat. For your biology, vision, inspiration, and creativity to charge back up, it needs more of a low-drip, slow-trickle charge. This cannot be done over a long weekend or even a vacation. It cannot be rushed.

This idea cooperates with a principle we've been majoring on to this point: The time on sabbatical must be commensurate to the amount of energy spent and damage done. If you've not been carried off the field on a stretcher with heavy endocrine and neurological degradation, maybe three months is responsible. If you're under heavy medical/health and wellness supervision and are likely to quit or can't leave the bed, maybe a year is more responsible. This is something for your surrounding leadership team and spouse to speak into heavily, because you'll likely want to short-change the duration due to feeling indispensable.

Some submit that a sabbatical should only occur after seven years of leadership. I would concur, but mainly because it takes approximately that long to get an endeavor (ministry, church plant, replant, etc.) to cruising altitude. I also see wisdom in long-term or tenured leaders scheduling a repetitive sabbatical every seven years thereafter. Some naysayers might react with, "*I do not understand why pastors and certain leaders need a sabbatical. I don't get one.*" It bears repeating something I mentioned earlier—ministry leaders rarely take a sabbath or day off, and most put in 8- to 12-hour days on Sundays. In the marketplace, most workers get at least a two-day weekend. Added to that, most employees in the secular marketplace get around six long weekends a year due to national holidays. This means they have paid time off from late Friday afternoon until Tuesday morning—six times a year. If you were to add up all the long weekends, holidays, sick days, vacation days, and any other paid time off over a seven-year span, you'll get—you guessed it— about what a responsible leader will end up taking in a true sabbatical. It's just math.

I hope you see the oscillation between work and rest something that God has designed to celebrate his work for us. It's as if he embedded a piece of his gospel story even into our finite capacities. "The death mark of the believer is deep restfulness. Jesus knew God would fulfill His work. As the believer advances, he learns to rest perfectly in his God."[16] Even as Andrew Murray says this, I can feel the blood pressure and anxiety wane. God has built us to work, and he has built us to rest— and both glorify him brilliantly. Recovering in the middle of your days, weeks, months, years, and long seasons is a celebration of God's gospel, and when we honor it, it creates resilience in us. As leaders, we can work harder when we work, and rest confidently knowing our rest is more than just not working. If you're interested in avoiding burnout, or are attempting to come out of burnout, you must find rest, find it often, and do it to the glory of God!

PIE HOLE
WE ARE WHAT WE EAT

There is no growth without change, no change without loss, and no loss without pain. You'll grow only to the threshold of your pain.
—Samuel Chand, *Leadership Pain*

I never really enjoyed PAC-MAN. Even when there was no other video game around, I found it boring, and the joystick never agreed with me. I do, however, like to eat like PAC-MAN. That guy eats whatever he wants, sometimes even eating what could kill him in those ghost-looking things. Just eats, eats, eats. Sounds like the life. My hope in this chapter is to convince you that you aren't PAC-MAN. You can't eat what you want, even if you jog a little and played soccer in college. Your food eventually becomes a part of you and makes up who you are. Think about that. Sitting there as you read this you are generally comprised of what you've been eating.

When I was tired of being sick, I had to seriously evaluate my nutrition. I was training and competing so much that I thought I had a free pass on whatever I wanted to eat, which I still find common among other leaders. We flip tires and visit the squat rack a couple times a week, viewing the exertion as penance for the Funyuns we had earlier. We figure as long as we burn calories, we can chow down indiscriminately. This may be a new concept for you, *but all calories are not created equal.* Your nutrition cannot be steered by calories in and calories out as if it were a mathematical equation. It's far beyond cold hard math. In addition to evaluating how my calories were sourced, I also had to face the fact that some of the foods I was eating actually contributed to and accelerated my burnout.

I know this might be the hardest chapter for you to read because I'm not suggesting you merely alter something (like sleep) or add something (like fitness). I'm suggesting you drop some things altogether, and no one likes to be told to stop something, even if it's killing them. How and what you eat is very likely leading you closer to burning out, not further from it. If the statistics are right, seven out of 10 of you reading this are at least 32 pounds overweight.[1] If you think that's no big deal, grab a 35-pound plate at the gym and carry it around for a few hours, and tell me how your back and knees feel. At our current clip, 33 percent of America will have type 2 diabetes by 2050, and 95 percent will be overweight.[2]

What concerns me most is not so much leaders who acknowledge being overweight, but those of us who aren't overweight and therefore feel exempt. Being thin doesn't mean you're anywhere near healthy. "You can be fat on the inside and skinny on the outside or metabolically obese with normal weight. It's very dangerous, and it leads to all the same consequences as being fat, such as heart attacks, strokes, cancer, dementia and diabetes."[3] Physician and neuroimager Jimmy Bell even gave this condition the acronym TOFI: Thin on the outside, fat on the inside.[4] As it turns out, whenever you slide someone into a DXA or MRI scanner, you can visually see not only their fat, but where it's distributed.[5] Many sick, but thin, patients are showing high levels of metabolic obesity, and guess where it sits? That's right, around the visceral organs in the midsection. Your gut.

I've never been overweight before. I've always fallen within the "healthy" metric of whatever test I was taking. My BMI and other various measurements never raised any alarms, yet I was dangerously close to breaking components vital to my body.[6] I was like 88 percent of you: driving through a fast food joint at least once a week and feeling great that onion rings were technically a vegetable and the iceberg lettuce buried under the not-meat was at least green.[7]

Upon my return from Doc Holliday back in 2011, I was immediately placed on a strict nutritional regimen. Actually, it was more of a cleanse. Any food I wanted badly was most likely on the "no fly" list. It was hell. The good doctor revealed to me that I was subsisting on food that cluttered my attempt to be healthy, and a cleanse would "wipe the slate clean" so that I could see what was problematic as I slowly added *some* foods back into my routine. Some foods made it back on my menu; some never will again. *The good news: I now feel better than food used to taste.*

I dumped all foods that needed to be freed from a sealed package. If it saw the south side of a deep fryer, I couldn't eat it. If it was passed through a window, I couldn't eat it. If a barista handed it to me, I couldn't consume it. I also ditched carbohydrates not gained from vegetables, *all* refined sugar, coffee, wheat, rice, beans, coffee, alcohol, coffee, fruit, pastries, coffee, and finally, coffee. I felt like an addict going through withdrawals because that is exactly what I was doing. I walked around highly distracted, very moody, tired, had a three-week headache, weird smelling sweat, and cravings I never thought possible. I felt as if I were losing my soul, and I am sure I was a delight to be around.

On the upside, I lost 18 pounds in three weeks with absolutely no fitness training. Eighteen pounds on a 190-pound frame is nearly 10 percent of my body by weight. You couldn't tell by looking at me because all of the weight was sitting in dangerous, less detectable areas. My body was detoxing, and my hunger was being trained. The very reason I was ready to pull a mask over my face and break the display glass at the local bakery was due to my furious reliance on sugar. The cravings were teaching me that I was eating mindlessly and that it was hurting me. My PAC-MAN days were over. Yours need to be as well.

Engineered for Failure

We don't really have hard cravings for broccoli or Brazil nuts. It might seem nice and welcome, but you don't get super grumpy when you don't get health food on demand in the same way you do with a MoonPie or pumpkin spice latte. When a food is taken away and you go a little crazy, it's because your body has developed an addiction-like state regarding that food. Saying no to unhealthy foods is not all about how disciplined you are. When it comes to our decision-making, food interacts with our brain chemistry. In other words, choosing healthy food is not as simple as turning right instead of left.

Our brains actually influence our decisions by reminding us where "peace" can be found as rewards in tough times. When we have particular foods, our brains release chemicals such as dopamine to give us the feeling of achievement, reinforcing future behavior. We're actually not much different than the dogs Pavlov used. For example, if I have a no-good, rotten, overwhelming, and difficult day capped off by a pint of Ben & Jerry's ice cream, chemicals communicate to my body a sense of reward. Studies have shown that when future pain comes the body then knows, "It's ice cream time!" not solely because it loves ice cream as much as it loves the perceived reward and semi-escape that it represents. The bad news is that there's a diminishing return to this when abused over the long haul, similar to those who struggle with drug addiction. A single pint a month turns into one a day.

Many researchers have noted a tangential relationship between the effect of some hard drugs and particular foods on our brains. Many of the foods you may enjoy are *literally* designed to unleash key chemicals in your body. Our fast food industry is well aware of the food-brain relationship and even manufactures food products to amplify the feelings. Sounds conspiratorial I know, but this is pretty much common knowledge now. Food companies are looking to hook you.

In addition to the strict chemical odds we're up against in today's diet, our nostalgic memories lead us to eat certain things at certain times, with stress being a common trigger. This is why coffee seems so much better in the morning or more appropriate when it's cold and rainy rather than when it's 96 degrees outside. It's pattern and memory driven. This is also why I'd never get a cheap beer or hot dog at home, but when watching the Rangers play the Red Sox, it would seem incomplete without it. When we slam into hard seasons as leaders, our memories and biology convince us only certain foods will work, and so we'll hunt those foods down and pay any amount of money for them. Nachos from a chain restaurant—no thanks. Nachos from a football stadium—*take all my money*.

I noticed over the *first few weeks* of my cleanse that the initial demands were abating and I was no longer tempted to cheat or destroy things.[8] My mind grew sharper, almost as if I had awaken from a long stupor. My energy didn't vaporize in the afternoon, my skin cleared up, my abs came back, my closest friends and bride noticed my attitude change, and about a dozen other very nice perks appeared. After only a couple months of this cleanse, I knew that I liked the way I felt more than I like the way some of the food I used to eat tasted.

After the whiteboard of my gut was cleaned, I slowly added some foods back in, looking for reactions. I learned that I can eat some foods all the time. Some foods I could eat moderately. And some foods I could no longer eat. I understand the controversy in "diets" and "fads," and I promise I won't push one on you.[9] We're all built differently with different budgets. A diet that works for me may not work so well for you. We're all also allergic to different foods, so maybe we can agree there is no "silver bullet" diet for everyone. God, in his brilliance and creativity, has designed us to have subtle differences in how we interact with food. There are, however, some foods that could and should be eradicated from all diets, regardless of individual chemistry. Basic structural changes can be made by all, regardless of whatever fine-tuning you apply to your final food plan.

Abusing Progress

A primary complication for leaders trying to be PAC-MAN is the ease and readiness with which we can get our hands on food. Count how many fast food drive-throughs there are on Main Street next time you get the chance. It's not like we have to go home and take 45 minutes to bake or cook the food we shouldn't be eating—we can do it in mere minutes for mere dollars. I'll even bet my next paycheck that within my lifetime, a drone can bring me my double meat double cheeseburger. I foresee efficiency in the food industry leading leaders to burnout faster and in greater numbers. Progress has made bad food easier to get, which I would argue is no longer progress. This accessibility has led to horrible diets which have accelerated pervasive fatigue.

Dr. Swenson speaks to the trade we make in technological advancement. "Gone are the old infectious foes, but replacing them are a variety of frustrating enemies variously known as 'the new morbidity,' 'the diseases of civilization,' and 'the diseases of lifestyle.' These ailments come as a result of our bad habits and poor choices."[10]

In other words, just as we say goodbye to the bubonic plague, we eat food that is begotten through high technology, and *half* of us will die due to lifestyle choices where food is a big player.[11] This isn't where our grandparents envisioned technology leading us back in their day. I can recall cheesy futuristic books and movies that portrayed an evolved human race—one where we have no toxins, wear slim, futuristic clothes, and are all shaped as if we hit the elliptical trainer every morning. We're not even close to that picture of humanity. Sure, we have technology making food more accessible and inexpensive, but as Swenson writes, we aren't really gifted with discipline by that same technology.[12]

On a brighter side, just as harmful food is cheaper and easier to get our mitts on now, so is better-sourced, healthier food. When steering my diet in a different heading, I was initially overwhelmed, feeling inconvenienced due to my new menu being so hard to find. Many of my primary meetings occurred over food, and so I ended up being "that guy" editing my food choice to the poor server to the point that it no longer looked like what was on their menu. It was also inconvenient to drive out of my way to go to the only healthy market to buy food. If you've already brought some course correction to your menu, you know exactly what I'm talking about. Yet, even in the last few years, I have seen greater ease and accessibility for healthy foods. Now, most grocery stores have an "organic" section, and most towns have a farm share program or farmer's market where you can get your hands on seasonal goods with little difficulty. Additionally, with the advent of certain outlets online, you can have a well-sourced and holistically healthy pantry for approximately the same cost you were paying in the Cocoa Puffs and Wonder Bread days. I hope to help with some practical methods to make your transition a bit easier, but no matter what hard application I can bring, the discipline to "apply" them rests on your shoulders.

Eating to Medicate
There's a time when eating feeds the flesh more than the body. When this involves Wild Turkey or Corona, we call it a drinking problem.

We all know that turning to alcohol, even in moderation, when life is overwhelming is medicating the flesh. It's attempting to remedy our felt need to escape. For those who struggle with abusing alcohol, it's not the taste of the alcohol they're addicted to—it's the hope of escape. Even in moderation, a tumbler of whiskey can promise escape from our out-of-control life, and when we believe that promise we've entered a drinking problem. Even a single glass of harmless red wine, when used to escape your hard work, is abuse. It has become a replacement for the peace Jesus brought us and promises us.

At this point, not many disagree, but the same line of reasoning holds true when applied to food. In fact, more people die from abusing food than from abusing alcohol. Eighty percent of type 2 diabetes is related to obesity and there has been a 76 percent increase in type 2 diabetes in middle-aged adults since 1990.[13] When it comes to medicating ourselves as a populace, food is doing far more damage than alcohol. Let me say that again with different words: *food is killing more leaders than booze.* I personally know leaders who declare scorched earth on the effects of alcohol abuse because of the damage it can do, yet are unable to say no to french fries. I know this may be an unpopular sentiment, but if we viewed dependence on food in ministry leadership as we did alcohol, we'd shrink the ranks of qualified leaders overnight. Certainly, you can't get drunk on Moon Pies (I only know this because I've tried), but abusing them for the express purpose of escaping difficulty is simply a different color of abuse, but abuse all the same. Eating to medicate is abandoning dependence on the Creator and requiring peace and reward from creation instead. Eating to medicate is not eating to the glory of God.

Eating to medicate is not a warning to those with a poor BMI or who are punching new holes in their belt, it's for the svelte and ordinary looking leader as well. *I think we've gone too long gauging our abuse of food by our weight on a scale. You can have a 32-inch waist and still abuse food heavily.* I did this my whole young life. Nowhere in God's word does gluttony equal overweight, and nowhere in God's word to us do we find scale readings to be the rudder for when we are eating for the body or eating for the flesh. It's very possible you're reading this and are within the parameters of weight given your height, yet you're making food to be a semi-Jesus that delivers rewards in tough times. *Food is great for eating, but makes a terrible Jesus.*

Fad Diets

Go to the food section of any bookseller and you'll see a wall of books in bright colors with skinny people in Lycra flexing on the front. Add to this the blogosphere full of people who swear eating Chipotle or bananas everyday helped them lose 50 pounds. They are working hard at convincing you that you'll look amazing if you follow their proprietary protocol. I'm not saying that some of these methods won't work, because some of them certainly will, but I'd like to put your mind at ease since food science and nutrition can be so overwhelming.

Avoid diets that are not based on nutrient density and balance. In other words, drinking only cayenne pepper and grapefruit juice instead of food in order to cleanse isn't a great direction. You'll lose weight but certainly won't gain health. Remember, the goal is to gain health, not carve out your biceps. There are numerous diet plans that will shed pounds but destroy your biochemistry at the same time. The '80s and '90s were full of diets that preached a single food or supplement to be the panacea for all shapes and sizes. Eat bacon but not bread, drink shakes instead of food, remove all meat, remove all fat, remove all carbs, etc. Many fads focus on eliminating some nutrients while favoring others. The trouble here is that your body actually runs best on a robust variety of macro/micronutrients. Being skinny isn't always healthy when your biology is looking for nutrients it'll never see.

Avoid diets that are overly simple or overly complex. I know this may sound unhelpful at first, but you shouldn't need a master's degree in nutrition to eat correctly, and neither should your food IQ be the same as your toddler's. You'll need to do some homework from time to time to make a good food plan work, yet not so much that it's only accessible to the scientific elite and requires six apps on your phone to track. I had to brush up on my biochemistry to write and coach others, but to be honest, I only needed to spend a small amount of energy accumulating knowledge that would lead my own body to health. It's likely you'll need to pick up another book or two in order to get serious. If you're like me, your bookshelf is full of books you've been wanting to read, and the thought of a "food book" outcompeting "real books" is hard to indulge, but remember, how you interact with food from here out displays your understanding of stewardship and worship. *Also, I'd contend that a book on nutrition for the frenetic leader may be worth 10 books on leadership that are saying very similar things.* At last count, I have read over 70 books specifically on leadership development or organizational leadership, and not one of them spoke deeply on how I handled food.

Avoid diets that require many specific purchases. Don't read what I'm not saying. It is very possible you'll have to learn where the supermarket keeps kale, and then proceed to the checkout with it in hand, but be wary of food plans that won't work *without* exact, particular, or proprietary food or supplements. The reason many people author and invent fad diets is to make buckets of money on the backend through extra purchases. Selling products with a service is more lucrative than just selling a service. Kind of like buying a cheap printer, only to keep sinking money into ink. You shouldn't have to do this with nutrition. Simply changing which foods are in your kitchen and which foods you pick from the menu will do the work you need. You won't need to have a GNC membership card or join an "elite" group with unlocked benefits on a website. Keep it simple.

Avoid diets where weight is the primary metric. As a personal trainer in college, I'd repeatedly have to convince clients that their weight gain was *good*. We're so enslaved to the digital readout on the scale that we make it the ultimate bar of progress. In all honesty, when pursuing health, you'll lose weight a bit slower than you'd like, but your health will increase. Change your metrics to sustained energy, better sleep, better sex drive, more strength, increased mental clarity, emotional stability, increased creativity, and a host of other intangibles. Learn to recast what your "marks" are as you alter your food lifestyle and leave both the scale's accusations and applause in 1950.

Food Discipline

A lack of discipline is what destroys many good intentions. It's moments of strength and resolve that forge goals and resolutions—and it's moments of weakness that tear progress down. Food provides us one of the best opportunities to develop internal discipline. With fitness training, we can "*see*" the results which strengthen our discipline. With sleep and rest, we can "*feel*" the results which in turn strengthens our discipline. With food restrictions, however, the results are deferred and less obvious, so it's easier to cheat. Food, in my opinion, is one of the best laboratories for forging good discipline.

Jerry Bridges rightly and simply defines discipline as "structured, planned training."[14] No real lasting alteration to your nutrition is going to come easily or quickly. It will take time to stave off certain cravings and temptations and, to be honest, after several years some of my cravings still haven't died. I haven't consumed a Coca-Cola in eight years, yet I could drink one right now. Same for doughnuts and calzones. I still haven't out-grown those cravings. Structure and planning, however, are the founda-tional elements that give discipline a fighting chance. The wise leader plans a structured food plan that will build health in hectic and stressful living.

Discipline begins now, not later. As V. L. Allineare rightly says, "When it comes to eating right and exercising, there is no 'I'll start tomorrow.' Tomorrow is disease."[15] Kicking the can down the same street as we promise to start the next day is a step toward indulgence. Every time we say yes, we make it more difficult to say no the next time. In his epic work *The Pursuit of Holiness*, Bridges comments on how holiness interacts with discipline around food:

> One more lustful look or one more piece of pie never satisfies. . . . We must recognize that we have developed habit patterns of sin. We have developed the habit of shading the facts a little bit when it is to our advantage. We have developed the habit of giving in to the inertia that refuses to let us get up in the morning. These habits must be broken, but they never will till we make a basic commitment to a life of holiness without exceptions.[16]

A key reason many struggle more than they should with food is that they have yet to be convinced that their actions may in fact be *sinful*. When we indulge in an extra pyramid of hot wings, we tend to see that as an innocent decision. For some, it may in fact be innocent, but for many it's a sin. Like with alcohol, if you aren't free to *not* indulge—then you aren't free *to* indulge. If it's sin, then repentance is in order. Food choices for you may no longer be a matter of discipline in an amoral area, but a crucial area with weighty implications in how you see God and his glory. Bridges continues, "We even joke about our overeating and other indulgences instead of crying out to God in confession and repentance. . . . Over 200 years ago Susannah Wesley wrote, 'Whatever increases the strength and authority of your body over your mind—that thing is sin to you.'"[17]

This is all very important in the larger discussion of overcoming burnout and having a good, functional understanding of self-care. Certainly, I believe that enjoying food is part of enjoying the grace of God toward us. I'm not a Spartan who ascetically views food as only utility and fuel not to be enjoyed. Yet, stewardship, worship, and even sacrifice also define how we should interact with food, not just pleasure. This might sound odd at first, but think about it, *if you cannot eat that plate of food to the glory of God, then why are you doing it? I think it's time for leaders to stop giving food a pass.*

Contagious Weakness

In Proverbs 27, Solomon shows us that our eyes and appetites are never satisfied. This is a statement true beyond food, but food is a bit of a softball. If there is room on the plate, then there is room for more food, right? Not only must we repent from any abuse of food in terms of escapism, we must be cautious of how being weak in our handling of food leaks to other areas of our life. If we cannot discipline the body regarding food, we'll find an uphill climb in other desires of the flesh. Obedience and discipline aren't a switch we can turn on and off depending on the subject. I cannot be impervious to lust when I'm unchained to eat whatever is in my sightline. *Weakness in one area is weakness in more than one area.* Thomas Boston once said a few centuries ago, "They that would keep themselves pure must have their bodies in subjection, and that may require, in some cases, a holy violence."[18] I know I'm in danger of overstating the obvious, but being soft and weak in our bodies inclines us toward weakness and softness in other areas as well. I'm not making this up, but remixing Paul.

> Every athlete exercises self-control in all things. They do it to receive a perishable wreath, but we an imperishable. So I do not run aimlessly; I do not box as one beating the air. But I discipline my body and keep it under control, lest after preaching to others I myself should be disqualified.[19]

Paul is connecting the discipline of the *exterior* man with its result in the *total* man. He knew that being weak in discipline regarding his physical body would drive him toward spiritual weakness and possibly disqualification. Bridges agrees with Paul: "When the body is pampered and indulged, the instincts and passions of the body tend to get the upper hand and dominate our thoughts and actions. We tend to do not what we should do, but what we want to do, as we follow the cravings of our sinful nature."[20] Andrew Murray, another trusted voice, says, "Overeating or eating for mere enjoyment, weights and makes the body heavy and unfit for prayer. That is the time the devil can come to you. A man may be living in victory over some sin but through the pleasure of eating the devil may get power over his flesh."[21]

"Pampered and indulged" and "eating for mere enjoyment" describe too many leaders in the church today. This is not a petition to be monkish in our food choices, but these men are wisely challenging us to stop retreating into a comfort food coma because our jobs are tough. When we do, we become targets for the devil and temptations of the flesh. In Paul's words, we dance closely toward the edge of disqualification. I don't know how much you weigh as you read this. But as we've already noticed, you can be thin as a Greyhound and be a glutton. An unfettered and unchecked use of food is abuse every bit as bad as the abuse of alcohol. It just hides behind cultural norms and collective toleration.

My goal has been to show that how we handle food is not an amoral issue outside of how we engage God, but a vital part of who we are as disciples of Jesus. As we get into practical strategies, remind yourself that you are not only overcoming bad self-care, but embarking on a life of worshipful stewardship where nothing is off the table, not even the size and contents of the plate in front of you.

Subtraction and Addition

In rebuilding leadership health, there will be some substantial changes to both your cabinet and frequent lunch dives. *This is typically an overwhelming process for most leaders, so we're going to focus on foods for leadership health alone.* My goal isn't to make you a Paleo distance runner or a vegan powerlifter. I'm only interested in your nutritional scheme as it aids your role, pace, and emotional load. I'm not even going to name this diet or try to patent it; there's way too much of that going around. Let's just look at some basic food items that need to be flushed immediately. This could be its own book, so I'm going to target the biggest influencers.

Foods to Flush

Coffee or anything caffeinated: You won't find an expert or a book on adrenal, neural, or endocrine health anywhere on earth that doesn't ditch coffee and other stout sources of caffeine. I'm including all stimulants in this category from the benign, well-sourced black tea and chocolate to sodas and the silver canned energy drinks truck drivers and college students buy at the gas station to stay awake. If you're sick and serious about long-term leadership health, buckle up and drop coffee.

Upon my recovery from burnout, I ditched coffee for a few years and only brought it back later under strict circumstances. Quitting coffee had true side effects for me in both irritability, perceived energy, and headaches, which should signal that there was an addiction my body wasn't excited about evicting. Just the smell of coffee was a therapy to me, and I couldn't imagine leaving it behind; yet it was accelerating my burnout.

Coffee does a great job of tossing us into a fight-or-flight posture. Caffeine, like all stimulants, convinces the pituitary gland that it's time to navigate an emergency. Cortisol and epinephrine flood the bloodstream, and this alertness and mental sharpness is exactly why many of us gravitate towards coffee. It's not so much the taste or smell as much as it is a habit we've developed and depend upon. We need it to erase fatigue and jumpstart our alertness. We even joke about not being able to function or contend with issues "until we've had at least a cup or two of coffee." The problem this presents for the hurry-up leader is that it brings an unnecessary taxation to our emergency system. Dr. James Wilson, who specializes in people who are burned out, notes, "As they continually kick their adrenals with over consumption of fast food and caffeine and deprive their bodies of certain restorative nutrients, their adrenal glands become more and more fatigued and difficult to stimulate."[22] So when we take in buckets of coffee, we bring degrading fatigue to our vital glands and hormones and develop a resistance.

Even after such an indictment, the common question I still get from the unconvinced is, "*So then how much coffee is too much?*" For the sick leader, *all* coffee is too much coffee. A Venti Blonde Roast at Starbucks has 475 milligrams of caffeine in it, which is much more than the recommended amount of caffeine for a *healthy* adult for the entire day.[23] *If you're sick, then you aren't healthy.* You shouldn't even be indulging in a cup of black tea (120 milligrams) while orbiting burnout. Any chemical that elicits a false emergency is a bad idea for the sick. We're not trying to find normal consumption from a healthy posture as much as we're trying to dig out of a deep hole. Every time you sense withdrawal, ask God for the grace to endure. Every time you get sleepy in the afternoon, take a short nap. After some time, the addiction goes away. Without the addiction, you'll be better able to discern whether it's something to be brought back when your health has improved.

Bulletproof, fat coffee, or keto has recently appeared on the scene and deserves treatment here. Fat coffee is where healthy fats such as unsalted and well-sourced butter, coconut oil, MCT oil,[24] and other variants are blended into a coffee for a more mentally alert, satiating, and thermogenic result.[25] I've been drinking these for years, and I personally find the hype to be true. They satisfy me until lunch and upregulate fat burning. All in all, it's a great innovation on coffee, but the sick leader has more options without the caffeine. You can achieve the identical effect by mixing the same healthy variants of fat with non-caffeinated teas, kale and coconut milk smoothies, "green" smoothies, or a ton of other "fat vehicles." For the sick leader, it should not be coffee that you are bulletproofing—pick something else. If you're on a high-fat, low carbohydrate nutritional scheme and are hoping to take healthy fats in the morning, don't use coffee to transport them.[26]

Once you've experienced increases in your health over a longer span of time, both subjectively and through various test panels, you may consider adding caffeine back in under strict parameters. As I said, it was a few years before I brought it back. Even now, as I have reassimilated coffee, I fast from it every month for a week or so. This is because we grow a tolerance to coffee and it begins to have a diminishing return after prolonged use. This is why you probably never push the "small" setting on your Keurig. You may have started small but are now likely closer to "Big Gulp" size.

Caffeine efficiently alters the chemistry and physiology of our brains. Being both fat-soluble and water-soluble, it easily crosses what is called the "blood-brain barrier."[27] The caffeine molecule hogs receptor sites built for something else entirely. It's like rude people who barge into a restaurant and sit at a reserved table. Our brain cells have receptors to receive a neurotransmitter called adenosine. Generally, adenosine causes feelings of sleepiness or being drowsy, and it looks very similar to the caffeine molecule, which means caffeine sequesters all the adenosine receptors in the brain. No adenosine on the brain equals no sleepiness, and that's how caffeine works in a nutshell.

Because your brain is so brilliantly fashioned, it just makes more adenosine receptors to accommodate the rude caffeine. This means we'll need more coffee to block the adenosine, though. It's like a bar owner adding more bar stools to make room for a particular kind of patron, yet the wrong kind of patron keeps hogging all the bar stools. Instead of the bar owner kicking the bad crowd out, the owner just adds more stools.

Wellness Coach Ben Greenfield researched what it takes to "reset" the barstool madness, and the answer might surprise you. In order to reset the receptor number, we only need brief and intermittent fasts from caffeine. A two-week hiatus from caffeine or other stimulants will go a long way to recalibrate your adenosine receptors.[28] This is why I ditch coffee a week or two per month to keep my brain physiology from adapting.

Booze: Even if your convictions provide you freedom to consume alcohol, doing so as a sick leader is unwise. When I jettisoned coffee, alcohol was on my hit list as well. Even though I'm more Malbec than Corona, those carbohydrates are naked carbohydrates in a highly refined form. Even more refined than sugar, these particular carbohydrates rapidly generate energy. This, as we've seen, sets off a blood sugar roller coaster, spending nutrients that the alcoholic beverage won't pay back. Our liver also experiences an upregulation, *but in the wrong direction.* When you drink a tumbler of whisky or a glass of wine, your liver is distracted from its task of leaching loose adrenaline from your system in order to process the alcohol. Your liver, a sort of adrenaline "sink," abandons its "tend and mend" posture for a "fight or flight" one.

Alcohol has fooled many, because the immediate effects mask the endocrine depletion occurring under the surface. Where we might feel relaxed and able to shift down a gear or two, the adrenals are manufacturing hormones to regulate the new energy and balance blood sugar levels. *We need to assume the same posture here that we take with coffee; if it's depleting reserves, we need to put it down until our body is healthy enough to re-assimilate it.* Even if dropping coffee and wine only contributes an increase of, say, six percent, we can stack that with everything else we've learned so far in our path toward health. If you are hurry-up sick, wine isn't where you want to cheat your recovery. In fact, it might be one of the most dangerous places to cheat.

The extra demands levied against the emergency system *exacerbates the craving for alcohol.* Drinking to relax oneself, even in moderation, can place the body in a sort of endocrine debt that increases the craving for even more alcohol. Does this sound familiar? Ever hear of leaders finding alcoholism within their hurried pace of leadership? Several studies depict a correlation between stress and alcoholism. If you're already struggling with flagging health and are knee-deep in burnout, alcohol is a very, very bad idea. Alcohol can fool you into feeling relaxed, when in fact your body is working overtime in the wrong direction, and it's increasing your desire for more alcohol. Even if you are free to drink—you may not be free to drink.

Sugar, in all its disguises: Sugar is toxic. It feeds cancer cells and hides within so much of what we eat. Since 1977, sugar use in America has *more than doubled*. This is why of the 30,000 different food items at your local supermarket, 74 to 80 percent of them have added sugar.[29] I know that sounds crazy, but because sugar shape-shifts into different names, it goes undetected. You'll see it also listed as lactose, sucrose, fructose, maltose, glucose, dextrose, table sugar, cane sugar, beet sugar, agave, maple syrup, honey, invert sugar, turbinado sugar, carbitol, concentrated fruit juice, corn sweetener, diglycerides, disaccharides, evaporated cane juice, erythritol, Florida crystals, fructooligosaccharides, galactose, glucitol, glucosamine, hexitol, inversol, isomalt, maltodextrin, malted barley, malts, mannitol, nectars, pentose, raisin syrup, ribose rice syrup, rice malt, rice syrup solids, sorbitol, sorghum, sucanat, xylitol, xylose, and the bigger public enemy, high-fructose corn syrup.

It has many passports, *but you'll absorb them exactly the same*. Metabolically, your body goes through the same mechanics to process all the sugar variants. Too much sugar in any form is dangerous, so replacing maltodextrin with honey in high amounts, for example, doesn't help you much. You'll need to increase your sugar fluency a bit.

Sugar is tricky in much the same way alcohol and coffee are. It can misdirect you from the downward trendline of your health by giving you an immediate surge of energy. This is why the donuts in the office are just as awesome in the afternoon as in the morning. Rivers of ink have been spilled on chronic sugar dependence, but for our purposes I want to focus on *why it's so hard to put down*. I know my work with sick leaders isn't in proving that sugar is unhealthy, it's in helping them leave it behind.

Whenever you drink a sweet tea or eat a cinnamon roll, the liver switches on in order to process the sudden appearance of sugar, namely the sweet fructose portion of sugar.[30] It's like when someone cleans up the house quickly when a surprise guest rings the doorbell. When the liver activates, the pancreas comes to help by flooding the bloodstream with insulin. Insulin's main job as a hormone is to store energy. Like a warehouse foreman, it decides where to put all the boxes. In this case, it takes the sugar from that pastry and stores it as fat. For men, this fat is most concentrated around the gut.

This much is basic biology, *but a flood of insulin also keeps the brain from feeling "full."* Insulin does its best work engaging complex carbohydrates, like broccoli or dark greens, not stuff we create, like a PowerBar or calzone. When simple sugars are absorbed faster than insulin can downregulate and disappear, the residual insulin sticks around hunting down more sugar, causing you to *feel* hungry still. This is why one donut doesn't really make us feel satisfied. No one eats one donut and says, "Man, I'm stuffed." Your brain thinks it's still hungry, so you keep eating donuts.

Do this for a decade or two and you can become *insulin resistant.* Without proper insulin activity (no warehouse foreman to place boxes), there is no place for the sugar to go—except gut storage. Are you beginning to see the spiraling trend? This has led some researchers to shift their philosophy from "patients are undisciplined with food so they are obese" to "patients are obese, and it may be making them less disciplined." When the brain says "keep eating," it's hard to say no.

Complicating our resolve even further, sugar is more addictive than even cocaine. Researchers at Princeton did a very revealing study in which they took over 40 rats and examined addiction tendencies. When given the choice of sugar water or cocaine, the rats *overwhelmingly* chose sugar.[31] In another study, rats on a sugar water diet showed common signs of addiction, binging, craving, and withdrawal when the sugar was removed. Their teeth would even chatter.[32] Sugar addiction is no joke and has the same effects on the brain's chemistry as hard drugs do. In all honesty, as hard as coffee was to quit, sugar refused to go silently. Since sugar was camouflaged in a long list of foods like barbecue sauce, soups, dressings, granola, sports drinks, anything low-fat, flavored coffee and water, protein bars, fruit juice, and baked beans, I realized how much of an overhaul my diet needed. My nutrition didn't need a quick biohack, but a sea change.

Processed or refined starches: It's not just sugar or naked carbohydrates that have the power to overload an already overtaxed body. These starches are contorted into simple glucose within the blink of an eye. Refined starches are grains that have been processed so that the nutrient and fiber-rich outer layers are removed, leaving only the starchy interior. Bread, white rice, white potato products, pasta, and breakfast cereals would fit in this category. Vitamins and minerals necessary to metabolize the inner starchy portion are contained in the outer portion of the grain that is milled away during the refining process. Now that the valued part of the grain is gone, your body has to figure out how to handle the refined starch. Sometimes, your body takes it from itself or sequesters it from other foods. If this were plotted on a spreadsheet, it would depict nutritional bankruptcy. Also, when all of the processed culprits hit the digestive tract, metabolically your body handles them the same as it does sugar. Dr. David Ludwig, a professor at Harvard Medical School, agrees: "You can eat a bowl of corn flakes with no added sugar or you could eat a bowl of sugar with no added corn flakes. They might taste different, but below the neck, they're metabolically the same thing."[33]

I'm not declaring war on all carbohydrates. Like all calories are not the same, so goes it with carbohydrates. Soon we'll look at better sources of more complex nutrient dense forms of carbs, but the simple processed forms have to go. If your body cannot distinguish and interact with them any differently than sugar, then they aren't helping you, only hurting.

Fast foods—of course: Of the 568 senior pastors surveyed by Ellison Research, 88 percent eat fast food at least once per week. Thirty-three percent eat fast food three or more times per week.[34] When sick, I was a 33-percenter, but I convinced myself it was okay because the restaurant didn't have a drive-through window. I'd be willing to bet these statistics have shifted upward since the advent of *fast casual* restaurants like Chipotle, Boston Market, Panera, and dozens more on their heels. They're a hybrid, promising (and sometimes delivering) better quality food. They also give the consumer the idea that *anything* they choose is healthy since it doesn't have a dollar menu. "If this is a healthy place, I can choose anything!" I love a burrito the size of a pillow as much as the next guy, but if it's a white flour tortilla the size of a party platter stuffed with cheese, white rice, and meat that has been grilled to carcinogenic perfection, I'm not much better off than had I grabbed a kid's meal down the street.

On a practical note, look ahead to where your meetings are over a shared meal and steer their location when possible. Currently, when my assistant sets up my lunch appointments, she offers only a handful of places as options. It allows me to plan around the meal and helps me make wise choices. If I have a meeting at the local pizza planet, I'm not always strong enough to choose a side salad over the meat lover's pizza.

Packaged and microwaved foods: Just as fast casual has lulled us into a false safety in our choices, so have some packaged foods. Packaged foods are adding descriptions to their labels promising health, but for a food to be "shelf stable," they often include a bunch of preservatives, further taxing the body's digestion. *When shopping at the grocery store, you're better off sticking to the border walls where there are perishable goods.* Cook at home, use real food, and avoid the microwave. If it comes in a package, box, or bag—read the ingredient label and ask critical questions. Interrogate your food.

Some fruits and juices: We grew up hearing all juice was great for us. If you're sick, this isn't true for you right now. Foods like grapefruits, bananas, figs, raisins, and dates are abrasive on the adrenals, partly due to their levels of *potassium*, and partly due to their high sugar content. Not even fruit is above scrutiny for you. Notice that some of those foods just mentioned make up the main ingredients for healthier snack bars. Figs, raisins, and dates add enough sweetness to a snack bar to avoid adding sugar. This is a great improvement, but the fructose content will still be too much for a recovering leader.

This bears even more weight when the fruit is dried. A dried fruit concentrates the fructose and makes it easier to gorge on more of it. Have you ever seen the difference in size between a fig or grape and the resulting dried fig or raisin? Nobody can eat a suitcase full of grapes, but everyone can eat the same amount of raisins. You might as well be eating candy. In fact, in one 12-hour race I completed, my only food strategy was to eat dried figs—all day. In a perpetual sugar rush, I was running on cheap fast fuel. The next day, however, my health was wrecked, not from racing, but from my middle school food strategy.

Juice is worse. When fruit juice is consumed, it's minus all the fiber that came with the natural fruit. This is the same problem we saw with refined carbohydrates mentioned earlier. When you turn nine large apples into a glass of juice, without the accompanying fiber, it's like throwing gas-soaked tinder on a fire. Your limping pancreas goes into hyperdrive. Most juices also contain a fair amount of potassium, which is a problem for those recovering from cortisol depletion. If you wake up and slam an orange juice, big banana, and oatmeal with raisins and brown sugar (typical hotel fare), your body doesn't perceive that as a "healthy, well-balanced breakfast," no matter what the commercials say. Flush these foods. They aren't helping; they're hurting.

Dairy, wheat, and other inflammatory foods: If you were to visit an endocrinologist savvy in overcoming hurry-up sickness, they'd certainly advise dumping any foods that you *may be* allergic or sensitive to. Most folks have no clue as to what they're allergic to, which is why you see many nutritionists and wellness experts advise "elimination diets" in order to find out.[35] Many who *eliminate* the usual suspects for a season find that upon adding them back, they react oddly. Maybe it's a rash, grumpy stomach, a tingling in the cheeks or forehead, itchiness, or just simple swelling. Upon this writing, the more commonly hidden allergens for people are dairy, wheat, corn, soy, chocolate, tomatoes, and peanuts. *No one is really allergic to sugar, but sugar is an amplifier to the allergic reaction, so it must be handled as an allergen of sorts.*

Regarding the controversial punching bag of lactose intolerance, even if you're not lactose intolerant, you might be intolerant to a protein called *casein.* The only way to know is to remove dairy for a period of time and see how you react. The same goes for wheat, particularly wheat high in *gluten.* Casein is a protein very similar in molecular structure to gluten, and most people who are gluten intolerant are casein intolerant too. On a personal note, I found out that dairy is on my "no fly" list. I'll chance it occasionally, but will later notice inflammation in the joints.

It's tough for me to stop orbiting the cheese tray at a football party, but I like the way my joints feel more than the taste of cheese. When the body is fatigued and trying to recover from being overstressed, *food allergies actually worsen the situation by putting additional unnecessary stress on the body.*

I don't think the whole world is gluten intolerant, but I think many will react with at least a slight sensitivity. Although the subject and controversy of gluten and dairy far exceeds this book, we can at least concern ourselves with the overlap between sensitivities and the sick leader. What's not controversial is that ingesting foods we're sensitive or allergic to begins a snowball of disaster in our stomachs. Because of gut dysregulation and leaky gut, we experience overactive histamine production and inflammation. Again, this is upregulating our immune system unnecessarily.

This is precisely what happened in my case. My gut lining had a poor biota (habitat) due to antibiotics and a horrible diet, and my gut was leaky. Leaky gut occurs when the intestinal lining is permeable, allowing undigested food particles into the bloodstream. The immune system, although already taxed, attacks the particles with vigor. It thinks the undigested particles to be dangerous pathogens, and preps for battle. This is where the high histamine levels and inflammation come from.

In order to reformat my gut, I spent a few months cultivating a better flora of bacteria, repairing my leaky gut. It was only after this master reset that I slowly reintroduced foods—one at a time. Dairy didn't pass the test. You could be different, but you won't know until you find out. Purposefully choosing foods our body is reacting poorly to is the opposite of leadership self-care—it's simple neglect.

Foods to Add

Stuff growing from the ground: You knew this was coming. It's the most obvious change, second to off-loading sugar. Almost two out of three Americans don't even eat one vegetable per day. [36] Not impressive. You'll need the nutritional density of well-sourced vegetables to reassemble your glands and hormonal balance. A multivitamin or green pill simply can't replace eating stuff from the earth. When I'm able, I'm consuming

10 to 15 servings of vegetables per day, which means I'm always eating something that grows from the ground. When traveling, I focus on salads, resolved to find vegetables every meal.

When you begin buying fruits and vegetables, pay special attention to whether or not it is organic. Not because you're a snob, but because you'll be on the lookout for pesticides and herbicides. It won't do you any good to munch on more kale if it's encrusted with Roundup or one of the other five billion pounds of pesticide ingredients the EPA reports on American crops every year.[37] That's enough pesticide to fill over 33,000 swimming pools. This doesn't even include the rampant GMOs, chemical fertilizers, synthetic junk, sewage, and harmful irradiation. I know the strawberries look so pure, but consider what they went through to get to the produce section.

Ben Greenfield in his book *Beyond Training* lists which foods are most spooky when it comes to human additives. In his "Terrible 20" list, he suggests *always* purchasing produce organically due to their susceptibility to synthetic chemicals. From highest pesticide content to lowest, this list consists of: apples, celery, sweet bell peppers, peaches, strawberries, nectarines, grapes, spinach, lettuce, cucumbers, blueberries, potatoes, green beans, kale/collard greens, sweet corn, Hawaiian papayas, zucchini, yellow squash, cherries, and hot peppers. When it comes to these produce items, they assimilate and retain sprays and chemicals more readily. If you cannot find these organically raised, *strongly reconsider.*[38]

If you're pinching pennies, you can purchase some foods with less discrimination, especially if you wash them well.[39] This includes onions, pineapples, avocados, cabbage, sweet peas, asparagus, mangoes, eggplant, kiwi, cantaloupe, sweet potatoes, grapefruit, watermelon, and mushrooms. By intelligently washing produce, you can reduce your pesticide exposure by up to 80 percent.[40]

When possible, avoid vegetables and fruits from a can, and target fresh, dark leafy greens or colorful produce due to the higher levels of polyphenols and other helpful compounds. If it's a vegetable, that's a win. If it's a fresh vegetable, that's a double win. If it is a fresh colorful vegetable, even better. Blueberries, blackberries, kale, purple cabbage, swiss chard, carrots (both orange and purple), yams, pomegranates, mustard greens, brussels sprouts, tomatoes, bell peppers, and spring mixes that contain darker foliage would be in this category of colorful vegetables. Seaweed would be in this category as well, with some of the greatest nutrient density you'll find in a food.

A good goal would be to get around three colorful vegetables with both lunch and dinner every day. To the average person, this may sound like overload. I'm not proposing you become a vegan, but when correcting your diet you will undoubtedly notice many more vegetables on your plate, and you'll discover the increase in health relatively fast. I'm not a vegetarian, but I noticed enough of a health change with this innovation that I quit making fun of vegetarians.

Carefully measured, sourced, and prepared meats: Become more discriminatory in choosing and measuring meat. Dr. Wilson teaches that abandoning meat altogether doesn't necessarily speed healing up. "Vegetarians who have suffered moderate to severe adrenal fatigue have tremendous difficulty recovering on a strictly vegan (no foods from animal sources) diet. If you are a vegetarian and you have adrenal fatigue, you will do much better if you modify your diet to include eggs, miso (Japanese bean pasta), sea vegetables, yogurt, as well as combining your grains with beans, seeds and nuts at every meal."[41] I live in the Deep South and grew up in Texas, so meat isn't something I'm going to give up unless death is the alternative. I've been able to keep meat on my plate by following a few key protocols.

First, I eat no more than *six* ounces per day. That's the size of a couple decks of cards. Whether it's in one meal or two, I don't cheat this amount. Over-consuming protein isn't like over-consuming vegetables; it actually stresses the strained body more. Ben Greenfield explains this with another round number: "Once you get close to about 1,000 calories a day of protein (about 250 grams), you can no longer convert ammonia to urea, and this toxin begins to build in your body. This is extremely stressful on your internal organs, especially your kidneys."[42] When people go on diets low in carbohydrates or low in fat, they typically treat protein as something they can eat in unlimited quantity. I watched the rise and fall of the poorly executed Atkins Diet in horror as people piled four days' worth of smoked brisket on a plate, covered it in cheese and looked forward to a slimmer figure. Don't do this. More is not better in animal protein.

Second, it can't be meat from anywhere. I want to know it was grown responsibly without unnecessary hormones. This means that I have to vet my restaurant's suppliers like I do my kids' babysitter. Be critical here and remember, *if the meat is cheap, it's likely as juiced with hormones as a '90s MLB slugger*. It may also be loaded with preservatives and nitrates to be more shelf stable. This is actually how you'll find a lot of lunch meat. Nitrates, typically a preservative found in deli meat, can be nasty for the recovering leader, so reexamine how great of a deal "$6 Tuesdays" is at the local deli. Inexpensive meat is rarely well-sourced. If it's well-sourced, it will cost you money because it cost the establishment and supplier more money. Pay the money.

Last, I pay attention to *how* it's cooked. This last one is a booger being that barbecue is a magical experience for me. When eaten raw or lightly cooked, protein in general is easier to digest and delivers more intact amino acids versus being denatured due to smoking, grilling, or flash frying. When meat is cooked with high heat methods, not only are the amino acids denatured and rendered inert, other more gruesome chemicals show up. Heterocyclic amines and polycyclic aromatic hydrocarbons are long nerdy words for the resulting mutagenic compounds we consume. *In other words, they cause genetic changes, increasing the risk of cancer immensely*. This is what you'd find on the tasty outer bark of a smoked brisket or blackened chargrilled chicken. It's super yummy, but is as healthy as chewing on a handful of Marlboros.

Better Carbohydrates: We've seen that when starches are processed or refined, they convert immediately to glucose, so what about whole or unrefined grains? These grains still harbor nutrients and are mini-mally processed. When your body processes these unrefined carbs, they metabolize the energy slowly. You get energy in a more stable for-mat as well as the vitamins and minerals that remained from the lack of refining and processing. Examples of these carbs would be brown rice, amaranth, whole oats, millet, quinoa, and buckwheat. You can prepare and consume these carbohydrates sources closely with how they're discovered in nature, maybe steaming them at the most.

In addition to unrefined starches, I'd add vegetables again. A large salad full of colored vegetables, maybe some seeds, and no dressing would render around 20 grams of carbohydrates. This is around the same number of carbohydrates a can of Coca-Cola has. I might not need to say this, *but those carbohydrates aren't the same.* The salad is loaded with fiber, nutrients, and a robust source of complex carbohydrates, whereas the cola is highly refined sugar. The body will handle them very differently. The salad will be metabolized for energy with no crash, but the cola will flood the body with free floating glucose, provoking a sugar crash. When designing your nutritional scheme for health, consider where the carbohydrates come from. If you are trying to come *under* a certain number of carbohydrates for the day, as in a nutritional ketogenic or low carb diet, source your carbohydrate load with vegetables.

Juice—but not from the mall: "Green juice," made primarily from vegetables, can be helpful for your immunity and micronutrient density. Due to current trends, franchises are popping up everywhere that make this juice periodically throughout the day, so you can always get a freshly made serving. Although expensive, this was a quick way for me to reclaim nutrition when I was having a hard time controlling where I ate. This was particularly true when traveling.

Be careful of juice establishments that dump a bunch of fruit into the recipe for sweetness. Bananas and apples are common culprits. These fruits won't endanger the micronutrient density you'll gain, but will raise your blood sugar like a rocket. Stay green. If you add a fruit, make it green apple due to its sugar being a bit healthier for us and not causing as much of a rise as a banana.

You can also make these at home with whatever greens and vegetables you can get your hands on. The benefit in this route is your control of additives such as coconut milk, MCT oil, nuts, seeds, etc. We personally found as a family, however, that after you purchase the blender and ingredients, the price differential wasn't always worth it. Even as members of a farm share, we were making juice for right around the same price as what the local shop could crank out. If you're looking for savings, do the math on how you get juice. If you're looking to add specific ingredients, juicing at home is the way to go.

Good fats: Healthy fats help the recovering leader due to their satiating effect (ability to make us feel satisfied), and their ability to prolong energy over a longer span of time. If sugar or refined carbohydrates are oily shop rags thrown on a fire, then healthy fats are the huge log that will burn slowly through the night.

Since the middle of the twentieth century, fat became a skulking villain in America. This is due to bad science, corrupt lobbying, and other governmental factors outside this book's aim.[43] The result of the "fat is evil" campaign of the '70s was a food revolution pitching low-fat options for just about everything. The essential problem with low-fat food, however, is that it tastes like carpet, so the only way to sell it was to dump in sugar. Now, we have a health epidemic. We have grown to naturally see "fat is bad" and "carbs are good," which has gifted us with the obesity rate we now have.

A two-year study in 2005 followed 322 obese subjects as they adhered to a Mediterranean diet, low-fat diet, or basic low-carb diet. Those following a high-fat, low-carb meal plan not only lost the most weight, but also drastically reduced their bad cholesterol levels.[44] It has only been in the last decade or two that science's double take on fat has become mainstream. Fat in and of itself isn't the cause of blocked and clogged arteries or increased chance of heart disease—it's rather the combination of poor fats and poor carbohydrates that's doing the damage. When this ugly partnership occurs, cholesterol oxidizes and can lead to risk of heart disease.[45] I took this same approach when cleaning out my gut, and not only did my blood pressure stabilize, but my cholesterol responded impressively, and my overall fat percentage dropped to the best levels I've ever had.

When I refer to "healthy" fats, I'm referring to sources such as avocados, organically sourced butter, ghee, extra virgin olive oil, coconut oil, omega-3s (especially from wild fish when possible), nuts and seeds,[46] well-sourced eggs, grass-fed and organically sourced beef, full-fat dairy (if you can have it), MCT oil, well-sourced dark chocolate, flax, chia seeds, and nut butters.[47] You can find various lists and preparations of healthy fats in many other sources. I highly recommend the helpful book *The Art and Science of Low Carbohydrate Living: An Expert Guide to Making the Life-Saving Benefits of Carbohydrate Restriction Sustainable and Enjoyable* by Dr. Jeff Volek and Dr. Stephen Phinney. They also wrote a version to accommodate athletes.

Timing and Fasting

You may recall that cortisol is key to regulating blood sugar, so our body has what it needs when it needs it. When cortisol levels are low from overuse, the body struggles to moderate blood sugar. This decline toward hypoglycemia (low blood sugar) is harsh on your body due to more cortisol being mustered to normalize the problem. The more the cortisol drains from overstressed adrenals, the more havoc occurs.

Because of this, the recovering leader needs to eat healthy foods at intervals throughout the day to avoid low blood sugar levels. This frequency cooperates with struggling glands and hormones by not requiring so much cortisol to be marshalled forth to moderate sugar levels. Starving your body will dig your hole deeper. *When* you eat is about as important as *what* you eat.

As a practical principle for those trying to come out of leadership sickness, it's important you eat before 10:00 a.m. Even if you aren't hungry before that time, it's important you eat at minimum a healthy snack. You need to replenish your vanishing sugar stores (glycogen) after your sleep when your body was doing so much of its reparative and restorative work. It's popular for many to fast during breakfast in a strategy called "intermittent fasting." This strategy places 16 to 18 hours between dinner and lunch the next day, but this is only a good strategy if you have strong functioning health and your cortisol levels are strong. If you have leadership sickness or symptoms of adrenal fatigue, you should not indulge in intermittent fasting—you'd only be doing more damage. If you don't want your body starting the day at a deficit level, eat something nutritious before 10:00 a.m.

An early lunch is better than a late lunch for pretty much the same reason. Your body cruises through the energy sources you gave it earlier and needs another investment. The closer to 11:00 a.m. you can get, the better. Same goes for snacking. You should find a nutritious snack in your schedule between 2:00 and 3:00 p.m. This nourishment sustains the sick leader through that most dangerous period between 3:00 p.m. and 5:00 p.m., when energy sources are lowest.

The evening meal should be no later than 6:00 p.m. This will set you up for solid resting and repairing through the evening. As a simple diagnostic, Dr. Wilson notes how we should *feel* after this evening meal. "If you are like most people suffering from adrenal fatigue, you will feel your best after your evening meal. If you do not feel your best after the evening meal, you may be eating the wrong foods for supper."[48] As you can tell, it looks like you're eating all day long, but the goal is to keep blood sugar at a healthy level—not sky high and not rock bottom, but stable so that our dwindling reserve of cortisol isn't overtaxed.

You may be thinking, "What about fasting for spiritual reasons?" If you are sick, my advice is to fast from something other than food until you find health again. There will be a day when you can return to fasting from food, but this is a poor time to stress the body even further. Juice fasts may be less harmful due to micronutrient intake and slight caloric increase, but juice fasts still place you in the high caloric deficit you cannot chance right now. If you're sick, don't pretend you aren't. Fast from your phone, media, or something else, but don't keep damaging your health by abandoning food.

Supplementation

If your food IQ is improving, and you're eating frequently in proper amounts, you'll notice improvements as the weeks roll on. Food is a fantastic medicine in itself. For those who are looking to physically train aggressively, you'll want to consider finding supplements that allow you to maintain health under harsher terms. You don't need a pill carrier that looks like you're 120 years old, but you'll need to target your supplementation for nervous system and endocrine health. As you begin to take supplemental help in pills and capsules, know it might take a few weeks or even months before you notice a difference. Don't get frustrated if you don't notice immediate improvements.

Several books have been written on this singular topic, discussing the science of how supplements interact with the body, how they're made, and how to spot good supplements when you see them. My goal is to get you at least thinking in this direction.[49] Because you're pressing your body beyond its limits, you'll need nutrition beyond what is normally accessible. Unnatural lifestyle and pace equals unnatural nutrient requirements.

You'll likely be fine securing a very good multivitamin. Supplementation beyond that might need the insight of additional reading or even a trip to an aware physician, nutritionist, or dietician. Anything you get beyond a good multivitamin will fine-tune your nutrition, but a multivitamin covers a lot of ground quickly. When you're shopping for multivitamins you can afford, make sure they contain as many of these ingredients as possible:

> Vitamin A, Vitamin C, Vitamin D3, Vitamin E, Vitamin K, Vitamin K2, Thiamin, Riboflavin, Niacin, Vitamin B6, Folate, Vitamin B12, Pantothenic Acid, Magnesium, Zinc, Selenium, Copper, Manganese, Chromium, Molybdenum, Green Tea, Choline Citrate, Boron, Lutein, Biotin, Calcium, and Iodine

Use this list as a checklist and try to hit as many as possible. I've even listed them in the rough order they should show up on the label. The more you find in one source, the more expensive it will likely be. This is especially true if it was prepared and sourced well. I take a formula with all of what's listed above (and more) and it's a serious investment but a vital part of my ongoing health.[50]

I also supplement with "adaptogenic herbs" such as licorice root (not the candy), ashwagandha, Korean and Siberian ginseng, ginger root, ginkgo leaf, holy basil, astragalus root, rhodiola, and cordycep mushrooms.[51] Many of these adaptogens are found hanging out together in not only the same section of a store, but even in the same bottle. You'll see the blends given names such as "Adrenal Health" or "Stress Help," or something similar. If you're able, these formulated blends would be a great addition to what you take every day.

We won't get sick with one meal. Heart disease and obesity don't work like that. But with a thousand meals (roughly what you'll eat in a year), you can create disease, metabolic syndrome, leaky gut, gut dysregulation, high levels of visceral fat, and a hundred other problems. This is a level of leadership health you can control. All the destruction we place on our finite frames can be avoided, but it will require a radical posture with food.

John Stott once said, "Becoming and being Christian involves a change so radical that no imagery can do it justice except death and resurrection—dying to the old life of self-centeredness and rising to a new life of holiness and love."[52] I find this to be brutally true. Death to what I want to eat when I am stressed out and anxious. Death to what my flesh demands to comfort itself. Self-care is not a way of escaping suffering, it is stepping into it. Self-care is self-denying as we've seen in functional fitness, resting, and even what we put in our mouths.

FIT FAT

FUNCTIONAL FITNESS FOR THE OVER-BUSY AND DESKBOUND

I always start these events with very lofty goals, like I'm going to do something special. And after a point of body deterioration, the goals get evaluated down to basically where I am now—where the best I can hope for is to avoid throwing up on my shoes.

—Ephraim Romesberg,
65 miles into the Badwater Ultramarathon

For the fitness industry, Valentine's Day is a magical day. Most of my time in college I made good money as a fitness trainer, and one thing I learned is that the industry makes enough money between January 1 and Valentine's Day to virtually cover the overhead for the whole year. You heard that right: Nearly everything from mid-February onward is profit. Sounds a bit fantastical, but you can actually see this phenomenon occur before your very eyes.

The first week of the year, lofty goals and shiny workout plans enter the glass doors while it's still dark outside. Covered in new breathable gear unwrapped during Christmas, everyone is determined. Resolve springs a leak, however, by week three, and by March resolutions have run their course, leaving a gym full of regulars staring at each other once again. On January 2, there is a line for the treadmill, but on April

4th, there's dust on it. The gym industry is the only business model that depends on its clientele *not* showing up, as it sells more memberships than the building could hold at any given time. More than doubling membership the first weeks of the year, the gym will decrease back to stasis, keeping the gym from ever having to grow the facility.

It's especially depressing to those who pulled the ripcord before meeting their goals. If this has been you, then I'm sure you can resonate with the crushing feeling of getting a bill from a gym you never attend. Forget the local gym for a minute. What about *any* physical fitness plan you've devised, whether it's CrossFit, running, weights, yoga, boxing, MMA, cycling, etc.? *Where* did it go? *Why* did it go? You're far from alone. Currently, 57 percent of ministry leaders don't have a regularly scheduled exercise routine.[1] Of the remaining minority that exercises, the preponderance is doing the *wrong thing* at the *wrong time*. Doing the wrong thing at the wrong time potentially accelerates burnout. One of the things I gathered quickly when having my own bottom-dwelling health measured was that my training regimen, as disciplined and intense as it was, actually contributed to my burnout. I was not only doing the wrong thing, but also doing it at the wrong time.

Even if you are able to form the discipline necessary to increase fitness, what do you do? Run? Flip tires? Swim? And what about stretching, or days off? Do you need a trainer? It can be confusing, and with all the different fads and camps out there, it feels easier to just do what you remember from high school. London and Wiseman, in their studies on pastoral trends, found exactly how many ministry leaders simply "forget about it" and leave fitness and health in the rearview mirror: 76 percent.[2] Three out of four pastors said they were either overweight or obese with lack of fitness being an assumed culprit.

Lumpy, Splotchy, and Misshapen

Being fit is *a part* of being healthy; yet, fitness and health aren't the same thing. There is no great health without at least a modicum of fitness, yet you can be fit without being very healthy. Some wellness experts call this being "fit fat" or "skinny fat." Fit fat folks are able to go to the gym daily and complete their workout-of-the-day (WOD), yet cannot seem to lose the flab around the middle. I've been around highly competitive triathletes and distance runners who usually find the podium, yet have perfected the muffin top flab handles around the waist. They have muscular limbs and the lungs of a racehorse, but they have a paunch making them look a bit blocky in the middle. *They may be fit, but they are nowhere near healthy.* My goal in this chapter isn't to make you competitive or to create a version of you that looks good naked, but to assess where you may be going wrong in functional fitness.

By this point, you've seen that our leadership roles can take a pretty nasty physical toll, but because our jobs are largely sedentary and deskbound, we also develop an ingrained posture that literally kills us slowly. Dr. James Levine, director of the Mayo Clinic at Arizona State University, believes we are "sitting ourselves to death" as sedentary deskbound knowledge workers. "Sitting is more dangerous than smoking, kills more people than HIV and is more treacherous than parachuting."[3] In 2008, Australian physicians found that for every hour adults over the age of 25 watch TV from their favorite futon, they've peeled almost 22 minutes off their life. Smoking a cigarette only drains 11 minutes away, making it twice as healthy as sitting for adults.[4] Dr. Levine has a more morose opinion of sitting: It claims two hours from our lifespan for every hour we sit.[5] Even if all these smart people don't agree with exactly how much time falls though the hourglass, it's unarguable that chronic sitting shortens our lives. What should scare you about this stat is that the average American knowledge worker (you) sits for 13 hours a day.[6] I realize how controversial this all sounds, but these are physicians who work at some of the most reputable establishments on earth. You should always be critical consumers about shocking statistics, but also consider the source. Even the mainstream WHO (World Health Organization) ranks physical inactivity as the fourth biggest *preventable* killer in the world. Over three million annual deaths can be prevented by a mindfulness of our sedentary living.[7]

This is typically where the overbusy leader flaunts their fitness routine in order to show that they are in fact *not* inactive, but very active. "But the cold, hard truth is that exercise will not reverse the potentially harmful and irrefutable effects that too much sitting has on our bodies."

Dr. Kelly Starrett, a physical therapist who works with professional athletes, and author of the book *Deskbound*, has been a sobering voice for knowledge workers. "Working out will certainly make you healthier overall, but it's not a time machine that can undo the sedentary choices that you make over the rest of the day."[8] By hitting the gym, we imagine it leveling out our day parked in front of a laptop and crammed into an office chair. But your quick 40- to 60-minute fitness credit isn't paying off the 8 to 12 hours of sedentary debit.

In earlier chapters, we saw recurring injuries as signs of encroaching burnout. Add tension headaches and overall joint pain to this, and it becomes clearer that sitting still (or standing incorrectly) all day is violently but slowly ripping our bodies to pieces. Dr. Starrett observes,

> When we sit for long periods, the muscles in our lower bodies literally turn off and become inactive. Simultaneously, we automatically adopt positions that don't utilize the critical muscles and connective tissues that stabilize and support our trunk and spine. The result is compromised body function, and it causes a multitude of common and pernicious orthopedic problems, like back and neck dysfunction, carpal tunnel syndrome, and pelvic floor dysfunction.[9]

Mouth Breather

Consider the average leader's posture, the one built over time through sedentary living. The natural standing posture typically exhibits what is called *anterior pelvic tilt*. Our tummies roll out, our butt slightly sticks out and our hips and pelvis rotate inward and downward. If you had a bowl of water inside of your hips, it'd be dumping water forward in front of you. This slouchy posture is pandemic among office workers. It was built over years of inactive glutes that come from sitting. When you sit in a chair all day, you are sitting on muscles (glutes and hamstrings) that weren't meant to bear weight, but to hold posture. Chairs disable those rear muscles, but also won't allow your trunk musculature to fire and set the spine in neutral, so the hips and pelvis move into unhelpful angles.

We also roll our shoulders inward (*internal rotation)* pulling our center of gravity forward. Because of this, we crane our necks without even thinking about it. *This is the ready-set-go position for keyboard pounding—and it's an orthopedic train wreck.* With the head drooping forward, it adds pressure on your compromised spine. In fact, for every inch your head droops in front of you, 10 pounds are added to a head that already weighs 10 pounds.[10] This means you have critical vertebrae bearing the weight of a toddler as you work hard at the desk. Nice.

So far this seems harmless. I mean, it might make you look unconfident or sickly, but what kind of immediate health ramifications are there for the oddly shaped leader? As it turns out, anatomically odd posture fires our "fight or flight" system unnecessarily. Remember, as leaders guarding our resilience, we are looking to downregulate how often this sympathetic nervous system activates. As we hunch forward in our chairs (or at our standing workstations) and our necks lunge even more forward, our jaws naturally open, leaving our mouths agape where we breathe shallowly through the mouth while not engaging our diaphragm. Being a shallow mouth-breather signals your body that you're entering a sort of semi-emergency which in turn triggers the cascade of chemicals we looked at earlier. Your posture might be sending unnecessary rescue flares to your brain.

By contrast, as we breathe both from the nose and the diaphragm, we downregulate our emergency system and upregulate its counterpart, the parasympathetic (rest and digest) nervous system. This is why it's common to hear people lead others to take a "deep breath" when they are panicking. Dr. Starrett notices the same phenomenon: "How you breathe—whether it is shallow neck breathing or powerful breathing initiated by the diaphragm—affects the ways in which your body interprets stressors."[11] So, for our purposes, we must be mindful of shallow neck breathing we find ourselves in when sedentary and seated in our normal days.

Beer Belly

Leaders who experience a decent amount of stress and pressure activate their emergency response system, which in turn drives the body to *store fat around the gut.* This is ultimately a beautiful design by God, but bad news for the sedentary knowledge worker. Your body thinks that in its current disaster you need fast burning sugar, so your adrenal glands release adrenaline, which tells the body to *stop* making insulin. With lower insulin, blood sugar can flood the blood stream and go where it's needed quickly. Remember from earlier chapters that this is a thoughtful consideration God made for us. We're able to move chemicals to desperate places in a flash.

Your body interacts with fat a bit differently. It takes that fat you get from food and stores it near your midsection for survival. In layman's terms, *when you live on stress, you get a beer belly.* When someone has too much of this *visceral fat*, they develop metabolic obesity, which is incredibly dangerous and many times imperceptible. Many who have seemingly low subcutaneous fat (just under the skin) can carry large amounts of deadly visceral fat.

This pendulated fat is more dangerous than the fat, say in the thighs, butt, or backs of your arms, because it surrounds your *visceral organs.* This beer belly is the most dangerous fat you can possibly have and no amount of sit-ups or classes on the sweaty spin bike are going to whittle it away. Your hurry-up pace of leadership is making you fat because your body is actually *resisting* the loss of fat. This particular fat also increases your risk for cardiovascular disease, type 2 diabetes, colorectal cancer, sleep apnea, high blood pressure, and a slew of other weird things you shouldn't be having. These risk factors don't increase if I'm carrying some triceps fat or a double chin or something of that nature, but when it's around the gut, it's dangerous.

Recently at a leader's conference populated with church planters, I caught myself scanning the room and noticing all the new faces. I was also caught off guard by their size. It wasn't the overweight arms or calves, but what was hugging the belly that betrayed their stress-driven weight gain. This makes sense as we saw earlier—church planters and younger leaders are much more prone to ignoring health and burning out. If this is you, you're in treacherous territory. No, you aren't big-boned. Stop saying that. You're letting stress and sedentary living drive you toward a quick end. It's difficult to lose this visceral fat and takes some time. You'll need patience and discipline.

I'm sure the apostle Paul and gang didn't struggle so much with the physical fallout of a sedentary work week. Of course, they had rocks thrown at them and had to doggie paddle through a few shipwrecks, but there was obvious activity involved in their rhythms. Their culture was pedestrian in nature, and physical labor was something even bivocational knowledge workers were busy with. There was no pointing and clicking within a cubicle or cafe. We must look at compensating for deskbound and sedentary lives if we want to lead for a long time and exhibit stewardship, discipline, and gospel fluency before others. So far, we've seen that office dwellers collect bad posture, neck and back injuries, hip and pelvic imbalances, and large bellies. I'd like to add another unimpressive development to the list: *immobility*.

Mobility Is Not an Option

Mobility is your ability to perform an action with no impeded range of motion. It's not the same thing as flexibility, but flexibility is needed for good mobility. Flexibility is merely your muscles and joints' ability to extend easily to their limit without tearing. Mobility is the ability to carry out functions over a full range of motion easily and fluidly. It's common among leaders to focus on training and breaking a sweat, but not mobility. You won't see them in isometric routines or wrestling with a foam roller. They will be doing sets, repeats, jumps, curls—and miles of running with grotesque form. This builds a rigid and immobile frame, making posture even worse and injuries likely.

Consider when you work out hard and tear some muscle or soft tissue. The next day you're pretty sore, but after a while the soreness ebbs because the damaged area has self-repaired. In the repairing aftermath, however, there can be a mess of soft tissue that knots or bunches in spider web inconsistency. Connective tissue spreads around and across the muscles and joints to stabilize the previously injured area. It heals into a firmer version of what it used to be, like a cast. This is part of God's brilliance showing our body's design to preempt future damage again like a cast or splint would. If this damaged area is left unattended, however, it becomes *immobile*. This immobility can cause imbalances over time, such as favoring one leg over another, or even sleeping only on one side. It's similar to putting your wallet in the opposite pocket and noticing how weird it feels. Your body has learned how to accommodate for that wallet's location. You likely don't even realize how much you favor certain parts of your body due to injuries and immobility collected over the years.

I recall my first real yoga class with a live instructor. It was humiliating how immobile I was. I was likely as *flexible* as the other folks and I'm also pretty sure I could run faster, longer, and lift more than most in the room, but I couldn't make my body do what everyone else was doing. I was like a plastic action figure that had four joints, with the rest being a stiff joke. I discovered tightness and impedance in areas I neglected over the years, and it was finally on display before all the yogis. When leaving leadership sickness, I had to make changes to my fitness protocol, but of all the additions, subtractions and alterations, *becoming more mobile gave the most noticeable change.*

So far, my goal has been to reveal the occupational dangers of your sedentary leadership to your physical frame. Because of your butt being glued to a chair with your hands on a phone, book, or mouse, you're an orthopedic nightmare. You may also be slowly evolving into a belly-fat mouth breather with rigid and inflamed joints. Immobility is claiming you slowly as your C-shaped spine and shoulders roll internally to make you look like you're 99 years old. Capped off with a craned neck, your body isn't sure if it should be panicked or not. *So, that's where we are. Next, we'll see how things can get even worse for us before they get better.*

Faulty Starts

In Track and Field, jumping from the blocks in a sprint event before the gun goes off will get you busted by the race official, earning everyone a frustrated trip back to the blocks to try it again. The fastest times recorded are from athletes who get a clean jump from the blocks. I'd be irresponsible to not speak to *how* we start the road back to fitness for the leader. Many times, it's full of false starts, bringing mounds of shame and discouragement. I realize that not everyone reading this enjoys fitness, and I can sympathize. I'll do the best I can to speak both to leaders who find fitness fun and those who don't.

Because this book is written directly to leaders, I'm going to just cut to the chase: *there is no such thing as picking up where you left off back in the day.* I'm a six-day-a-weeker and if I miss over four days in a row, I have to ratchet everything back about 10 percent in intensity and duration just to stay alive and not blow a gasket. There are studies that posit a potential drop-off that occurs after a couple weeks of sedentary living in the normally consistent *athlete.* If this is true for those who are consistent athletes, then your six years of not exercising definitely counts. *You'll need to start small, work slow, and practice quality.*

When coaching runners, I'd always teach, "slow is fast!" Going too hard in the beginning can lead to injury for a slew of reasons, like cruddy form from overexertion. Injury means you're back on the sideline for the foreseeable future, not getting more fit. Whether or not you're "into" fitness, taking it slow and easy at first will get you to functional fitness far faster than trying to pick up where you left off when you were 16. I'm not anti-CrossFit by any means, but the spike in joint injuries since the advent of CrossFit has been widely recognized. It's not CrossFit breaking leaders in half; the injuries come from trying to do too much with lagging form. No matter what you do to find fitness, start small and slow, and practice quality.

DOMS: Delayed Onset Motivation Soreness

Inspiration has a shelf life. After some time, our motivation gets sore. As a trainer, I'd tell clients that they'd have to agree up front to give me six to eight weeks before quitting. I picked this time because that's how long it would take to see measurable results in the mirror. By then, they wouldn't want to quit. Before that time, they would want to quit a thousand times. When you begin a fitness journey, it will feel odd and awkward, and none of the new movements will feel natural. It will seem like everyone around you is a pro while you look like a doofus. "The change should be awkward," Christopher McDougall admits. "You should go through a period where you're no longer good at doing it wrong and not yet good at doing it right. You're not only adapting your skills, but your tissues; you're activating muscles that have been dormant most of your life."[12] Traditionally, results are slow and convince us that we aren't changing, so it's easy to drop fitness like a hot rock. When the mirror and clothes tell us we aren't changing, we weigh the profit and loss statement of time and decide it isn't worth the investment.

Functional fitness can quickly become an optional category for those not seeing impressive results quickly. *When fitness is only an option, then the threshold of motivation sits even higher.* If you view fitness as extracurricular, you'll end up with a gym membership that never gets used and running shoes only worn to Costco. Fitness can't be expendable, even if you don't see big results. Visible results can take months, and they can be so slow you may not notice a serious difference for even longer. You must see the *urgency*, results aside, for a healthy fitness regimen to stick. You cannot rely on the mirror.

I realize some readers have no problem grabbing the gym bag and clocking in at the gym. In fact, you wait for it all day. Repetitions finished and miles logged serve as a sort of sanctum. You probably wear workout gear all the time, track your fitness on all your devices, and don't panic in the supplement aisle. You take "no days off" and likely wanted to skip this chapter because you're never tempted to miss "leg day." *My goal isn't to increase your maximum output athletically or help you win medals, but to recast what fitness for a leader looks like.* Even with undergraduate work and certifications for fitness, I had to recast everything to accommodate for a leader's unique biological demands. Otherwise, my "no pain, no gain" theory would facilitate repeated burnouts. Whether you're a fitness freak or a fitness not-so-much, ask yourself a couple of questions.

1. Why do I want to be fit? What motivates me?
2. How important is this to me? Do I sense a deep urgency?

Our *motivation* to be fit unveils our heart's desire and values, and our *urgency* displays resolve. These questions help us analyze both ends of the leader's fitness spectrum.

For example, if you want to be fit so you look like Thor, you could be struggling with a need for approval. God has given approval to you vertically, but you hunger for it horizontally. This might also show up if you video or livestream your gym sessions to everyone so they can admire you. Or, if you never miss a training day, maybe it's because the gym is the only place you can "win," having mastery over an environment. If this describes you, fitness may be a good thing made into an ultimate thing. You may have a six pack yet are abusing fitness as a medication. Maybe your motivation is to win medals and climb podiums, subtly building glory. After taking emotional punches and feeling like a loser all day, there is something enticing about box jumping better than everyone else. After feeling insignificant and invisible all day, there is something soothing to feeling not-invisible as you sculpt a perfect frame. The byproduct for such gospel fractures is not only that fanatics like us struggle in our satisfaction with God, we are likely denting our health at the same time. "No days off" reads tough on a shirt, but is actually a pretty dumb strategy.

Maybe you answer the questions with a, "Well, I don't want to be fit. It's not important to me. It's not like I have cancer or can't tie my shoes or something like that." Your motivation bends in a different direction as you may be motivated to *avoid discomfort*. Your satisfaction in God's good news is no more impressive than it is to the fanatic. Chasing comfort at the cost of functional fitness is barely better than eating corn dogs all day. Or maybe, you too struggle with value and approval and the thought of looking silly or remedial in a gym full of supplement-slurping muscleheads is too much.

I vividly recall whisking my father to the hospital after his first heart attack. I heard him gasping as he was trying to eat his third Stouffer's Chicken Pot Pie, and I rushed him downtown. After his surgeries, he had to gain fitness, doctor's orders. My dad was a *not-so-much* fitness enthusiast before the attack, but he followed the doctor's orders. No more pot pies, no more sitting still. He worked on his fitness, starting small and slow and not quitting. He did it because he was able to answer those questions for himself honestly. He saw the *urgency* and was *motivated*. He wanted fitness so he could meet his grandkids. He saw the urgency because of how close he came to death. *Motivation is important. Perceived urgency is crucial.*

You must wrestle with those questions in order to adopt a leader's functional fitness lifestyle. I don't care if you have a drawer full of spandex or not, if you have hurry-up sickness, you must be intentional with *how* you achieve fitness.

Bro, Do You Even Lift?

There has been a civil war brewing for eons: weights versus cardio. I still hear it in the locker room and read it in forums. I'm personally bored with the controversy, but still today resistance training and cardiovascular training are pitted against each other as the yin and yang of all fitness. They even form camps, with websites pointing to the benefits of one over the other. "Weights are better for your joints." "Cardio is better for your heart." Everyone sounds so resolute and scientific. I think this adds to the confusion for leaders.

> What if the answer to this civil war was both—and none— depending on the day? What if your local gym-in-the-box isn't even the answer?

I'd like to cut through the confusion and make things a bit simpler. If you happen to be an active athlete and enjoy competition and a heavier training routine, I have some comments toward the end of this chapter that may help you balance your training with your workload to prevent burning yourself out. There are some considerations you need to take in developing where you place your hard and easy training sessions.

Meat Markets

When I work with leaders on their fitness, they automatically assume I'm going to tell them to get a gym membership or a personal trainer. That may be the case depending on the fitness IQ of the leader, but going to the gym doesn't always end in fitness. I'm not against gyms and have had a membership somewhere since 1991, but I don't think gyms are the panacea for all who are unfit. To prove my point, consider the rate of climbing obesity in America and then consider the rate of growth in health club revenues—they are the same at about two percent.[13] Something is obviously broken. People are joining gyms in hordes, but no one is staying except for those who enjoy it already. *Gyms are making tons of money, but obesity didn't get the memo.* Many things can be found at a local gym, but not always fitness. Squat racks, battle ropes, and spin bikes are positioned efficiently within walls of mirrors, but the fitness we hunt at the local gym doesn't always bring the fitness we need as sedentary leaders.

Fitness wasn't born in the 24-hour centers flanking us today. Look through ancient Grecian artistic renderings of athletic training back in the day, and you'll likely find naked guys running, jumping, sparring, doing plyometrics, balancing, and other movements that are more like today's plank than bench press. In fact, if you were to "go to the gym" before the early 1970s as a non-athlete, it meant going to a boxing gym. All the athletes of the day were fighters at sweaty warehouses like you see in the movies. Very different from today, you'd not find a line for the elliptical machine, but a random set of parallel bars that showed years of use. Grunting was allowed, but flexing in the mirror might have gotten you ridicule and a new nickname. What we currently know as the "gym" didn't find its genesis until the Terminator made his grand appearance in 1977. Journalist Chris McDougall noticed the cultural shift.

> *Pumping Iron* was released and, thanks to Arnold Schwarzenegger's swaggering charisma and chemically-enhanced physique, bodybuilding was transformed from underground entertainment into a worldwide phenomenon. Arnold would become Hollywood's most bankable star, and bodybuilding—*a form of male modeling that has nothing to do with agility, endurance, range of motion, or functional skill*—became the new gold standard for gym training. Just like that, the best-conditioned athletes in the world were being replaced by some of the worst.[14] (emphasis added)

When you see the cover of *Men's Fitness*, you don't really see a guy celebrated for his mobility. Foam rolling and yoga is back page material. Instead, you see articles on new ways to do the same boringly predictable exercises to make your six-pack come "back from hibernation." How-to articles on sculpting the physique are everywhere, but not much is taught in the way of postural control or what a recovery day ought to look like. *Fitness has morphed into boutique muscles advertising a fitness that often isn't there.*

It was after that curtain drop in 1977 that the fitness industry was born. Soon after, the first Nautilus machine showed up, and machine locations were springing up all over that would allow you to use these machines within their four walls for a fee. There wasn't even a need for trainers or instructors, just someone to wipe the sweat off when you were finished pushing the bar back and forth 4 x 12 times. Gone were the days of using medicine balls, bounding, sparring, balancing—in were the days of sitting on a machine in the local meat market. "The Greek ideal of a supple, balanced, useful physique was out. Massive McBodies were in."[15]

I'm taking you through a brief history of the gym as we know it because of that last key phrase McDougall uses: *useful physique*. This is the bar I'm holding for us as leaders. I'll also be using the phrase *functional movement* or *functional fitness* to describe the best way to gain a *useful physique*. Supple, balanced, useful, mobile, flexible—I believe these to be a better description of fitness than how many bricks or plates we can lift.

To explain what I mean by functional movements, I turn again to Theodore Roosevelt, who was way ahead of his time as a fitness guru. A guy who understood the stress of constant leadership and crisis, his résumé paints a picture of someone likely to feel the smoldering wick of burnout. He was lousy at football and still knew the pain of defending against a hurry-up offense. Roosevelt leveraged functional movements and holistic training to gain a *useful physique* that allowed him to lead well. *This is what we're after.*

As a young man, Roosevelt was wheezy, weak, and had cruddy eyesight. Imagine Peter Parker before the spider bit him. His dad brought him to Wood's Gymnasium in East Manhattan, knowing that his kid was in danger of continuing to skulk around only to get pounded by bullies. As Roosevelt grew in athleticism, leadership began to emerge in him and he found a taste for competitive functional movements. Historians agree as to how he'd later, as president, make functional fitness a hallmark of how leaders around him were built as well. His goal was never to sculpt horseshoe triceps, but to increase performance—and therefore leadership capacity. He and his father shared the same philosophy on building the *whole leader.*

Roosevelt was known for challenging aids and nearby soldiers to wrestling matches, just to get their heart rates up. He'd also be known to strip down to nothing and swim the freezing Potomac late at night. He'd even sometimes grab a pair of cudgels and challenge someone simply standing close by to a duel. (Just so you know, cudgels were sticks.) He was stick fighting his cabinet to stay in shape. This is a different kind of WOD[16] for certain.

Especially insightful for us are the tales of Roosevelt's training regimen of selecting a distant landmark and trekking toward it, keeping as straight of a line as possible. If there was a barn in the way, he'd climb over it. If there was a lake in the way, he'd swim across it. He was known for dragging advisors and other diplomats with him. Straight line. Stop whining. No excuses. The president was inventing Spartan courses long before you'd pay to do one for a medal or tattoo. He once said, "We liked Rock Creek for these walks because we could do so much scrambling and climbing along the cliffs. Of course under such circumstances, we had to arrange that our return to Washington should be when it was dark, so that our appearance might scandalize no one."[17] Translation: The course was so rough, they were trading clothes for wounds.

Functional useful movement was key for this leader. Range of motion, cardiovascular fitness, strength, mobility, flexibility, endurance, challenge—all of these were a part of his routine. From what the historians tell us, he was more parkour and less beach body. What if we borrowed from Roosevelt's program? He was a leader who understood stress, pressure, and crisis. What would it look like for us to take his approach? Would we be more resilient and functionally fit leaders?

As I mentioned earlier, I know that not every leader has the same wiring and therefore shouldn't adopt the same training regimen. I personally love "Rock Creek" type workouts and love trashing my clothes, getting cuts and scars, and overcoming obstacles, fears, and doubts. I've done some of the toughest races in the world and love the pain, fight, and finish. The more people that drop out, and the more it makes me dig into the pain cave, the more I want to do it. It's a huge release for me. Some of my closest friends, though—not so much. They think I'm dumb and hide the cudgels when I'm around. They're incredible and highly skilled leaders, however, and I've been inspired by their consistent investment in fitness, knowing that for them one minute of breaking a sweat feels like 10 minutes. They are doing what it takes to have a *useful physique* and lead God's people well. They are the truly disciplined leaders, in my opinion, because they have to gear up every time they grab the gym bag. Whether you are the swim-through-an-icy-creek kind of leader, or not so much, there are some nonnegotiables that will help you lead from a better posture, literally.

Posture IQ

Our posture is the first thing under attack as deskbound leaders. For double-digit hours every day, we slouch, stare, talk, or type. Done long enough, this lifestyle deforms our bodies. On top of our sedentary contribution to a weirdly shaped body, the popular fitness routines of the day don't help. We attempt to make our chests huge, further curling our shoulders inward due to tighter pectorals and an underdeveloped back. We do a billion crunches from various positions, further curling our body inward and forward without a lower back and pelvic floor to balance the load. Instead of strengthening our glutes and hamstrings for proper posture, we sit on them all day. *This is called lamination.* We laminate or stack layers of connective tissue so that our posterior musculature looks like thick immobile beef jerky.[18] These are parts of our body not meant to passively bear weight.

Instead of building our bodies to resemble a tall and neutral "I" shape, we assemble a muscular hunched "C" shape. Dr. Eric Goodman, author of *Foundation: Redefine Your Core, Conquer Back Pain, and Move with Confidence*, notes how your workout later in the day may be throwing gas on the fire. "All that time hunched in our cars and at our desks means we spend much of our lives internally rotated—otherwise known as computer syndrome—which is only exacerbated by all those crunches."[19]

We choose to develop our showcase muscles, sending our posture in the wrong direction. I'm convinced we do this because when we get the wild hair to work out, we want to spend time on muscle groups we can see. After all, who wants to tone their invisible pelvic floor musculature?

When it's been a long time since we've worked out, "chest and triceps" seem as good of a place to start as any. Interestingly, when I go to the gym, I never need to wait for a station targeting hip musculature. In all honesty, since my sickness, much of my fitness time is spent on muscles difficult to see or measure. In changing the muscles I focus on, I've been able to build a better chassis to hold the rest of my fitness and endure the rigors of a sedentary job.

When I was sick several years ago, I injured my lower back playing racquetball. I know I'm not special, and everyone tweaks their back, but the chiropractor told me something I'd never seriously considered. *"Luke, you have a great engine in the upper body and a great engine in the legs, but the linkage that connects them is severely weak and couldn't hold the load. This will keep happening if you don't strengthen the connection point of your midsection and posterior chain."* My posterior muscles and midsection made a bad transmission, and I couldn't get my northern and southern hemispheres to cooperate. This was largely due to my sedentary and primarily seated desk job.

Learning to Stand

I know what you're thinking at this point. *"But Luke, I have a standing desk and don't sit all day, so I'm not really sedentary."* It's true, I've been in your offices and have seen your cool desks. One of the biohacks becoming viral in recent years is the standing desk, or even the treadmill desk (don't do this to yourself). The idea is that since sitting is so bad for you and even considered the new smoking, standing cancels it out and improves posture. I agree that standing all day is an improvement on sitting all day, but it does not fix the odd curvature of our hips, neck, and shoulders. *The best working position is not the standing position, it's the next position, whatever that may be.* You should be changing positions often: sitting, standing, shifting from one leg to another, walking, leaning, etc. But even with an ever-changing position, we're still just touching the tip of the iceberg of functional fitness. For us to have useful physiques, we have to begin at the core. It's from a developed core and neutral collected spine that all fitness springs.

Standing seems like such a minor improvement that the innovation is laughed off, but consider that our bodies utilize energy differently when standing. Dr. Levine discovered how standing burns and stores calories differently when we stand instead of sit. The acronym he give this phenomenon is NEAT, which stands for Non-Exercise Activity Thermogenesis. *Thermogenesis* simply refers to how we churn through calories to make heat. "Non-exercise activity' is what you do when you're not exercising at high intensity—things like standing, walking, gardening, cooking, running to catch an elevator, and even fidgeting."[20] In Dr. Levine's research, someone who is sitting and sedentary for eight hours per day burns about 300 NEAT calories. That's not total calories, only calories above your basal metabolic rate that didn't come via a workout. This obviously slides on a scale depending on the size and efficiency of the body. Construction workers or food servers burn more NEAT calories, even up to 1,300 by their measurements. "That's a difference of 1,000 calories! Over time, that calorie variance can be the difference between being thin and being obese."[21] In layman's terms, when you stand versus sit, you are ahead of the game to the tune of one burrito per day. That adds up. This variance in caloric expense is even reflected in some of the latest activity trackers. As of this writing, my watch records not only total calorie burn for the day per heart rate, but how the calorie expenditure varies between active and non-active.

You don't need an expensive desk to work in this fashion—in fact, for quite a while I was using a filing cabinet at the church office. The only rubric you need to apply regards the elbow angle and the eyeline when looking at a monitor. It's important that you're able keep a neutral and collected spine, or as Dr. Starrett calls it, an "aerobic spine" and make sure that you aren't provoked to hunch or droop over the keyboard or laptop. Slouching while standing isn't much better than slouching while sitting. In fact, your standing might need a tune-up.

Upon my walk back to health, I literally had to learn how to *stand* correctly. One of the major critiques of the standing workstation is that it reinforces poor standing posture. I'm not sure how that is worse than poor sitting posture, but it is true how fast I realized I was standing with poor mechanics. After several hours at the standing desk, my back would begin to bark at me for my poor standing posture. If you're considering a standing option to sitting all day, I highly recommend Starrett's book, *Deskbound: Standing Up to a Sitting World*. He not only teaches you how to organize a neutral spine or stand correctly, but he guides you on how to breath, walk, squat, and sit correctly. As a man in his 40s who has been schooled in upper level kinesiology, I thought I was competent in something like walking across the room, hinging at the hips, and picking up a book. Turns out, we reinforce what is easiest, not what is proper mechanics. This wrecks the office worker.

Redefining the Core

Ask the average person walking down the street to name the muscles in their core, and they'll likely point to their abs. Some may even mention the obliques and lower back. Traditional wisdom has defined the core as the wide band that wraps around our midsection—the powerhouse of all our activity. Therefore, a conventional core workout has sit-ups, throwing heavy balls around, leg raises on a Roman Chair, and crunches—endless crunches. This idea of the core is highly dated, however, and needs a revolution for the sick leader.

Dr. Eric Goodman, an expert in performance and movement, has been a pioneer in shifting attention from the core being "abs and gang" to what he calls the posterior chain. His insight can help us lay down a foundation for better movement and fitness. The posterior chain—call it the *new* core—begins in the neck, of all places.

The neck interfaces with the upper back, which does the same with the lower back. Traveling farther south, our posterior chain contains our butt, hammies, calves, all the way down through the heels. Consider your posterior chain (*core*) to be a spider web in which touching one area affects the rest, diminishing the further out it goes. This explains why when you've hurt your lower back, it even limits how much power you can deliver through the hamstrings and constrains how wide you can swivel your neck. Injuries can have both upstream and downstream effects on mobility and function. Also, try to bend over and touch your toes. You can literally feel the entire posterior chain working together—or not— in concert. Any good chiropractor or physical therapist will look for deficiencies *around* the damaged area in the back to see if it contributed to the back pain. When I raquetballed my lower back to shreds, it turned out that my pelvic muscles and adductors were underdeveloped, not pitching in when needed. I wasn't able to activate and stabilize my core to transfer power correctly. One small group of torn muscle, probably the size of a deck of cards, shut me totally down for two weeks and affected everything from my lower legs to my neck.

According to Goodman, we're wildly underdeveloped in the posterior chain and for every exercise we do for the front of our bodies, we should do *four* in the posterior department. Those are the muscles that influence our mobility the most. All our main movements originate in our posterior chain, yet we tip the scales in the wrong direction when we go to the gym or do push-ups on the floor. Goodman has been effective redeveloping busted up posterior chains in what he calls Foundation Training,[22] the thrust of which is beyond the scope of this book, but I highly endorse and personally use his training in my functional fitness.

I bring Dr. Goodman into our conversation because he's helping folks build a foundation for all activity. With a healthier, more developed posterior chain, you can branch out into whatever physical activities interest you, anything from yoga to CrossFit.[23] After adopting portions of his regimen, I found improvement in (1) my posture, whether I was standing or sitting, (2) my mobility and ability to have unimpeded range of motion, (3) fewer injuries, and (4) an ability to deliver more strength or speed in key training blocks. It did more than round me out, it built a functional frame. "Once your back muscles are stronger, your spine will relax, your hamstrings will lengthen, your glutes will function more powerfully, and you will naturally open up."[24]

In our quest to develop functional movements and leadership fitness, the basement level investment needs to be in the core, or posterior chain. If you only have time to do one thing, work on your new core. No, it might not show up in the mirror, but when you're working and leading, it will allow you to live unimpeded and have a posture that isn't falling victim to your sedentary lifestyle. The best part about working on your core—you don't need a gym.

Downward Dogs and Baby Cobras

In the quest for functional fitness or a *useful physique,* yoga stretches and postural holds ought to be mentioned at the minimum. I already know what you're thinking: *"Isn't yoga demonic or full of ancient chanting and weird stuff?"* I've noticed many heavy voices and bloggers herald yoga holds as virtual cult worship. Others just avoid it due to the controversy. It might be helpful to redefine yoga in much the same way we have had to redefine what the core is.

Yoga is in fact an ancient practice that combines elements of fitness and spirituality, and yes, it can get weird and distinctly demonic if you choose to go certain routes. Kind of like Netflix. It's also possible to leverage elements of yoga to serve the sick leader who has crumbling fitness. I practice a particular set of yoga stretches aimed at runners and triathletes that help me keep my core straight and toned, hips open, and it meets other needs my body has due to how I train and my sedentary proclivity. I inject *zero* spirituality into my various yoga routines. To be honest, I don't even throw an obligatory scripture into it to make it feel Christian. I just hit my poses, hold them, sweat and tremble, and breathe from the diaphragm. Yoga stretches are virtually isometric holds and positions that focus on mobility and muscular and postural balance. I know that a ton of yoga classes online and in studios will insert measures of eastern spirituality from time to time and show off their fluency in Sanskrit, but I typically don't go to those classes or videos.

You can certainly chant and burn incense doing just about anything if you wanted. Conversely, you can perform an isometric yoga hold doing nothing but listening to Run DMC and eating a Slim Jim.[25] In other words, I don't chant an ancient language when under the squat rack when I am doing reps, so why would it be necessary when stretching the spine and opening up the shoulder joints. One of the instructors I've benefited from greatly, Dean Pohlman, founded Man Flow Yoga under this same idea: *"Chanting, incense-burning, ohm-ing, calling out poses in an ancient language that nobody in the room speaks, and one-minute, public meditations all drive me insane. When I first started yoga, I did not understand why any of the aforementioned activities were part of the workout. . . . For me, yoga was just another form of fitness. The chanting and spiritual stuff made no sense."*[26]

I don't blame anyone for being nervous around yoga. I've seen some men far more brilliant than me even submit the exchanging of the *word* yoga for something less scandalous, like stretching. That's fine—after all, the controversy is semi-new. It's only been in the last decade or so that it's being used by non-spiritual practitioners divorced from a spiritual component. It's only been in the last few years I've heard male leaders mention yoga to be a part of their fitness routine. Also, 80 percent of yoga instructors are females; so, there's that. No male leader wants to go to a class at the YMCA and take a yoga class that has 32 women and no men. It just feels creepy. The high female constituency of yoga has led to men avoiding it like they would a nail salon.

The reason I'm including yoga in this conversation is its gentle and restorative nature. When we're injured or over-cooked, holding particular yoga poses and combining certain routines speed recovery time dramatically. Controlled breathing through mobility work increases blood flow while the heart rate stays nominally low. Yes, yoga holds can be tough, and there are some routines that shred me pretty good, but for the most part, they build our fitness through functional movements that we don't normally catch ourselves doing. Go ahead and try Downward Dog or knock out some Sun Salutations. Look them up on Dean's website and give it a shot. Yes, you'll be tired when you're done if you move and breathe correctly, and you will have a very difficult time naming one or two exercises that do the same thing with the same intensity. If what we're building is a *useful physique* comprised of practiced quality *functional movements*, then yoga holds belong in the conversation.

Foam Tube Aisle

I'm sure you can tell by now that I'm aiming for areas you probably don't spend much time considering. I'd like to throw one more thing into the mixed bag that you're unlikely to be doing: active mobility work. Earlier, we defined mobility as the *ability to perform an action with no impedance to range of motion.* Greenfield defines it as "your ability to move your body and limbs freely and painlessly through your desired movement."[27] Mobility isn't a priority for the typical leader, and honestly we can be a bit lost when wandering through the back aisle of Academy Sports trying to discern what the different tubes, balls, straps, and other torture devices are supposed to do, as well as trying to get over how much they all cost. And even if we did drop a small fortune on different shaped bright colored foam implements and straps, what do we do with them?

Habitually, we move about, sit, work out, and even sleep the same way all the time. Because we're a pattern-oriented people, our bodies succumb to predictability. A largely inactive and predictably routine life will yield:

- Limited range of motion, because stillness isn't dynamic in nature
- Singular plane movements, utilizing only major muscle groupings
- Imperceptible imbalances due to accommodating injuries over time
- Confining movement due to joint problems and soft-tissue limitations
- Bad form when we exercise, jeopardizing our body further
- Overusing certain muscle groups while underusing others

Mobility work counteracts the confining and calcifying aspects of an inactive lifestyle. It's an antidote to a leader's imprisoned desk-driven routine. *Even if you're fairly active or athletic,* a lack of mobility will eventually catch up with you. No one is genetically impervious to immobility. Becoming stiff, rigid, and imbalanced is simply a part of the fall where we come apart.

As an example of the effect of mobility, the first seven years I coached high school runners I juggled teenage injuries. As the season progressed, more injuries would appear. It was reality, not just for me but for all coaches. With elite runners putting in so much mileage, injuries seemed inevitable. All we could do was get them to an athletic trainer and cough up a plan to mitigate further damage. By season's end, the team picture was much smaller because many were on the trainer's table getting iced. It wasn't until I added ballistic stretching (as opposed to static), foam rolling, PNF stretching, [28] and various trigger point work to the routines that I sensed a massive difference. During my last season as a coach, *we didn't have a single season-ending injury out of 24 high school distance runners, each averaging 50 to 60 miles per week.* In fact, a magazine article was written on our championship team, and the headline was "Team Foam Rolls Their Way to Championship." It was unheard of 10 years ago, but now most elite teams use their stingy budgets to bring in mobility experts or yoga instructors to work with athletes for sports-specific mobility.

As an example for non-athletes, I've noticed great relief for those with pain in the upper back and neck after trigger point work, especially as they focus on areas up and downstream from where the pain radiates. Whether by foam roller, lacrosse ball, or something bought exclusively for trigger point work, I've known many to find improvement in the neck's range of motion, release of headaches, and decreased pressure in the lower back due to daily mobility work. Also, for the classic *anterior pelvic tilt* mentioned above, I've seen mobility unlock pent-up hip flexors and quadriceps, allowing the hips to mobilize and roll back so the spine can collect itself properly. In short, you stand more like the Marlboro Man and less like the Hunchback of Notre Dame.

The rabbit hole of mobility tools and routines is second only to yoga. So, for our purposes in developing a *useful physique,* I'll list the most helpful ways I've been able to use mobility to care for self and help others lead from a healthier place. There are more options within the mobility universe than what I've listed, but these are the basics.

- *Dynamic/Ballistic Stretching:* Ballistic stretching is best employed pre-workout and throughout the day. Different than static stretching, where a muscle is moved to its limits and held for a set amount of time, ballistic or dynamic stretching incorporates movements that place the stretch "in context" within activity. Consider that when you train your body under resistance (running or lifting), you are functionally *shortening* the muscles repeatedly. Static stretching is doing the opposite, and is therefore not very helpful pre-workout. When you see folks touch their toes and hold the stretch for 30 seconds before they hit the elliptical, all they have done is statically hold an unprepared muscle for a long time in a shape it won't see at all on the machine. This is why you don't see wild animals stretching right before they chase a fat moose down. If you perform static stretching, it's best performed after your easier recovery sessions. Ballistic stretching, on the other hand, promotes muscle readiness and should be done before you train.[29]

A riff on this type of stretching is PNF stretching. Short for Proprioceptive Neuromuscular Facilitation, it incorporates resisting the stretch actively for a few seconds, only to resume the deep stretch again. If you're stuck and cannot gain mobility in key areas, I've known PNF stretching to get people through the sticking point. Resource Kelly Starrett's instruction on his various websites and video channels for instruction on how to properly perform PNF stretching.

- **Trigger Point Therapy:** Trigger points, or muscle knots, are areas in the muscle that are irritable and not begging to be manhandled. By applying pressure to these knots, you can restore mobility and possibly alleviate pain. You can even find stores online that sell nothing but trigger point tools with routines. For instance, I have a spikey looking ball that I use on a trigger point near my hips, and it helps not only loosen me up and erase the pain, it also opens my range of motion so I can train safely. At first, I cussed and cried my way through the session due to the breaking up of knotted tissue, but after a while, the muscle turned from beef jerky to rare flank steak. Because of the spiderweb of connective tissue holding everything together, working on the areas around an injury is help the injury as well. In order to attain functional mobility, pain must be handled before any additional flexibility. Pain immobilizes the body even more than disuse. Fix the areas of throbbing or piercing pain, and watch mobility improve.

- **Deep Tissue Massage:** Nobody likes this, and if they say they do—they're likely doing it wrong or not paying enough money. Unlike other forms of massage, like Swedish or family-gifted neck rubs, this species of massage goes for the deeper muscle tissue underneath the more superficial tissue. Deep muscle, surface muscle, tendons, fascia, and laminated layers of knotted connective tissue are kneaded and broken down. I get one of these at the end of hard race seasons and as much as it hurts, it's incredibly effective in producing better mobility. This is why it's typically an upgraded massage at a spa. Pay the extra money because it's worth it, but if you aren't wincing or saying "*whoa*" often, it might not be deep enough. It needs to feel like the masseuse hates you. If you find one, keep them on speed dial.

Because the world of fitness is embracing this level of mobility more wholesale, you can now get tools and instruction on how to do all of this on yourself. Dr. Starrett calls this "smashing" yourself and has excellent work in his book, *Becoming a Supple Leopard*, regarding how to drive mobility into your frame. On a practical note, I've learned to do the bulk of "smashing" on non-key training days due to the teeth-gritting pain it can bring and the inflammation that sometimes comes with it. Drink lots of water before and after this work to hydrate your tissues so they can handle the manipulation, and schedule this for a day when you'll have adequate time to recover. You may also sense some nausea afterward due to the increase in inflammation.

- Foam Rolling: Realistically, this should be considered part of deep tissue massage, but due to its virality and acceptability, it might be good to mention it separately.[30] These rollers mimic what you'd get in a deep tissue massage without the expense and quality. If you can only afford one roller, aim for the mid-firm smooth roller and don't get trapped into the demonic looking advanced ones. You can get plenty of work done on a basic roller. In fact, you may have things lying around the house (rolling pin, PVC pipes, softballs, etc.) For instructions and guidance on how to use the rollers, simply look online at the work Dr. Starrett and others have done.

As an added bonus for those who aren't afraid of crying, when rolling tougher areas that are slow to respond to mobility work, consider what some call active-release treatment (ART).

Once you've rolled across a noticeably painful or stuck area, stop on that area and then move your limbs so that you contact and elongate the tissue and muscles directly where the "hot spot" is. This has helped me in key posture influencers such as my iliotibial band (IT band) and glutes.

Both And

When considering the content of your fitness routine, *there are some things you'll need to include whether or not you're super excited about them, and other things you'll need to include because you like them and will continue to do them.* Earlier, we looked at the Republican/Democrat-like discussion of strength training versus cardiovascular training. Both are effective, and you'll need to insert them into your daily rhythms in such a way that you're able to lead from health. In fact, recent research suggests that strength training is also highly cardiovascular, so maybe it's time to retire the old categories we've grown to use over time. As an example, Roosevelt was able to include both types of training. He was swimming and cudgeling. Boxing and running. What you do in your cardiovascular work (elliptical, swimming, running, biking, rowing, etc.) and what you do in your strength or resistance training (Crossfit, HIIT training, machines, free weights, plyometrics, etc.) exceed the scope of this work. My goal is to get you doing both without prejudice, while adding mobility work, foundational core work, and postural holds. My goal is to help you create a useful physique.

Cardiovascular work and strength training aren't compartmentalized in such a way as to work on different portions of the body exclusively anyway. When we run, it develops the balance and muscular development of the legs, and when we do something like Spartan training or CrossFit, it will undoubtedly test our cardiovascular limits, VO2 capacity, and lactate threshold. Both training formats overlap and increase overall systemic health and fitness. Think holistically and know that you'll need an assortment of movements and strategies.

Fitness has inertia to it, and keeping variety in your regimen will speed that inertia up and keep it high. What's of value is that you don't favor one group of movements to the point of excluding others. If 90 percent of your time gaining fitness revolves around a machine with cables, you'll never really gain the functional fitness you'll need to be a fit leader. Conversely, swimming is fantastic for you, but if you don't work on those heavily-used shoulder joints via mobility work and also strengthen your core, you'll end up incomplete and damaged. *So, how do you know what to do and when to do it?*

Timing Is Everything

We're finally at the point where we can apply our exploration of oscillation theory to how we spend energy in fitness. We've seen that not all days are equal, and not all fitness sessions are equal. In fact, neglecting how we see and spend the finite quantum of energy we have can potentially wreck leadership health faster than not training our fitness at all. This is where my ignorance accelerated my sickness and where I needed an overhaul. If you are naturally drawn to training, you'll need to make similar adaptations.

Some days, like Monday for example, I wake up and can feel the residue from yesterday's oil spill. I'm fatigued and feel under-resourced. It's on those types of days when I can literally "*feel*" the lack of energy that I alter what kind of functional fitness I work on that day. Although I have a strategic plan to my fitness regimen, it flexes around how healthy my nervous system is. *In short, I plan intentionally, but I do as I feel.*

Your nervous system is somewhat like a battery to your body, and as we've seen, it can be taxed and "drained" as you incur both emotional punches and celebrate huge wins. Going back and forth from Disneyland and the battlefield drain the battery. Leadership is a roller coaster, and your responsive nervous system requires rest like any battery. This neural fatigue must be accounted for in the leader's fitness strategy and likely explains why some days you leave the gym and feel like you may have gone backwards. Greenfield explains, "This is why you can still be theoretically overtrained or under recovered even if you're not overdoing it at the gym, but are perhaps partying too much, working too much, or not sleeping enough."[31] This is what we've implied throughout the whole book. Leadership stress affects the body as much and even more than physical stress. This is why we must honor energy management via oscillation. *Hard days at work shouldn't be punctuated with hard days of physical training.* Too often, I hear the Sunday leader express how they feel energized after a Sunday service, and so they start setting records at the local gym on that same day. *This is simply unwise.* You must account for the neural expenditure and fatigue to avoid burning out. Greenfield continues, "It's important to know that your central nervous system does not differentiate between muscle groups. If it's fatigued, it's fatigued."[32]

Calling Audibles

Functionally, this looks like packaging (or repackaging) your fitness load according to how you experience leadership stress. For instance, Sunday afternoon or even Monday morning may be an unwise time to flip monster truck tires or run hill repeats. Your body has been in various shades of fight-or-flight for the majority of Sunday, and the battery needs to trickle charge. Those days are better suited for movements like an easy swim (if you know how to swim, else you're back to fight or flight) or easy elliptical and mobility work. You can camp under a squat rack on those days if you want, but don't expect your body to conform to the challenge, because it's trying to recuperate from the previous day's stress load. You'll just damage your overall health.

This sounds like common sense, but so many "feel better" after a hard workout session, so they fail to calculate the toll it is taking on their health. The exhaustion after a rigorous session may feel like you've accomplished a great feat, but it doesn't mean you've improved your health. You may have gained in various physical metrics (VO2 max, lactate threshold, muscle mass, etc.) but have also set yourself back internally and placed your body in a rampant search for rest and reset. *Bigger biceps, but shriveling adrenal glands is a bad tactic.* Greenfield agrees, "I see the biomarker values of many, many CrossFitters each week—and they tend to be some of the most hormonally depleted folks I work with. If you don't want to suffer adrenal fatigue, which is where hormonal depletion leads, my first piece of advice is typically to back off CrossFit and add in more recovery sessions, easy swims, yoga, sleep, rest, and calorie intake."[33] Think long term. Sometimes, the best way to advance all of your health metrics is to either take the day off, or do something that looks unimpressive on Strava, like walk around the block.

As an example of how this works from the other end, I have personally found Friday to be a great day to dig hard physically because Thursday is a bit easier for me emotionally, and I have my family day the next day. Sandwiched between days of neural recovery, I am able to accommodate the hard training session. *Maybe now, you can see why it's important to get your training calendar to have an honest conversation with your work calendar.* Greenfield suggests, "Low-level aerobic cardio doesn't really create as much neural fatigue as high-intensity cardio and sprints, which is why you should alternate aerobic and anaerobic sessions during the week if you want to allow for prime neural recovery."[34]

As a final note on timing, consider also what we saw in earlier chapters regarding your body's response to the circadian rhythm. We learned that if you schedule your training sessions for the morning hours, you'll find a body not quite ready for hard physical taxation. It's not until the afternoon hours that your heart rate is highest, your body temperature primed, and your musculature ready for stress. Reserving mobility or yoga holds for the morning is wiser than running bleachers. Sometimes, the best thing you can do for your functional leadership fitness is simply reschedule *when* you train. Doing the right thing at the wrong time is simply doing the wrong thing.

I realize that getting it done early in the morning means it won't get skipped and allows you to work later into the day, but you may need to innovate your rhythms to serve you better. Again, as an example, I "clock in" very early, which means I'm able to train hard in the afternoons and before I go home for the day. This single innovation helped greatly and allowed me to build a threshold as well between work and home. As a side note, training hard past 5:00 p.m. has always made it difficult for me and others to fall asleep in a timely manner. Return to the chapter on sleep to see why this happens, but an overactive neural grid and elevated heart rate doesn't make for great sleep. Try to hit your hardest sessions, whatever they may be, between 3:00 and 5:00 p.m., and you'll be fine. Go past that and you're simply asking for it.

HRV

I've been cautious to mention too many tech tools due to the speed of technology dating anything I write, but I'd be remiss to not speak about HRV applications to the recovering leader. Mentioned briefly in an earlier chapter, I've found this to be an active part of my self-care dashboard and have recommended it to other leaders. As a reminder, HRV stands for *Heart Rate Variability* and is a measure of the variability between heartbeats. Not to be confused with heart rate, which is the rate per amount of time, variability is a reflection of the regularity *within* that time. For instance, if your heart beats 60 times per minute as you sit and read this, there will be variability in those 60 individual beats. They don't come exactly 1 second apart but look more random, like 1.05 - .95 - 1.1 - 1 - .88 and so on. What we know for a fact is the more regular or precise the rate (less variability), the more your nervous system is trying to regulate itself and find recovery from neural stressors. It's your body demanding regularity to charge the battery efficiently. The more variability we see, the more rested your neural framework, and the more stress you can apply. This should sound counterintuitive at first read, but experimenting with and paying attention to this metric will be a big step in the right direction for the fit leader, especially if you train hard.

The technology for this goes back to the '60s as the Soviet Union would experiment with it to build the better athlete. They didn't have phone apps back then, and I've heard the machines were pretty cumbersome. From then until the early 2000s, HRV would show up exclusively in clinical and research realms generally out of reach for all but professional sports teams. Now, HRV technology has been made to interact with the everyday person through their phone or activity tracker. When I first signed up for help in HRV measurements in 2012, there were only two companies offering it—now there are dozens of ways to get this measurement. It's too accessible to ignore now.

The idea is simple: Early in the morning, you measure your HRV and the result gives you vital information to make decisions on how you can shape your fitness work to your neural health. The information may be delivered in a number, or a color (red, yellow, green, etc.), or even some quick advice depending on the company you use, but this helpful measurement will help you map or remap your day. I found this to be helpful personally due to how I "felt" in the morning not being an accurate depiction of what was actually happening under the hood. There would be mornings I'd feel fine and ready to tackle a tough day, only to find I was in neural fatigue and needed to make changes or even cancel any fitness work. HRV taught me I can't always trust how I feel.

Also, using HRV is what helped me see which specific stressors held the most weight. For instance, looking back over a several-month period of HRV results I was able to see what it was that "stressed me out" the most. This is incredibly valuable information if you are building your rhythms to recover and lead well. There have been mornings when I've taken my HRV measurement and then texted my assistant to reschedule my appointments that day. I'd also make sure my fitness plan for that day cooperated with my neural load and stress health.

If you are serious about being a fit leader and are running an up-tempo and heavy load, you may consider grabbing an app or heart rate strap to do this on your own. In fact, watches and even rings are coming with more accurate sensors to measure this in real time during the course of the day.[35] This tech is made for athletes, but because of what we know regarding emotional stress eclipsing even physical stress on the body's limits, we can use it to our advantage as leaders. As with any activity tracking, it is more effective and helpful the longer you use it. Using it for a few months yields better data than using it for a few weeks. Be patient.

Principles

I've spent more time on *when* to train than *how* to train because when you train properly is defined by biology, but what you do in that time is defined by your passions and interests. I think the best way to approach the content of your training session is to ask: *"Am I growing my functional fitness in a way I enjoy?"* As a personal trainer, I never lost a client because they were having a blast. What can you do that you look forward to? Paddleboard, run, Judo, racquetball, powerlifting? But to bring balance to the equation, is there enough variety so that your functional fitness is improving?

See how simple that is? No arguing over whether CrossFit is better than Step Aerobics or whether you should lift using machines or free weights. If you enjoy powerlifting but you're noticing that you don't do anything to accommodate for a deskbound lifestyle, then you're honoring the second part of the principle but not the first. If you are Lord of the Spin Bike yet hate every second of it, then you may successfully accommodate for being in an office all day, but you'll eventually quit because you hate it.

To honor the overly basic principle, make sure mobility and core strengthening are part of your new normal. Without this adaptation, it won't matter how impressed your friends are with your fitness level, you're not fighting against a sedentary lifestyle properly. Make sure the bulk of your training is in a context you enjoy. In addition to this obvious principle, I'd love to introduce another way to accelerate fitness and improve your office experience—especially if you have a lot of ground to cover.

Greasing the Groove

Ben Greenfield, whom I've quoted often in my work, is one of the most sought after fitness experts in America and has been a great help to me in my recovery. An industry leader and avid Ironman triathlete himself, he too has felt the stress and pressures of balancing all the spinning plates. As a business starter, coach, and traveling conference speaker, he originated the phrase "*greasing the groove*," and I think it may be helpful for you, the leader looking to develop a useful physique that can hold on through the rigors of leadership life.

Greasing the groove is creating moments in the midst of your workflow to step away from the desk and do something active. You might recall this moment in the middle of work when we looked at how to change gears between ultradian bursts. For instance, you may break to do six 30-second lunges,[36] and then go back to work. You could do 30 push-ups, air squats, a wall sit, a set of planks, or even some pull-ups. Nothing that would take more than a moment to do, but something that is noticeable. You'll burn NEAT calories without even loading up the car to go to the gym. When I have heavy office days, I'll set a timer to go off every 30 minutes, at which point I'll do a variety of movements that incorporate multiple joints and functional movements. I know this sounds goofy, but when you do the math, it truly makes a difference.

The average sedentary desk job has you burning between 50 and 100 calories per hour with the large variance determined by your size and metabolic efficiency. I noticed for me it was closer to 100 calories per hour for the whole day. When greasing the groove, however, the calories per hour is lifted to 125 to 150 per hour for the day. So after eight hours of this, I burn around 400 extra calories without really breaking a sweat. Four hundred calories is the equivalent of four Moon Pies or two Krispy Kreme donuts. After a five-day week of this, you burn 2,000 calories that you weren't burning before. Extra credit if you're standing and changing positions as you work as opposed to sitting.

Greasing the groove doesn't need to be intense, but it needs to be something active and consistent. I have a number of things around my office that I can do quickly, and I even substitute in yoga poses and active-release therapy foam rolling. Just introduce something to keep the heart rate above the metabolic baseline, muscles ready and warm, and fat burning. I also noticed anecdotally that this practice increased my creativity and productivity, as we've already touched on in other chapters. I'm a big believer in greasing the groove, and it has kept my functional fitness at a high level.

The alternative is being still all day, only to work out later for an hour or two, only to go back to more sitting and standing. I'm seeing more and more reports and studies comparing those who are 100 percent sedentary versus those who have sedentary jobs yet hit the gym daily. *There seems to only be a slightly elevated fitness level in those who hit the gym compared to those who don't.* The studies are painting a picture that the effects of sitting all day are greater than the benefits of going to a gym daily. Greasing the groove can be a great way to lead from a healthier place even though you may have what is widely considered a desk job.

✵ ✵ ✵

To this point, my goal has been to make you functionally fit and mobile, so you can carry out the work God has put before you. Think of this chapter as more of a starter kit, but not a complete statement on high fitness. If you are interested in achieving high or competitive fitness, take a look at the endnotes for this chapter, and you'll find an ocean of resources. If this chapter is as far as you'll investigate leadership fitness, then stay consistent and know that it may take several months for substantial and noticeable changes to occur. You may even need to secure a knowledgeable expert or coach in your fitness work.

ACKNOWLEDGMENTS

I began researching and writing material with the single goal of helping a few random sick leaders find health. It seemed so many others were experiencing the same thing I had. At that time, I was also surrounded by many voices that encouraged me to produce this book, speak, and coach others orbiting burnout and overall leadership sickness.

Along this path, I was greatly shaped and held together by my friend John Fooshee. For years, he has been both a heavy voice and a good friend, and he knew when to be which.

I also couldn't have done this without the support and prodding of Elliot Grudem and the men of the Leaders Collective: Elliot, Jamey Nettles, Rick Gilmartin, Jason Tucker, Bubba Jennings, and Jerome Gay. Without Elliot's life-altering guidance and shaping through the Leaders Collective, I'd still be meandering in sickness.

Finally, I'm thankful for the people and pastors of Legacy Church. Not only did they afford me the time to write this and coach other pastors, they encouraged and expected it. I couldn't have done this without all of you.

ENDNOTES

Introduction

1. Samuel Chand, *Leadership Pain: The Classroom for Growth* (Nashville: Thomas Nelson, 2015), 56.

Play Hurt

1. George Schroeder, "At SEC Meetings, Calm Voices on Roiling Football Debate," *USA Today*, May 29, 2014, https://www.usatoday.com/story/sports/ncaaf/sec/2014/05/29/college-football-pace-of-play-hurry-up-no-huddle/9747947/.
2. Bucky Brooks, "Up-Tempo Offense Catching On As Quick Path to NFL Success," NFL.com, September 17, 2014, http://www.nfl.com/news/story/0ap3000000377868/article/uptempo-offense-catching-on-as-quick-path-to-nfl-success/.
3. Schroeder, "At SEC Meetings."
4. Dan B. Allender, *Leading with a Limp: Take Full Advantage of Your Most Powerful Weakness* (Colorado Springs: WaterBrook Press, 2006), 1.
5. There is a simple physiological reason behind shin splints, but for many years it was a kind of mystical ailment that had equally mystical remedies.
6. Mark 6:31, 32
7. Liminality is the place of disorientation that finds us in the middle of big changes. We no longer hold the deep values we once had. We can never return, but we haven't completely transformed into what we want to become. We're stuck in the middle.
8. Psalm 69:1–3
9. Michael Casagrande, "How Do HUNH Offenses Impact Alabama's Defense? Tide Linebackers Get Their Say after Coaches Spar," AL.com, March 20, 2014, http://www.al.com/alabamafootball/index.ssf/2014/03/how_do_hunh_offenses_impact_al.html.
10. Yes, that's my third sports analogy in one chapter, completing the trifecta.
11. "The processes that take place in chronic diseases from arthritis to cancer pull on the adrenals as more and more demand is made upon the body by

the disease. Therefore, take it as a general rule that if someone is suffering from a chronic disease and morning fatigue is one of their symptoms, the adrenals are likely involved." James L. Wilson, *Adrenal Fatigue: The 21st Century Stress Syndrome* (Petaluma, CA: Smart Publications, 2017), Kindle.

12. Wayne Cordeiro, *Leading on Empty: Refilling Your Tank and Renewing Your Passion* (Bloomington, MN: Bethany House Publishers, 2009), 14.

13. As of this writing, AFS, or hypoadrenocorticism, isn't officially recognized by major medical associations but is widely recognized and treated by most educated and credentialed health and wellness doctors. Conventional medicine in general only recognizes AFS when it is at the furthest reaches of degradation, known as Addison's disease.

14. H. B. London Jr. and Neil B. Wiseman, *Pastors at Greater Risk* (Ventura, CA: Regal Books, 2003), 20.

15. London and Wiseman, Pastors at Greater Risk, 172.

16. "Adrenal Fatigue Symptoms," The Institute for Effective Diagnosis and Treatment, http://effectivediagnosis.org/adrenal-fatigue-symptoms/.

17. This metaphor is used by numerous teachers on this subject. Wayne Cordeiro does a great job in his book *Leading on Empty*. It's been very helpful for me and those I work with. I'll explain more thoroughly later in this book.

18. Timothy Keller, *Walking with God through Pain and Suffering* (New York: Riverhead Books, 2015), 252.

19. Richard A. Swenson, M.D., *Margin: Restoring Emotional, Physical, Financial, and Time Reserves to Overloaded Lives* (Colorado Springs: NavPress, 2004), 98.

Bent Trees

1. James L. Wilson, *Adrenal Fatigue: The 21st Century Stress Syndrome* (Petaluma, CA: Smart Publications, 2017), 12 Kindle.

2. C. H. Spurgeon, *The Devotional Classics of C.H. Spurgeon: Morning and Evening I & II* (Lafayette, IN: Sovereign Grace Publishers, 1990), 18, Google Books.

3. Swenson, *Margin*, 47.

4. Caroline Alexander's epic book *The Endurance: Shackleton's Legendary Antarctic Expedition* has helped me greatly in leadership. I also give it to staff and pastors that we train. It's a book that CEOs buy by the crate.

5. Joshua Horn, "Shackleton's Ad—Men Wanted for Hazardous Journey," *Discerning History*, http://discerninghistory.com/2013/05/shackletons-ad-men-wanted-for-hazerdous-journey/.

6. A liger is half tiger and half lion. There! Now you don't need to watch the movie.

7. Jason Ankeny, "A Winning Personality: Why Ambiverts Make Great Entrepreneurs," *Entrepreneur*, March 5, 2015, https://www.entrepreneur.com/article/242502.

8. If this is a new concept for you, I strongly recommend Alexander Strauch's *Biblical Eldership: An Urgent Call to Restore Biblical Church Leadership* (Colorado Springs: Lewis and Roth Publishers, 1995).

9. Cordeiro, *Leading on Empty*, 58.

10. Brennan Manning, *Abba's Child: The Cry of the Heart for Intimate Belonging* (Colorado Springs: NavPress, 2002), 34.

11. A. W. Tozer, *The Pursuit of God* (Harrisburg, PA: Christian Publications, 1948), 12.

12. Anne Jackson, *Mad Church Disease: Overcoming the Burnout Epidemic* (Grand Rapids: Zondervan, 2009), 49.

13. "Had my six" means "had my back," six o'clock being behind me if twelve o'clock is in front.

14. Cordeiro, *Leading on Empty*, 21.

15. I see EQ and EI used interchangeably, depending on the source, but as far as I can discern, they refer to the same general idea.

16. Brennan Manning, *Abba's Child*, 71.

17. Swenson, *Margin*, 46.

18. Tim Chester, *The Busy Christian's Guide to Busyness* (Westmont, IL: InterVarsity Press, 2008), referenced in Kevin DeYoung, *Crazy Busy: A (Mercifully) Short Book about a (Really) Big Problem* (Wheaton, IL: Crossway, 2013), 26.

19. Walter Carter Tucker, *Men Who Fought. . . . Boys Who Prayed: A Combat Chaplain's Story: Vietnam* (Mustang, OK: Tate Publishing & Enterprises, 2013), 104.

20. In about 12 hours, I burned more than 12,000 calories and lost 12 pounds. To my understanding, this particular race is the most strenuous single-day, single-stage race you can do. It takes about three weeks to totally recover. Still, it paled in comparison to some very average days in ministry leadership.

21. You can find more about HRV testing in "Fit Fat."

22. Roland H. Bainton, *Here I Stand: A Life of Martin Luther* (New York: Penguin Books, 1995), 42.

She-Bear

1. If you don't know who Jack Bauer is, put the rollerblades down and watch *24* with Kiefer Sutherland.

2. Hans Selye, *The Stress of Life* (New York: McGraw-Hill, 1984), 430.

3. Swenson, *Margin*, 45.

4. London and Wiseman, *Pastors at Greater Risk*, 20.

5. London and Wiseman, *Pastors at Greater Risk*, 172.

6. Ben Greenfield, *Beyond Training: Mastering Endurance, Health, and Life* (Las Vegas: Victory Belt Publishing, 2014), 162. I'm using Greenfield's four-stage model of adrenal digression from his book *Beyond Endurance*. I found it to be the simplest and most helpful tool, and I highly recommend it to any active person looking to optimize their overall health. It's one of the most marked-up books I own.

7. Sometimes, adrenaline and noradrenaline are also referred to as epinephrine and norepinephrine, respectively. Don't panic. They are the same thing.

8. Christopher McDougall, *Natural Born Heroes: How a Daring Band of Misfits Mastered the Lost Secrets of Strength and Endurance* (New York: Alfred A. Knopf, 2015), 23.

9. Some of the communication between the brain (hypothalamus) and adrenal glands occurs electrically through nerves via the spinal column, but the other primary pathway is through the blood supply. Both modes of communicating with the adrenal glands are seemingly instantaneous.

10. James L. Wilson in his book *Adrenal Fatigue: The 21st Century Stress Syndrome*, defines adrenal fatigue as non-Addison's hypoadrenia, subclinical hypoadrenia, neurasthenia, adrenal neurasthenia, and adrenal apathy. The most commonly used term is simply *adrenal fatigue*.

11. At the time of this writing, Garmin and other wearable activity trackers use your heart rate and other factors to address your recovery time. Interestingly, the amount of time for recovery is always much longer than you would guess.

12. Don't do this because the bear is faster and a better climber than you are.

13. ATP (adenosine triphosphate) is a small molecule that's key to energy transfer.

14. Greenfield, *Beyond Training*, 162.
15. When tight pants are worn, sometimes the skin of the abdomen overflows above the waistline like the top of a muffin. It's an awesome look.
16. Greenfield, *Beyond Training*, 163.
17. Greenfield, *Beyond Training*, 163.
18. It's important for me to repeat that I am not medically trained, nor am I a physician. You should never abandon a path your physician has you on unless you dialogue with him or her on how to come off of medications safely. That is especially true for antidepressants.
19. Brad Hambrick, *Burnout: Resting in God's Fairness* (Phillipsburg, NJ: P&R Publishing, 2013), 8.
20. Archibald D. Hart, "Depressed, Stressed, and Burned Out: What's Going on in My Life?" *Enrichment Journal*, http://enrichmentjournal. ag.org/200603/200603_020_burnout.cfm.
21. Once you hit midlife, the adrenal glands gradually become the major source of the sex hormones circulating throughout the body. That is true for both women in menopause and men in general.
22. Cordeiro, *Leading on Empty*, 25–26.
23. The doctor and researcher was Dr. Rick Cohen, who was very helpful when I looked into sleep and adrenal testing. You can find some of his helpful materials at http://core4nutrition.com.

My Crimes

1. Timothy Chester, *You Can Change: God's Transforming Power for Our Sinful Behavior and Negative Emotions* (Wheaton, IL: Crossway, 2010), 73–74.
2. For the record, I think everyone has a daddy issue. I know this term has been used for those who have particularly horrible fathers, but I'm not sure how one gets to adulthood even with a good father figure who is not affected by sin.
3. Kevin DeYoung, *Crazy Busy: A (Mercifully) Short Book about a (Really) Big Problem* (Wheaton, IL: Crossway, 2013), 34.
4. DeYoung, *Crazy Busy*, 353.
5. Hambrick, *Burnout*, 6.
6. Bainton, *Here I Stand*, 26.
7. Bainton, *Here I Stand*, 30.
8. I strongly suggest *Dangerous Calling* by Paul David Tripp, *On Being a Pastor*

by Derek J. Begg and Alistair Prime, *Glory Hunger* by J.R. Vassar and Matt Chandler, and *The Imperfect Pastor* by Zack Eswine.

9. Zack Eswine, *The Imperfect Pastor: Discovering Joy in Our Limitations through a Daily Apprenticeship with Jesus* (Wheaton, IL: Crossway, 2015), 74.

10. Raymond C. Ortlund, *The Gospel: How the Church Portrays the Beauty of Christ* (Wheaton, IL: Crossway, 2014), 80–81.

11. Ortlund, *The Gospel*, 81.

12. Ortlund, *The Gospel*, 103.

13. Roger Bannister, quoted in Christopher McDougall, *Born to Run: A Hidden Tribe, Superathletes, and the Greatest Race the World Has Never Seen* (New York: Vintage Books, 2009), 13.

14. Eswine, *The Imperfect Pastor*, 127.

15. Matt Perman, *What's Best Next: How the Gospel Transforms the Way You Get Things Done* (Grand Rapids, MI: Zondervan, 2016), 264.

16. If you are interested in the Leaders Collective, contact them at http://leaderscollective.com. Without a doubt, working with them was the most helpful and formative thing I have done as a leader. I cannot overstate the value to pastors who are fatigued, lonely, and in need of help. What I learned and the friendships I made truly altered my leadership going forward.

17. Ortlund, *The Gospel*, 83.

18. If this is you, you might want to read Anne Marie Jackson's book *Mad Church Disease*. It's written from a burned-out perspective that's not from a lead position.

19. Phil Knight, *Shoe Dog: A Memoir by the Creator of Nike* (New York: Simon & Schuster, 2017), 296.

20. Mark Sayers, *Facing Leviathan: Leadership, Influence, and Creating in a Cultural Storm* (Chicago: Moody Publishers, 2014), 103.

21. 1 Corinthians 10:12

22. Jerry Bridges, *The Pursuit of Holiness* (Colorado Springs: NavPress, 2016), 99–100.

Your Remedy

1. Spoiler alert! Snipes are mythical creatures.

2. Acts 12:1–8

3. Simon Guillebaud, *More Than Conquerors: A Call to Radical Discipleship* (Grand Rapids, MI: Kregel Publications), 47, Google Books.

4. McDougall, *Natural Born Heroes*, 86–87.
5. Psalm 46:1–11
6. Mark 4:39–41
7. John 14:1–4
8. Bob Kellemen, "Guard Your Relationship with God Your Guard: Faith in Your Father," October 21, 2011, accessed December 18, 2018, https://www.rpmministries.org/2011/10/guard-your-relationship-with-god-your-guard-faith-in-your-father/.
9. J. R. Vassar, *Glory Hunger: God, the Gospel, and Our Quest for Something More* (Wheaton, IL: Crossway, 2015), 20.
10. Genesis 3:24
11. 2 Samuel 4:4
12. 2 Samuel 9:1–6
13. 2 Samuel 18:1
14. 2 Samuel 9:7–11
15. 2 Samuel 10:12
16. "The Anguish and Agonies of Charles Spurgeon," *Christian History Institute*, https://christianhistoryinstitute.org/magazine/article/anguish-and-agonies-of-charles-spurgeon.
17. Hambrick, *Burnout*, 14.
18. 2 Corinthians 4:7
19. Andrew Murray, *The Spiritual Life* (Philadelphia, PA: George W. Jacobs & Co., 1897), 164–165, Google Books.
20. Murray, *The Spiritual Life*, 147–148.
21. 1 Corinthians 3:6
22. Luke 10:38–42
23. Paul David Tripp, *Dangerous Calling: Confronting the Unique Challenges of Pastoral Ministry* (Wheaton, IL: Crossway, 2012), 35.
24. 2 Corinthians 4:16
25. 1 Samuel 30:6
26. Murray, *The Spiritual Life*, 243.
27. Psalm 139:23–24
28. William Gurnall, *The Christian in Complete Armour: Volume* 1, Abridged Edition (Carlisle, PA, The Banner of Truth Trust, 1986), 30.
29. Detoxing is a booger. Nobody enjoys it, but it is the sign your body has been in a bad place and is demanding more of what had been normal. We are robbing it of that, and the body is answering by revolting. Renewing a commitment to fitness has a similar feel.

The Walking Dead

1. Swenson, *Margin*, 100.
2. Bainton, *Here I Stand*, 138.
3. Charlie Wardle, *How to Sleep Better* (Bath, UK: Brown Dog Books, 2015), Kindle file, location 266.
4. Greenfield, *Beyond Training*, 228.
5. Greenfield, *Beyond Training*, 442.
6. Swenson, *Margin*, 97.
7. Swenson, *Margin*, 113.
8. Swenson, *Margin*, 114.
9. Wardle, *How to Sleep Better*, loc. 352.
10. Wardle, *How to Sleep Better*, loc. 369.
11. Wardle, *How to Sleep Better*, loc. 352.
12. Wardle, *How to Sleep Better*, loc. 398.
13. Ben Greenfield, "The Terrifying Condition of Sleep and Why You'll Die Earlier If You Don't Experience It," *Ben Greenfield Fitness*, October 10, 2017, https://bengreenfieldfitness.com/article/sleep-articles/the-terrifying-condition-of-sleep-and-why-youll-die-earlier-if-you-dont-experience-it/.
14. DeYoung, *Crazy Busy*, 95.
15. Kelly Clay, "Didn't Get Enough Sleep? You Might As Well Be Drunk," *Forbes*, September 4, 2013, https://www.forbes.com/sites/kellyclay/2013/09/04/didnt-get-enough-sleep-you-might-as-well-be-drunk/.
16. Rusty Lindquist, "Sleep Deprivation: How You Sabotage Your Own Success," *Life Engineering*, April 5, 2014, http://life.engineering/sleep-deprivation-like-being-legally-drunk/.
17. Fatigue Science, "Why Athletes Should Make Sleep a Priority in Their Daily Training," September 4, 2013, https://www.fatiguescience.com/blog/infographic-why-athletes-should-make-sleep-a-priority-in-their-daily-training/.
18. Grant Hill, quoted in David Murray, "50 Good Reasons to Sleep Longer," *HeadHeartHand*, May 14, 2014, http://headhearthand.org/blog/2014/05/14/arrogance-of-ignoring-our-need-of-sleep/.
19. Steve Nash, quoted in Tom Sunnergren/Philadunkia, "The Science of Sleep," ESPN, March 3, 2012, http://www.espn.com/blog/truehoop/post/_/id/37958/the-science-of-sleep.
20. Go back to Chapter 3 to see what cortisol does.

21. Wilson, *Adrenal Fatigue*, 124.
22. REM stands for Rapid Eye Movement, not the very average American band from the 1990s.
23. Wardle, *How to Sleep Better*, Location 271.
24. There's been adequate research to suggest that nasal and diaphragmatic breathing provokes the parasympathetic nervous system to be more active, which means our fight-and-flight sympathetic nervous system is cycling down. I've found this to be true. It may only be slight, but slight is all I need.
25. I seldom use Kindle screens because of the blue light they emit. If I do, I use an app that suppresses it through a blue light filter. You can find it for free on any platform.
26. EMF stands for electromagnetic field, not to be confused with the very average British 1990s band.
27. Wardle, *How to Sleep Better*, loc. 611.
28. Wardle, *How to Sleep Better*, loc. 1035.

Floor Sander

1. The bullies all looked six years older than Daniel Larusso, so okay, I guess there is a flaw.
2. DeYoung, *Crazy Busy*, 94.
3. James E. Loehr and Tony Schwartz, *The Power of Full Engagement: Managing Energy, Not Time, Is the Key to High Performance and Personal Renewal* (New York: The Free Press, 2005), 28.
4. A two-minute drill is an up-tempo, high-pressure strategy in which a football team has very little time to accomplish a lot. They are focused on clock management and stuffing as many plays in the finite time left in order to score one last time.
5. Bruce Miller, *Your Church in Rhythm: The Forgotten Dimensions of Seasons and Cycles* (San Francisco, CA: Jossey-Bass, 2011), 143.
6. Mark 6:30–34
7. Matthew 11:28–30 (The Message)
8. I have heard several coaches and pastors use this analogy and wouldn't know where to attribute credit, but these men have taught it very thoroughly.
9. Jackson, *Mad Church Disease*, 44.
10. Swenson, *Margin*, 81–82.

11. DeYoung, *Crazy Busy*, 98.
12. Psalm 127:2
13. Cordeiro, *Leading on Empty*, 126.
14. C. H. Spurgeon, *Lectures to My Students, Volume 1* (Grand Rapids: Zondervan, 1954), 51, Google Books.
15. Swenson, *Margin*, 198.

Stop Start

1. Sayers, *Facing Leviathan*, 132.
2. Loehr and Schwartz, *The Power of Full Engagement*, 97.
3. Loehr and Schwartz, *The Power of Full Engagement*, 32–34.
4. Perman, *What's Best Next*, loc. 350.
5. James L. Wilson, *Adrenal Fatigue: The 21st Century Stress Syndrome* (Petaluma, CA: Smart Publications, 2017), Kindle, loc. 282.
6. Ecclesiastes 10:10.
7. Martin Moore-Ede, quoted in Loehr & Schwartz, *Power of Full Engagement*, 37.
8. Loehr & Schwartz, *Power of Full Engagement*, 39.
9. Swenson, *Margin*, 128.
10. Burst-oriented movements such as box jumps or burpees can communicate "alert" and "execute" a bit more than a slow 20-second lunge. Our goal here is to find rest, not establish a new record.
11. When laughing, your felt stress diminishes, and your body naturally relaxes. It's in this relaxed state that our adrenals and other internal mechanisms recover and reset.
12. As mentioned in the chapter on sleep, box breathing is inhaling over four counts, holding for four counts, exhaling for four counts, and holding for four counts. It's widely used with our military's various special forces and also Olympic athletes. Although this is very calming, it requires practice. It's not a normal way to breathe all day, but helpful in tight moments. Now, I've noticed many wearable activity trackers are guiding you in literal box rhythms.
13. Dr. James Wilson in his book *Adrenal Fatigue* comments on this phenomenon within his commentary on meditation. I cite it here due to the physical efficacy only. *"The body shifts from sympathetic to parasympathetic nervous system dominance; breathing, heart rate, and oxygen consumption slow down; muscles relax; the brain predominantly generates the slower alpha waves;*

and blood pressure may drop. These changes occur within a few minutes of beginning an activity that produces the relaxation response, whereas they happen very gradually over hours while sleeping and often not at all while engaging in a leisure activity. Of particular relevance to adrenal fatigue recovery is that during the relaxation response, stimulation of your adrenal glands diminishes so they can rest and, in addition, all the tissues in your body become less sensitive to stress hormones secreted by your adrenal glands. This means that every part of your body has a chance to return to normal and recuperate instead of being constantly on red alert." (Kindle, loc. 1374)

14. Loehr and Schwartz, *The Power of Full Engagement*, 98.

15. Loehr and Schwartz, *The Power of Full Engagement*, 102.

16. Dean Karnazes, *The Road to Sparta: Reliving the Ancient Battle and Epic Run That Inspired the World's Greatest Footrace* (New York: Rodale, 2017), 46.

17. Friedrich Nietzsche, quoted in Jean-Marc Pascal, "On the Virtues of Peripatetic Philosophy," November 24, 2011, accessed December 18, 2018, https://blogs.osc-ib.com/2011/11/ib-teacher-blogs/dp_philosophy/on-the-virtues-of-peripatetic-philosophy/.

18. Jean-Marc Pascal, "On the Virtues of Peripatetic Philosophy," November 24, 2011, accessed December 28, 2017, https://blogs.osc-ib.com/2011/11/ib-teacher-blogs/dp_philosophy/on-the-virtues-of-peripatetic-philosophy/.

19. Allen Taha, "Physical Self-Care Practices for Sustainable Pastoral Leadership in Local Church Ministry," abstract (PhD diss., Covenant Theological Seminary, St. Louis, 2010).

20. Swenson, *Margin*, 69.

21. Swenson, *Margin*, 69–70.

22. Cal Newport, *Deep Work: Rules for Focused Success in a Distracted World* (New York: Grand Central Publishing, 2016), 6–7.

23. Newport, *Deep Work*, 42.

24. I've heard and read wide variation in how long it takes to regain focus after a distraction, but those are the furthest bounds I have heard in either direction.

25. Newport, *Deep Work*, 52.

26. Perman, *What's Best Next*, 242.

27. See Allen's work, particularly in his book *Getting Things Done*. Also see Matt Perman's comments on this concept in his book *What's Best Next*.

28. Perman, *What's Best Next*, 275.
29. Craig Groeschel, quoted in Jackson, *Mad Church Disease*, Kindle, loc. 2047.
30. It's actually a setting on my phone (Do Not Disturb) that will only allow calls or alerts from my wife and one elder. All other notifications of any kind are kept quiet depending on the settings I establish.
31. Newport, *Deep Work*, 149.
32. Newport, *Deep Work*, 149.

French Resting
1. London and Wiseman, *Pastors at Greater Risk*, 188.
2. DeYoung, *Crazy Busy*, loc. 1005.
3. Mark 2:27
4. Dollywood is the Disneyland of East Tennessee, complete with tourists, under-disciplined kids, overpriced everything, and a long walk to the car. I also heard somewhere that it is fun.
5. Remember, it's been scientifically proven that emotional distress wrecks the internal chemistry and health of someone more than physical stress.
6. I took a month to measure my glucose activity and heart rate before, during, and after a 40-minute sermon. I found that my heart rate rose from a resting heart rate of under 48 beats per minute (bpm) all the way to 100 bpm for the entirety of the sermon. Also, my body saw a rise in blood sugar and blood pressure as it perceived stressors. Even with 20 years of experience in an arena where I felt totally calm, I found myself in an alarm reaction state. Other public speakers outside of the ministry have commented on the same phenomena. You can see why leading multiple services and/or meetings and being in the trenches all day Sunday *without an answer* to the stress response in the form of recovery is not such a brilliant idea. You must accommodate for the load.
7. London and Wiseman, *Pastors at Greater Risk*, 175.
8. Martin Luther, quoted in Roland H. Bainton, *Here I Stand*, 191.
9. Marjorie Greenbie, *In Quest of Contentment* (New York: McGraw-Hill, 1936), 57.
10. Pastor Mark Driscoll has spoken deeply on this type of reflective work, and Wayne Cordeiro has also done great work writing on his PRD or personal retreat days. You can read more from Cordeiro on this in his book *Leading on Empty*.

11. London and Wiseman, *Pastors at Greater Risk*, 203.

12. Perman, *What's Best Next*, loc. 3634.

13. Loehr and Schwartz, *The Power of Full Engagement*, 6.

14. Manning, *Abba's Child*, 39.

15. Cordeiro, *Leading on Empty*, 190.

16. Andrew Murray, *The Spiritual Life: Undeniable Ways to Conquer the Flesh and Grow in Christ* (Chicago: George W. Jacobs & Company, 1897), Kindle, loc. 2666.

Pie Hole

1. Anne Jackson, *Mad Church Disease*, Kindle, loc. 693.

2. *Fed Up*, directed by Stephanie Soechtig, produced by Katie Couric and Laurie David, January 19, 2014, accessed January 27, 2018, http://fedupmovie.com.

3. *Fed Up*.

4. *Fed Up*.

5. DXA or DEXA (Dual-energy X-ray absorptiometry) scanners are used to measure bone mineral density but have been adapted to detect fat distribution, and have been accurate to a higher degree than conventional methods. MRI (Magnetic resonance imaging) is a medical imaging technique used in radiology to form pictures of the anatomy and the physiological processes of the body in both health and disease.

6. BMI stands for Body Mass Indicator and is used by many to determine optimal weight, yet the scale is rarely helpful when it comes to the quality of the weight on a person according to their height, or even how the weight is composed. In other words, you can have an acceptable BMI and be in poor shape.

7. Jackson, *Mad Church Disease*, loc. 700.

8. Yes, weeks. It took a long time to overcome some cravings, but I have to say that after two years, I would just as quickly drink a green juice over a milkshake if both were put before me. Your cravings can be reprogrammed.

9. I have lived on a particular nutrition plan for the last few years and am a big believer in it, but have found other healthy leaders (ministry and non-ministry) using a variation of my nutrition scheme that worked very well for them. I've found that most of the better nutrition plans curbing the damage we do in a hurry-up lifestyle focus on (1) drastically decreasing poorly sourced carbohydrates, (2) moderate protein intake, and (3) increased healthy fats.

10. Richard A. Swenson, *Margin: How to Create the Emotional, Physical, Financial & Time Reserves You Need* (Colorado Springs: NavPress, 1992), 95.
11. Swenson, *Margin*, 95.
12. Swenson, *Margin*, 95.
13. Jackson, *Mad Church Disease*, loc. 2410.
14. Bridges, *The Pursuit of Holiness*, 139.
15. V. L. Allineare, quoted in Dr. Asa Andrew, *Empowering Your Health: Do You Want to Get Well?* (Nashville: Thomas Nelson, 2007), 261.
16. Bridges, *The Pursuit of Holiness*, 128.
17. Susannah Wesley, quoted in Bridges, *The Pursuit of Holiness*, 148.
18. Thomas Boston, quoted in Bridges, *The Pursuit of Holiness*, 151.
19. 1 Corinthians 9:25–27.
20. Bridges, *The Pursuit of Holiness*, 152.
21. Murray, *The Spiritual Life*, loc. 396.
22. Wilson, *Adrenal Fatigue*, loc. 1602.
23. A Venti can also hold close to a bottle of wine. Ironic that no Christian leader would have a bottle of wine every night because of how it would impair our leadership and health, yet we'd indulge in the same 20-plus ounces of coffee, which also alters our leadership and health.
24. MCT stands for medium chain triglycerides. This healthy oil is highly thermogenic. It accelerates the production of ketone molecules and brings both sharp thinking and faster fat burning. You can buy pure MCT oil and many variants of it pretty much anywhere.
25. A thermogenic substance increases base metabolism, predominantly burning fat.
26. This is not a recipe book, but to get a look at an example of a smoothie that can carry fat and high nutritional density at the same time, refer to Ben Greenfield's iconic morning smoothie. He has raised the smoothie to an art form. Check out https://bengreenfieldfitness.com/article/nutrition-articles/the-best-smoothie-ingredients/.
27. The blood-brain barrier (BBB) is a selective semipermeable membrane consisting of capillaries forming tight junctions that don't really show up in other parts of the body. It acts as a gate, only allowing certain things past, such as some gases, water, caffeine, ketone molecules, glucose, and pertinent amino acids.
28. Greenfield, *Beyond Training*, 434.

29. Dr. Lustig in the film *Sugar Coated* states that of all "packaged" foods in grocery stores, 74 percent have sugar added. Researchers in the documentary *Fed Up* state that 80 percent of all food items have added sugar. It's not impossible that the difference between expert numbers simply be the baked goods or other non-packaged foods containing added sugar.

30. Dr. Wilson notes in his book *Adrenal Fatigue*, "Approximately three feet of sugar cane makes one tablespoon of white sugar. That means that three feet of nutrients and fiber are lost to produce one tablespoon of naked calories. Continually consuming these naked (energy without nutrients) calories leads to nutrient deficiencies. Nutrient deficiencies lead to impaired physiological function. Impaired physiological function leads to the structural and pathological changes we know as chronic illnesses." (Loc. 1723)

31. "Intense Sweetness Surpasses Cocaine Reward," National Center for Biotechnology Information, August 1, 2007, accessed February 5, 2018, https://www.ncbi.nlm.nih.gov/pmc/articles/PMC1931610/.

32. Kitta MacPherson, "Sugar can be addictive, Princeton scientist says," Princeton University, December 10, 2008, accessed February 5, 2018, https://www.princeton.edu/news/2008/12/10/sugar-can-be-addictive-princeton-scientist-says.

33. Alice Park, "7 Not-So-Sweet Lessons about Sugar," *Time*, May 9, 2014, accessed February 5, 2018, http://time.com/92545/7-not-so-sweet-lessons-about-sugar/.

34. Jackson, *Mad Church Disease*, loc. 700.

35. I'd suggest these books on reformatting a diet through elimination: (1) Robb Wolf, *Wired to Eat: Turn Off Cravings, Rewire Your Appetite for Weight Loss, and Determine the Foods That Work for You*; (2) Mark Sisson and Brad Kearns, *The Keto Reset Diet: Reboot Your Metabolism in 21 Days and Burn Fat Forever*; and (3) Tom Malterre and Alissa Segersten, *The Elimination Diet: Discover the Foods That Are Making You Sick and Tired—and Feel Better Fast*.

36. Wilson, *Adrenal Fatigue*, loc. 397.

37. Greenfield, *Beyond Training*, 397.

38. Greenfield, *Beyond Training*, 397.

39. Greenfield and others suggest a light rinse of a 9:1 ratio of water to white vinegar. Then, rinse with water, and there you go.

40. See previous note.
41. Wilson, *Adrenal Fatigue*, loc. 1692.
42. Greenfield, *Beyond Training*, 105.
43. If this is of interest to you, look into Dr. Volek and Dr. Phinney's books, *The Art and Science of Low Carbohydrate Living* and *The Art and Science of Low Carbohydrate Performance*, as well as Gary Taube's books, *Good Calories, Bad Calories* and *Why We Get Fat*.
44. "Weight Loss with a Low-Carbohydrate, Mediterranean, or Low-Fat Diet," *The New England Journal of Medicine*, July 17, 2008, accessed February 5, 2018, http://www.nejm.org/doi/full/10.1056/NEJMoa0708681.
45. Ben Greenfield, *The Low-Carb Athlete: The Official Low-Carbohydrate Nutrition Guide for Endurance and Performance* (n.p.: Archangel Ink, 2015), 5.
46. We have found that soaking nuts, salting them, and then dehydrating them makes them easier on the stomach. It takes some work but is a better route. Avoid nuts and seeds that are soaked in some dumb flavoring or roasted in a bad oil.
47. Anecdotally, I currently favor nut butters for my long distance racing due to their prolonged energy release. They have far outperformed most supplements I used to take for races longer than six hours. I have found that this also is the case during a typical workday.
48. Wilson, *Adrenal Fatigue*, loc. 1620.
49. For more robust discussions on supplements and vitamins, be sure to look at Dr. Wilson's book *Adrenal Fatigue*. He gives the most detailed treatment I've seen for the sick leader exclusively. If you are an athlete, you may consider adding Ben Greenfield's *Beyond Training* to the list. He does an equally helpful job.
50. I currently use Multi Vitamin Elite by Thorne Nutrition (https://www.thorne.com/products/dp/multi-vitamin-elite) but also saw great lists and sources from multivitamins formulated by Dr. Mercola (https://shop.mercola.com/search?filter=&search=multivitamin&type=q&keywordoption=CUSTOM&cid=0&fltrdesc=) and Mark Sisson's Primal Blueprint (https://www.primalblueprint.com/primal-master-formula/). In terms of cost, Thorne's supplement will be in the middle of those mentioned.
51. An adaptogenic herb is a plant known for its healing attributes. They help

regulate, restore, and guard the body as it responds to stressors. They help normalize our body's physiological reactions.

52. John Stott, *Through the Bible, Through the Year* (Oxford: Candle Books, 2006), 210.

Fit Fat

1. London and Wiseman, *Pastors at Greater Risk*, 172.
2. London and Wiseman, *Pastors at Greater Risk*, 172.
3. Dr. James Levine, quoted in Kelly Starrett, Juliet Starrett, and Glen Cordoza, *Deskbound: Standing Up to a Sitting World* (Las Vegas: Victory Belt Publishing, 2016), 8.
4. Starrett, Starrett, and Cordoza, *Deskbound*, 8.
5. Starrett, Starrett, and Cordoza, *Deskbound*, 8.
6. Starrett, Starrett, and Cordoza, *Deskbound*, 9.
7. Starrett, Starrett, and Cordoza, *Deskbound*, 8.
8. Starrett, Starrett, and Cordoza, *Deskbound*, 17.
9. Starrett, Starrett, and Cordoza, *Deskbound*, 10.
10. Starrett, Starrett, and Cordoza, *Deskbound*, 46.
11. Starrett, Starrett, and Cordoza, *Deskbound*, 66.
12. McDougall, *Born to Run*, 206.
13. McDougall, *Natural Born Heroes*, 209.
14. McDougall, *Natural Born Heroes*, 211.
15. McDougall, *Natural Born Heroes*, 213.
16. WOD stands for Workout of the Day.
17. McDougall, *Natural Born Heroes*, 215.
18. Posterior simply means backside. The front of our bodies is the anterior.
19. Dr. Eric Goodman and Peter Park, *Foundation: Redefine Your Core, Conquer Back Pain, and Move with Confidence* (New York: Rodale Books, 2011), 20.
20. Starrett, *Deskbound*, 18.
21. Starrett, *Deskbound*, 18.
22. I highly recommend Goodman's book *Foundation*. It can be read in a few hours and is loaded with pictures to guide someone at any skill level through his program. You can also find some great material and videos from Dr. Goodman online.
23. Goodman and Park, *Foundation*, 11.

24. Goodman and Park, *Foundation*, 65.
25. Feel free to listen to Run DMC, but substitute almonds for the Slim Jim.
26. Dean Pohlman, "My Personal Story: How I Got Started with Yoga," *Man Flow Yoga*, accessed December 30, 2017, http://manflowyoga.com/the-story/.
27. Greenfield, *Beyond Training*, 123.
28. PNF (Proprioceptive Neuromuscular Facilitation) is a fancier way of doing static form stretching while incorporating the brain in a way that immediately opens up range of motion.
29. Feel free to visit Kelly Starrett's or Dean Pohlman's YouTube accounts for dynamic/ballistic stretching. Now that it is becoming more conventional, the number of teachers online is growing.
30. I just left an indoor track meet where college athletes had their own rollers personalized and carried them everywhere like their babies. Rollers are now accessories.
31. Greenfield, *Beyond Training*, 152.
32. Greenfield, *Beyond Training*, 152.
33. Greenfield, *Beyond Training*, 59.
34. Greenfield, *Beyond Training*, 59.
35. The later Garmin products are recording HRV and giving adequate data, and the Oura ring (https://ouraring.com/) is another route. If you go the phone app route, I'd suggest looking at BioForce and Joel Jamieson (http://www.bioforcehrv.com/) or Elite HRV (https://elitehrv.com/)
36. Yes, isometric lunges can be slothfully slow, but try a 30- to 60-second slow lunge and notice it only takes 18 seconds for whining to start.

BIBLIOGRAPHY

Allender, Dan B. *Leading with a Limp: Take Full Advantage of Your Most Powerful Weakness*. Colorado Springs: Waterbrook Press, 2008.

Andrew, Asa. *Empowering Your Health: Do You Want to Get Well?* Nashville: Thomas Nelson, 2007.

Ankeny, Jason. "A Winning Personality: Why Ambiverts Make Great Entrepreneurs." *Entrepreneur*. March 05, 2015. Accessed December 28, 2017. https://www.entrepreneur.com/article/242502.

Bainton, Roland H. *Here I Stand: A Life of Martin Luther*. New York: Penguin Group, 1950. Kindle.

Bridges, Jerry. *The Pursuit of Holiness*. Colorado Springs: NavPress, 2016. Kindle.

Burns, Bob, Tasha Chapman, and Donald Guthrie. *Resilient Ministry: What Pastors Told Us about Surviving and Thriving*. Downers Grove, IL: IVP Books, 2013.

Brooks, Bucky. "Up-tempo Offense Catching On As Quick Path to NFL Success." NFL.com. September 17, 2014. Accessed December 28, 2017. http://www.nfl.com/news/story/0ap3000000377868/article/uptempo-offense-catching-on-as-quick-path-to-nfl-success/.

Casagrande, Michael. "How Do HUNH Offenses Impact Alabama's Defense?" AL.com. March 20, 2014. Accessed December 28, 2017. http://www.al.com/alabamafootball/index.ssf/2014/03/how_do_hunh_offenses_impact_al.html.

Chester, Timothy. *You Can Change: God's Transforming Power for Our Sinful Behavior and Negative Emotions*. Wheaton, IL: Crossway, 2010.

Clay, Kelly. "Didn't Get Enough Sleep? You Might As Well Be Drunk." *Forbes*. September 04, 2013. Accessed December 28, 2017. https://www.forbes.com/sites/kellyclay/2013/09/04/didnt-get-enough-sleep-you-might-as-well-be-drunk/.

Cordeiro, Wayne. *Leading on Empty: Refilling Your Tank and Renewing Your Passion*. Minneapolis: Bethany House, 2009.

DeYoung, Kevin. *Crazy Busy: A (Mercifully) Short Book about a (Really) Big Problem*. Wheaton, IL: Crossway, 2013.

"Adrenal Fatigue Symptoms." EffectiveDiagnosis.org. 2014. Accessed December 28, 2017. http://effectivediagnosis.org/adrenal-fatigue-symptoms/.

Eswine, Zack. *The Imperfect Pastor: Discovering Joy in our Limitations Through a Daily Apprenticeship with Jesus*. Wheaton, IL: Crossway, 2015.

"Why Athletes Should Make Sleep a Priority in Their Daily Training." *Fatigue Science*. September 11, 2017. Accessed December 28, 2017. https://www.fatiguescience.com/blog/infographic-why-athletes-should-make-sleep-a-priority-in-their-daily-training/.

Fed Up. Directed by Stephanie Soechtig and Laurie David. Produced by Katie Couric. Performed by Katie Couric. *Fed Up*. January 19, 2014. Accessed January 27, 2018. http://fedupmovie.com

Gerber, Michael E. *The E-myth: Why Most Businesses Don't Work and What To Do About It*. New York: HarperCollins, 2012.

Goodman, Eric, and Peter Park. *Foundation: Redefine Your Core, Conquer Back Pain, and Move with Confidence*. New York, NY: Rodale, 2011.

Greenbie, Marjorie Latta Barstow. *In Quest of Contentment*. Freeport, NY: Books for Libraries Press, 1970.

Greenfield, Ben. *Beyond Training: Mastering Endurance, Health, and Life*. Las Vegas: Victory Belt Publishing, 2014.

———. *The Low-Carb Athlete: The Official Low-Carbohydrate Nutrition Guide for Endurance and Performance*. N.p.: Archangel Ink, 2015.

———. "The Terrifying Condition of Sleep and Why You'll Die Earlier If You Don't Experience It." Ben Greenfield Fitness. October 10, 2017. Accessed December 28, 2017. https://bengreenfieldfitness.com/article/sleep-articles/the-terrifying-condition-of-sleep-and-why-youll-die-earlier-if-you-dont-experience-it/.

Gurnall, William. *The Christian in Complete Armour.* Abridged ed. Edinburgh: Banner of Truth Trust, 1986.

Hambrick, Brad. *Burnout: Resting in God's Fairness.* Phillipsburg, NJ: P & R Publishing, 2013.

Hart, Archibald. *Adrenaline and Stress.* Nashville: W Pub. Group, 2003.

————. "Enrichment Journal." *Depressed, Stressed, and Burned Out: What's Going on in My Life?* Accessed December 28, 2017. http://enrichmentjournal.ag.org/200603/200603_020_burnout.cfm.

"Intense Sweetness Surpasses Cocaine Reward." National Center for Biotechnology Information. August 1, 2007. Accessed February 5, 2018. https://www.ncbi.nlm.nih.gov/pmc/articles/PMC1931610/.

Jackson, Anne. *Mad Church Disease: Overcoming the Burnout Epidemic.* Grand Rapids: Zondervan, 2009.

Karnazes, Dean. *The Road to Sparta: Reliving the Ancient Battle and Epic Run That Inspired the World's Greatest Footrace.* New York: Rodale, 2017.

Keller, Timothy. *Walking with God Through Pain and Suffering.* New York: Riverhead Books, 2015.

Knight, Phil. *Shoe Dog: A Memoir by the Creator of Nike.* New York: Simon & Schuster, 2017.

Lear, Chris. *Running with the Buffaloes: A Season inside with Mark Wetmore, Adam Goucher, and the University of Colorado Men's Cross Country Team.* Guilford, CT: Lyons Press, 2011. Kindle.

Lindquist, Rusty. "Sleep Deprivation: How You Sabotage Your Own Success." *Life Engineering.* April 05, 2014. Accessed December 28, 2017. http://life.engineering/sleep-deprivation-like-being-legally-drunk/.

Loehr, James E., and Tony Schwartz. *The Power of Full Engagement: Managing Energy, Not Time, Is the Key to High Performance and Personal Renewal.* New York: Free Press, 2005.

London, H. B., and Neil B. Wiseman. *Pastors at Greater Risk.* Ventura, CA: Regal Books, 2003.

Manning, Brennan. *Abba's Child: The Cry of the Heart for Intimate Belonging.* Colorado Springs: NavPress, 2015.

MacPherson, Kitta. "Sugar Can Be Addictive, Princeton Scientist Says." Princeton University. December 10, 2008. Accessed February 5, 2018. https://www.princeton.edu/news/2008/12/10/sugar-can-be-addictive-princeton-scientist-says.

McDougall, Christopher. *Born to Run: The Hidden Tribe, the Ultra-runners, and the Greatest Race the World Has Never Seen.* London: Profile Books, 2014. Kindle.

———. *Natural Born Heroes: How a Daring Band of Misfits Mastered the Lost Secrets of Strength and Endurance.* New York: Alfred A. Knopf, 2015.

Miller, Bruce B. *Your Church in Rhythm: The Forgotten Dimensions of Seasons and Cycles.* San Francisco: John Wiley & Sons, 2011. Kindle.

Murray, Andrew. *The Spiritual Life: Undeniable Way to Conquer Flesh and Grow in Christ.* Chicago: George W. Jacobs & Company, 1897. Kindle File.

Murray, David. "50 Good Reasons to Sleep Longer." *HeadHeartHand.* May 14, 2014. http://headhearthand.org/blog/2014/05/14/arrogance-of-ignoring-our-need-of-sleep/.

Newport, Cal. *Deep Work: Rules for Focused Success in a Distracted World.* New York: Grand Central Publishing, 2016.

Ortlund, Raymond C. *The Gospel: How the Church Portrays the Beauty of Christ.* Wheaton, IL: Crossway, 2014.

Park, Alice. "7 Not-So-Sweet Lessons About Sugar." *Time.* May 9, 2014. Accessed February 5, 2018. http://time.com/92545/7-not-so-sweet-lessons-about-sugar/.

Pascal, Jean-Marc. "On the Virtues of Peripatetic Philosophy." OSC IB Blogs. June 12, 2017. Accessed December 28, 2017. https://blogs.osc-ib.com/2011/11/ib-teacher-blogs/dp_philosophy/on-the-virtues-of-peripatetic-philosophy/.

Perman, Matt. *What's Best Next: How the Gospel Transforms the Way You Get Things Done.* Grand Rapids: Zondervan, 2016. Kindle.

Pohlman, Dean. *"My Personal Story: How I Got Started with Yoga."* Man Flow Yoga. Accessed December 30, 2017. http://manflowyoga.com/the-story/.

Prime, Derek J., and Alistair Begg. *On Being a Pastor: Understanding Our Calling and Work.* Chicago: Moody Publishers.

Sayers, Mark. *Facing Leviathan: Leadership, Influence, and Creating in a Cultural Storm.* Chicago: Moody Publishers, 2014.

Schroeder, George. "At SEC Meetings, Calm Voices on Roiling Football Debate." *USA Today.* May 29, 2014. Accessed December 28, 2017. https://www.usatoday.com/story/sports/ncaaf/sec/2014/05/29/college-football-pace-of-play-hurry-up-no-huddle/9747947/.

Spurgeon, C. H. *Lectures to My Students, Volume 1.* Grand Rapids: Zondervan, 1954.

———. *Morning and Evening Daily Readings.* Seaside, OR: Merchant Books, 2013.

———. *The Devotional Classics of C.H. Spurgeon: Morning and Evening I & II.* Lafayette, IN: Sovereign Grace Publishers, 1990.

Starrett, Kelly, Juliet Starrett, and Glen Cordoza. *Deskbound: Standing Up to a Sitting World.* Las Vegas: Victory Belt Publishing, 2016.

Stott, John. *Through the Bible, Through the Year.* Oxford: Candle Books, 2006.

Sunnergren, Tom. *Philadunkia.* "The Science of Sleep." *ESPN.* March 3, 2012. http://www.espn.com/blog/truehoop/post/_/id/37958/the-science-of-sleep.

Swenson, Richard A. *Margin: How to Create the Emotional, Physical, Financial & Time Reserves You Need.* Colorado Springs: NavPress, 1992. Kindle.

Taha, Allen. "Physical Self-Care Practices for Sustainable Pastoral Leadership in Local Church Ministry." PhD diss., Covenant Theological Seminary, St. Louis, 2010.

Tozer, A. W. *The Pursuit of God.* Harrisburg, PA: Christian Publications, 1948.

Tucker, Walter Carter. *Men Who Fought. . . . Boys Who Prayed: A Combat Chaplain's Story: Vietnam.* Mustang, OK: Tate Publishing & Enterprises, 2013.

Tripp, Paul David. *Dangerous Calling: Confronting the Unique Challenges of Pastoral Ministry.* Wheaton, IL: Crossway, 2012.

Vassar, J. R. *Glory Hunger: God, the Gospel, and Our Quest for Something More.* Wheaton, IL: Crossway, 2015.

Wardle, Charlie. *How to Sleep Better!* Bath: Brown Dog Books, 2015. Kindle.

Wilson, James L. *Adrenal Fatigue: The 21st Century Stress Syndrome.* Petaluma, CA: Smart Publications, 2017. Kindle.

"Weight Loss with a Low-Carbohydrate, Mediterranean, or Low-Fat Diet." *The New England Journal of Medicine.* July 17, 2008. Accessed February 5, 2018. http://www.nejm.org/doi/full/10.1056/NEJMoa0708681.

LEADERSHIP
DURABILITY
COACHING

Are you in danger of leadership fatigue? I would love to help you gain leadership health just as I've done for many other leaders. Through Leadership Durability Coaching, you will:

- **Audit** and debug your current rhythms and practices.
- **Build** a better sleep, nutrition, and fitness IQ that makes sense for you individually.
- **Create** work/rest rhythms that give you the margin you need.
- **Discern** what it looks like for you personally to drift toward danger.

Let me help you lead from a place of confidence, rest, and creativity.

For coaching and consulting, contact me at **leadershipdurability.com** to set up a free call that will assess your needs and discuss solutions. I also work with groups, teams, and in conference settings.

PEOPLE
LAUNCHING

People Launching helps boost your character and leadership to launch your redemptive cause.

- Gain clarity on your calling through our **relational assessments**.
- Increase your emotional intelligence and pastoral care with our **gospel-centered Enneagram training**.
- Focus your direction and organization with one-on-one **leadership coaching**.
- Get trained to launch your ministry with a **peer network** of like-minded nonprofit founders.

peoplelaunching.com
919.818.7609

LEADERS**COLLECTIVE** ◥

"My time in a Leaders Collective cohort was transformative for me, my family, and my leadership in the church. It's the resource I recommend for pastors who want to thrive in ministry for the long haul." —Luke Thomas

Leaders Collective helps pastors and church planters sustain healthy, fruitful ministry so they—through Jesus's Church—can advance the gospel throughout the world. It does this by facilitating lead pastor cohorts of six pastor-peers that spend two years considering the characteristics necessary to promote healthy, sustainable ministry.

These cohorts meet together once a quarter for two years to consider these characteristics through unique experiences, time with recognized experts in the field, and time giving one another the encouragement we all need to sustain fruitful ministry.

- 2-year lead pastor cohorts offered annually
- Themes: spiritual formation, self-care, emotional intelligence, marriage & family, leadership, and management
- Year-long church planter cohort also offered annually

Interested in growing in the characteristics necessary for pastoral longevity—in a way that's good for you, your family, and your church?

Contact Leaders Collective about their cohorts or find an alumni pastor near you who can tell you about their experience. Alumni pastors and information about cohorts can be found at **leaderscollective.com**.

LEADERS**COLLECTIVE** ◥
Healthy Pastors for Healthy Churches
leaderscollective.com

www.ingramcontent.com/pod-product-compliance
Lightning Source LLC
Chambersburg PA
CBHW070529090426
42735CB00013B/2917

* 9 7 8 1 6 3 2 9 6 2 9 5 9 *